Frommer's®

S0-BDM-854

PORTABLE

Puerto Vallarta, Manzanillo & Guadalajara

6th Edition

by David Baird & Lynne Bairstow

Here's what critics say about Frommer's:

"Amazingly easy to use. Very portable, very complete."
—*Booklist*

"Detailed, accurate, and easy-to-read information for all price ranges."
—*Glamour Magazine*

"Hotel information is close to encyclopedic."
—*Des Moines Sunday Register*

"Frommer's Guides have a way of giving you a real feel for a place."
—*Knight Ridder Newspapers*

BICENTENNIAL
1807
WILEY
2007
BICENTENNIAL

Wiley Publishing, Inc.

Published by:

WILEY PUBLISHING, INC.

111 River St.
Hoboken, NJ 07030-5774

ISBN: 978-0-470-14571-5

Editor: Melinda Quintero
Production Editor: Jana M. Stefanciosa
Photo Editor: Richard Fox
Anniversary Logo Design: Richard Pacifico
Cartographer: Guy Ruggiero
Production by Wiley Indianapolis Composition Services

Front Cover Photo: View over Banderas Bay from the cupola of Nuestra Señora de Guadalupe church.

For information on our other products and services or to obtain technical support, please contact our Customer Care Department within the U.S. at 800/762-2974, outside the U.S. at 317/572-3993 or fax 317/572-4002.

Wiley also publishes its books in a variety of electronic formats. Some content that appears in print may not be available in electronic formats.

Manufactured in the United States of America

5   4   3   2   1

Contents

List of Maps   v

1 Planning Your Trip to Mid-Pacific Mexico   1

  1 The Region in Brief 1
  2 Visitor Information 2
  3 Entry Requirements 4
  4 When to Go 5
       Calender of Events 6
  5 Getting There 10
  6 Money & Costs 13
  7 Travel Insurance 17
  8 Health 19
       The Curse of Montezuma 21
  9 Safety 23
  10 Specialized Travel Resources 24
  11 Sustainable Tourism/Ecotourism 30
       Frommers.com: The Complete Travel Resource 32
  12 Staying Connected 32
       Online Traveler's Toolbox 35
  13 Packages for the Independent Traveler 36
  14 Getting Around 38
  15 Tips on Accommodations 44
  16 Tips on Dining 46
       Fast Facts: Mexico 47

2 Settling into Puerto Vallarta   57

By Lynne Bairstow

  1 Puerto Vallarta Essentials 58
       Fast Facts: Puerto Vallarta 64
  2 Where to Stay 67
  3 Where to Dine 74

3   Exploring Puerto Vallarta & Beyond   86

By Lynne Bairstow

1 Beaches, Activities & Excursions 86
2 Shopping 100
  A Huichol Art Primer: Shopping Tips 103
3 Puerto Vallarta After Dark 109
4 Side Trips from Puerto Vallarta 115

4   Costa Alegre: Puerto Vallarta to Barra de Navidad   126

By Lynne Bairstow

1 Along Costa Alegre (from North to South) 126
2 Barra de Navidad & Melaque 131

5   Manzanillo   140

By Lynne Bairstow

1 Essentials 140
  Fast Facts: Manzanillo 144
2 Activities On & Off the Beach 144
3 Where to Stay & Dine 148
4 Manzanillo after Dark 154

6   Settling into Guadalajara   155

By David Baird

1 Orientation 155
2 Getting Around 159
  Fast Facts: Guadalajara 160
3 Where to Stay 161
4 Where to Dine 167

7   Exploring Guadalajara & Beyond   173

By David Baird

1 What to See & Do 173
  Guadalajara Bus Tours 177
2 Shopping 180

3 Guadalajara After Dark 184
   Tequila: The Name Says It All 185

Appendix: Useful Terms & Phrases   187

1 Basic Vocabulary 187
2 Menu Glossary 192

Index   196

   General Index 196
   Accommodations Index 203
   Restaurant Index 203

List of Maps

Mexico's Mid-Pacific
   Coast   3
Puerto Vallarta: Hotel Zone
   & Beaches   59
Downtown Puerto
   Vallarta   87
Costa Alegre & Central
   Pacific Coast   127

Barra de Navidad
   Bay Area   133
Manzanillo Area   141
Downtown Manzanillo   145
Greater Guadalajara   157
Downtown Guadalajara   175
Tlaquepaque   181
Tonalá   184

ABOUT THE AUTHORS

A writer, editor, and translator, **David Baird** has lived several years in different parts of Mexico. Now based in Austin, Texas, he spends as much time in Mexico as possible.

Lynne Bairstow has lived in Puerto Vallarta for most of the past 16 years. Her travel articles on Mexico have appeared in numerous publications, including the *New York Times, Los Angeles Times, Private Air* magazine, and *Luxury Living* magazine.

AN INVITATION TO THE READER

In researching this book, we discovered many wonderful places—hotels, restaurants, shops, and more. We're sure you'll find others. Please tell us about them, so we can share the information with your fellow travelers in upcoming editions. If you were disappointed with a recommendation, we'd love to know that, too. Please write to:

Frommer's Portable Puerto Vallarta, Manzanillo
& Guadalajara, 6th Edition
Wiley Publishing, Inc. • 111 River St. • Hoboken, NJ 07030-5774

AN ADDITIONAL NOTE

Please be advised that travel information is subject to change at any time—and this is especially true of prices. We therefore suggest that you write or call ahead for confirmation when making your travel plans. The authors, editors, and publisher cannot be held responsible for the experiences of readers while traveling. Your safety is important to us, however, so we encourage you to stay alert and be aware of your surroundings. Keep a close eye on cameras, purses, and wallets, all favorite targets of thieves and pickpockets.

FROMMER'S STAR RATINGS, ICONS & ABBREVIATIONS

Every hotel, restaurant, and attraction listing in this guide has been ranked for quality, value, service, amenities, and special features using a **star-rating system.** In country, state, and regional guides, we also rate towns and regions to help you narrow down your choices and budget your time accordingly. Hotels and restaurants are rated on a scale of zero (recommended) to three stars (exceptional). Attractions, shopping, nightlife, towns, and regions are rated according to the following scale: zero stars (recommended), one star (highly recommended), two stars (very highly recommended), and three stars (must-see).

In addition to the star-rating system, we also use **seven feature icons** that point you to the great deals, in-the-know advice, and unique experiences that separate travelers from tourists. Throughout the book, look for:

Finds	Special finds—those places only insiders know about
Fun Fact	Fun facts—details that make travelers more informed and their trips more fun
Kids	Best bets for kids and advice for the whole family
Moments	Special moments—those experiences that memories are made of
Overrated	Places or experiences not worth your time or money
Tips	Insider tips—great ways to save time and money
Value	Great values—where to get the best deals

The following **abbreviations** are used for credit cards:

AE	American Express	DISC	Discover	V	Visa
DC	Diners Club	MC	MasterCard		

FROMMERS.COM

Now that you have the guidebook to a great trip, visit our website at **www.frommers.com** for travel information on more than 3,600 destinations. With features updated regularly, we give you instant access to the most current trip-planning information available. At Frommers.com, you'll also find the best prices on airfares, accommodations, and car rentals—and you can even book travel online through our travel booking partners. At Frommers.com, you'll also find the following:

- Online updates to our most popular guidebooks
- Vacation sweepstakes and contest giveaways
- Newsletter highlighting the hottest travel trends
- Online travel message boards with featured travel discussions

Planning Your Trip to Mid-Pacific Mexico

Along the Pacific coast of Mexico, palm-studded jungles sweep down to meet the deep blue of the Pacific Ocean, providing spectacular backdrops for three modern resort cities, as well as smaller coastal villages. This lovely stretch of coastline, which extends from Puerto Vallarta down to Manzanillo, is known as the Mexican Riviera. Modern hotels, easy air access, and a growing array of activities and adventure tourism attractions have transformed this region into one of Mexico's premier resort areas. And for those who would like to explore the inland region, the bustling city of Guadalajara, home to some of Mexico's greatest artisans and mariachis, is only a few hours drive away.

A little advance planning can make the difference between a good trip and a great trip to these popular destinations. When should you go? What's the best way to get there? How much should you plan on spending? What festivals or special events will be taking place during your visit? What safety or health precautions are advised? These questions and others will be answered for in this chapter.

In addition to these basics, we highly recommend taking the time to learn a little about the culture and traditions of Mexico. It can make the difference between simply "getting away" and coming back with an enriched understanding.

1 The Region in Brief

Puerto Vallarta, with its traditional Mexican architecture and gold-sand beaches bordered by jungle-covered mountains, is currently the second most visited resort in Mexico (trailing only Cancún). Although it has grown rapidly in recent years, Vallarta (as the locals refer to it) still maintains a small-town charm despite sophisticated hotels, great restaurants, a thriving arts community, an active nightlife, and a growing variety of ecotourism attractions. **Manzanillo** is surprisingly relaxed, even though it's one of Mexico's most active commercial ports; it also offers great fishing and golf. And along the **Costa Alegre,** between Puerto Vallarta and Manzanillo, pristine coves are home to unique luxury and value-priced resorts that cater to travelers seeking seclusion and privacy. Just north of Puerto Vallarta is **Punta Mita,** home of the first Four Seasons resort in Latin America and a Jack Nicklaus golf course. With a new St. Regis Resort and a second Jack Nicklaus Signature course slated to open in early 2008, it is emerging as Mexico's most exclusive address. For a more essentially Mexican experience, head inland over the mountains to **Guadalajara,** Mexico's second-largest city and the birthplace of many of the country's traditions.

International airports at all three cities make getting to each easier; Guadalajara and Puerto Vallarta have the most frequent connections. Distances in the region are easily managed by car and the roads are in generally good condition. **Barra de Navidad,** for example, is so close to Manzanillo that it's easy to combine several days there with a stay in Manzanillo. From Puerto Vallarta, **Bucerías, Yelapa, San Sebastian,** and **Sayulita** all offer a change of pace and scenery. Hotelito Desconocido and Las Alamandas are both closer to Puerto Vallarta, with the remainder of the luxury coastal resorts between Manzanillo and Puerto Vallarta, nearer to Manzanillo. More frequent flights fly to and from Puerto Vallarta, and many people find that Puerto Vallarta provides the best access to the coastal area.

2 Visitor Information

The **Mexico Hot Line** (© 800/44-MEXICO) is an excellent source for general information; you can request brochures and get answers to the most common questions from the exceptionally well-trained and knowledgeable staff.

More information (15,000 pages worth) about Mexico is available on the official site of Mexico's Tourism Promotion Board, **www.visitmexico.com.** The **U.S. State Department** (© 202/647-5225; www.travel.state.gov) offers **Travel Warnings** and a **Consular Information Sheet** on Mexico with consistently updated safety, medical, driving, and general travel information gleaned from reports by its offices in Mexico. You can also request the Consular Information Sheet by fax (© 202/647-3000).

The **Mexican Government Tourist Board** has offices in major North American cities, in addition to the main office in Mexico City

Mexico's Mid-Pacific Coast

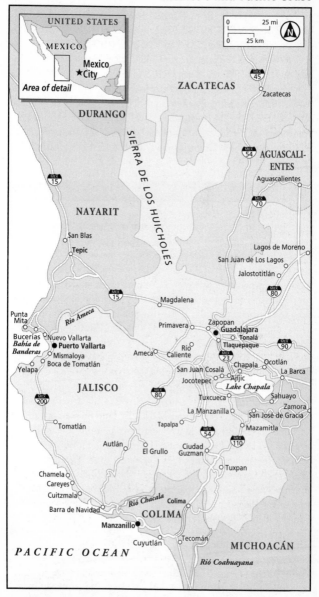

(📞 555/203-1103). In the **United States:** Chicago (📞 **312/606-9252**), Houston (📞 **713/772-2581**, ext. 105, or 713/772-3819), Los Angeles (📞 **310/282-9112**), and New York (📞 **212/308-2110**).

The **Mexican Embassy** in the United States is at 1911 Pennsylvania Ave. NW, Washington, DC 20005 (📞 **202/728-1600**). In Canada: 2055 Rue Peel, suite 1000, Montreal, QC H3A 1V4 (📞 **514/288-2502**); Commerce Court West 199 Bay St., Suite 4440, Toronto ON M5L 1E9 (📞 **416/368-2875**); 710-1177 West Hastings St., Vancouver BC V6E 2K3 (📞 **604/684-3547**). Embassy office: 45 O'Connor St., Suite 1000, Ottawa, ON, K1P 1A4 (📞 **613/233-8988;** fax 613/235-9123).

3 Entry Requirements

PASSPORTS

All travelers to Mexico are required to present **photo identification** and **proof of citizenship,** such as a valid passport, naturalization papers, or an original birth certificate with a raised seal, along with a driver's license or official ID, such as a state or military issued ID. Driver's licenses and permits, voter registration cards, affidavits and similar documents are not sufficient to prove citizenship for **readmission into the United States.** If the last name on the birth certificate is different from your current name, bring a photo identification card *and* legal proof of the name change, such as the original marriage license or certificate. *Note:* Photocopies are *not* acceptable.

Effective January 23, 2007, **all U.S. citizens** traveling by **air** to Mexico are required to have a valid passport to enter or reenter the United States. As early as January 1, 2008, U.S. citizens traveling between the United States and Mexico by **land** or **sea** may also be required to present a valid U.S. passport or other documents as determined by the Department of Homeland Security.

For information on how to get a passport, go to "Passports" in the "Fast Facts" section of this chapter—the websites listed provide downloadable passport applications as well as the current fees for processing passport applications. For an up-to-date, country-by-country listing of passport requirements around the world, go to the "Foreign Entry Requirement" Web page of the U.S. Department of State at **http://travel.state.gov.**

VISAS

You must carry a **Mexican Tourist Permit (FMT),** the equivalent of a tourist visa, which Mexican border officials issue, free of charge, after proof of citizenship is accepted. Airlines generally provide the necessary forms aboard your flight to Mexico. The FMT is more important than a passport, so guard it carefully. If you lose it, you may not be permitted to leave until you can replace it—a bureaucratic hassle that can take anywhere from a few hours to a week.

The FMT can be issued for up to 180 days. Sometimes officials don't ask but just stamp a time limit, so be sure to say "6 months," or at least twice as long as you intend to stay. If you decide to extend your stay, you may request that additional time be added to your FMT from an official immigration office in Mexico.

U.S. citizens do not require a visa or a tourist card for tourist stays of 72 hours or less within "the border zone," defined as an area from 20 to 30km (12–19 miles) of the border with the U.S., depending on the location.

Note: Children younger than age 18 who are traveling without parents or with only one parent must have a notarized letter from the absent parent(s) authorizing the travel. Mexican law requires that any non-Mexican younger than age 18 departing Mexico must carry notarized written permission from any parent or guardian not traveling with the child. This permission must include the name of the parent, the name of the child, the name of anyone traveling with the child, and the notarized signature(s) of the absent parent(s). The child must carry the original letter (not a copy) as well as proof of the parent/child relationship (usually a birth certificate or court document) and an original custody decree, if applicable.

MEDICAL REQUIREMENTS
For information on medical requirements and recommendations, see "Health," p. 19.

CUSTOMS
For information on what you can bring into and take out of Mexico, go to **"Customs"** in the **"Fast Facts"** section of this chapter.

4 When to Go
SEASONS
Mexico has two principal travel seasons: high and low. High season begins around December 20 and continues through Easter, although in some places high season can begin as early as mid-November. Low season begins the day after Easter and continues through mid-December; during low season, prices may drop 20% to 50%. In beach destinations, the prices may also increase during

the months of July and August, the traditional national summer vacation period. Prices in inland cities, such as Guadalajara, seldom fluctuate from high to low season, but may rise dramatically during Easter and Christmas weeks.

CLIMATE

From Puerto Vallarta south, all the way to Huatulco, Mexico offers one of the world's most perfect winter climates—dry and balmy with temperatures ranging from the 80s during the day to the 60s at night. From Puerto Vallarta on south, you can swim year-round. High mountains shield Pacific beaches from *nortes* (northers—freezing blasts out of Canada via the Texas Panhandle).

Summers are sunny, with an increase in humidity during the rainy season, between May and October. Rains come almost every afternoon in June and July, and are usually brief but strong—just enough to cool off the air for evening activities. In September, heat and humidity are least comfortable and rains heaviest.

The climate in inland Guadalajara is mostly mild. During the winter, it's a good idea to carry a sweater when going out in the evenings. The city also receives summer afternoon showers, although the rest of the day is usually hot and dry.

CALENDAR OF EVENTS

For an exhaustive list of events beyond those listed here, check http://events.frommers.com, where you'll find a searchable, up-to-the-minute roster of what's happening in cities all over the world.

During national holidays, Mexican banks and governmental offices—including immigration—are closed.

January

New Year's Day (Año Nuevo). National holiday. Parades, religious observances, parties, and fireworks welcome in the New Year everywhere. January 1.

Three Kings Day (Día de los Reyes). Commemorates the Three Kings' bringing of gifts to the Christ Child. Children receive gifts, and friends and families gather to share the *Rosca de Reyes,* a special cake. Inside the cake is a small doll representing the Christ Child; whoever receives the doll in his or her piece must host a tamales and atole party the next month. January 6.

February

Candlemas. Music, dances, processions, food, and other festivities lead up to a blessing of seed and candles, a ritual that mixes pre-Hispanic and European traditions marking the end of winter.

All those who attended the Three Kings' Celebration reunite to share atole and tamales at a party hosted by the recipient of the doll found in the Rosca. February 2.

Carnaval. Carnaval takes place the 3 days preceding Ash Wednesday and the start of Lent. It is celebrated with special gusto in Mazatlán. Here, the celebration resembles New Orleans's Mardi Gras, with festivities and parades. Transportation and hotels are packed, so it's best to make reservations 6 months in advance and arrive a couple of days ahead of the beginning of celebrations.

Ash Wednesday. The start of Lent and time of abstinence. It's a day of reverence nationwide, but some towns honor it with folk dancing and fairs. Lent begins on February 6 in 2008, and February 25 in 2009.

March
Benito Juárez's Birthday. National holiday. March 21.

April
Holy Week. Celebrates the last week in the life of Christ, from Palm Sunday to Easter Sunday, with somber religious processions almost nightly, spoofings of Judas, and reenactments of specific biblical events, plus food and craft fairs. Businesses close during this week of Mexican national vacations.

If you plan on traveling to or around Mexico during Holy Week, make your reservations early. Airline seats on flights in and out of the country are reserved months in advance. Buses to almost anywhere in Mexico will be full, so try arriving on the Wednesday or Thursday before Good Friday. Easter Sunday is quiet.

May
Labor Day (May Day). Nationwide parades; everything closes. May 1.

Holy Cross Day (Día de la Santa Cruz). Workers place a cross on top of unfinished buildings and celebrate with food, bands, folk dancing, and fireworks around the work site. May 3.

Cinco de Mayo. A national holiday that celebrates the defeat of the French in the Battle of Puebla. May 5.

June
National Ceramics Fair and Fiesta, Tlaquepaque, Jalisco. This pottery center outside Guadalajara hosts crafts demonstrations and contests, mariachis, dancers, and parades. June 14.

Día de San Pedro (St. Peter and St. Paul's Day). Celebrated wherever St. Peter is the patron saint, and honors anyone named

Pedro or Peter. It's especially festive at San Pedro Tlaquepaque, near Guadalajara, with numerous mariachi bands, folk dancers, and parades with floats. In Mexcatitlan, Nayarit, shrimpers hold a regatta to celebrate the season opening. June 29.

September

Mariachi Festival, Guadalajara, Jalisco. Public mariachi concerts, with groups from around the world (even Japan!). Workshops and lectures are given on the history, culture, and music of the mariachi. Plans for an extension of this festival in Puerto Vallarta are being worked out—call © **800-44-MEXICO** or click on www.mariachi-jalisco.com.mx to confirm dates and performance schedules. August 31 to September 10.

Independence Day. Celebrates Mexico's independence from Spain. A day of parades, picnics, and family reunions throughout the country. At 11pm on September 15, the president of Mexico gives the famous independence *grito* (shout) from the National Palace in Mexico City, which is duplicated by every *presidente municipal* (mayor) in every town plaza in Mexico. Both Guadalajara and Puerto Vallarta have great parties in the town plaza on the nights of September 15 and 16.

October

Fiestas de Octubre (October Festivals), Guadalajara. This "most Mexican of cities" celebrates for a whole month with its mariachi music trademark. A bountiful display of popular culture and fine arts, and a spectacular spread of traditional foods, Mexican beers, and wines all add to the celebration. All month.

November

Day of the Dead. The Day of the Dead is actually 2 days, All Saints' Day (honoring saints and deceased children) and All Souls' Day (honoring deceased adults). Relatives gather at cemeteries carrying candles and food, and often spend the night beside the graves of loved ones. Weeks before, bakers begin producing bread shaped like mummies or round loaves decorated with bread "bones." Decorated sugar skulls emblazoned with glittery names are sold everywhere. Many days ahead, homes and churches erect special altars laden with Day of the Dead bread, fruit, flowers, candles, and favorite foods and photographs of saints and of the deceased. Children, dressed in costumes and masks, carry mock coffins and pumpkin lanterns through the streets at night, expecting people to drop money in them. November 1 and 2.

The Puerto Vallarta Film Festival, Puerto Vallarta, Jalisco. Featuring a wide range of North American independent and Latin

American productions, this elaborate showcase includes galas, art expos, and concerts, with celebrity attendees. Check local calendars; call © **800/44-MEXICO** or go to www.vallartafilmfestival. com for details. First week of December.

Gourmet Festival. Puerto Vallarta, Jalisco. In this culinary capital of Mexico, chefs from around the world join local restaurateurs to create special menus, as well as host wine and tequila tastings, cooking classes, gourmet food expos, and other special events. Dates vary; contact the Tourism Board (© **888/384-6822** in the U.S.; www.festivalgourmet.com) for a schedule.

Revolution Day. Commemorates the start of the Mexican Revolution in 1910 with parades, speeches, rodeos, and patriotic events. November 20.

December

Feast of the Virgin of Guadalupe. Throughout the country, the patroness of Mexico is honored with religious processions, street fairs, dancing, fireworks, and Masses. It is one of Mexico's most moving and beautiful displays of traditional culture. The Virgin of Guadalupe appeared to a young man, Juan Diego, in December 1531, on a hill near Mexico City. He convinced the bishop that he had seen the apparition by revealing his cloak, upon which the Virgin was emblazoned. Children dress up as Juan Diego, wearing mustaches and red bandannas. December 12.

In Puerto Vallarta, the celebration begins on December 1 and extends through December 12, with traditional processions to the church for a brief *misa* (mass) and blessing. Businesses, neighborhoods, associations, and groups make pilgrimages (called *peregrinaciones*) to the church, where they exchange offerings for a brief blessing by the priest. In the final days, the processions and festivities take place around the clock, with many of the processions featuring floats, mariachis, Aztec dancers, and fireworks. Hotels frequently invite guests to participate in the walk to the church. The central plaza is filled with street vendors and a festive atmosphere, and a major fireworks exhibition takes place on December 12 at 11pm.

Christmas Posadas. On each of the 9 nights before Christmas, it's customary to reenact the Holy Family's search for an inn, with door-to-door candlelit processions in cities and villages nationwide. Most business and community organizations host them in place of the northern tradition of a Christmas party. December 15 to 24.

Christmas. Mexicans extend this celebration, often starting 2 weeks before Christmas, through New Year's. Many businesses close, and resorts and hotels fill up. December 24 and 25.

New Year's Eve. As in the rest of the world, New Year's Eve is celebrated with parties and fireworks.

5 Getting There

BY PLANE

The airline situation in Mexico is rapidly improving, with many new regional carriers offering scheduled service to areas previously not served. In addition to regularly scheduled service, charter service direct from U.S. cities to resorts is making Mexico more accessible.

THE MAJOR INTERNATIONAL AIRLINES   The main airlines operating direct or nonstop flights from the United States to Mexico include **Aero California** (© 800/237-6225; www.aero california.com), **Aeromexico** (© 800/237-6639; www.aeromexico. com), **Air France** (© 800/237-2747; www.airfrance.com), **Alaska Airlines** (© 800/252-7522; www.alaskaair.com), **American Airlines** (© 800/433-7300; www.aa.com), **Continental** (© 800/ 523-3273; www.continental.com), **Frontier Airlines** (© 800/432-1359; www.frontierairlines.com), **Mexicana** (© 800/531-7921; www.mexicana.com), **Northwest/KLM** (© 800/225-2525; www. nwa.com), **Taca** (© 800/225-2272; www.taca.com), **United** (© 800/538-2929; www.united.com), and **US Airways** (© 800/ 428-4322; www.usairways.com). **Southwest Airlines** (© 800/435-9792; www.southwest.com) serves the U.S. border.

The main departure points in North America for international airlines are Atlanta, Chicago, Dallas/Fort Worth, Denver, Houston, Las Vegas, Los Angeles, Miami, New York, Orlando, Philadelphia, Phoenix, Raleigh/Durham, San Antonio, San Francisco, Seattle, Toronto, and Washington, D.C.

BY CAR

Driving is not the cheapest way to get to Mexico, but it is the best way to see the country. Even so, you may think twice about taking your own car south of the border once you've pondered the bureaucracy involved. One option is to rent a car once you arrive. Rental cars in Mexico are generally new, clean, and well maintained. Although they're pricier than in the United States, discounts are often available for rentals of a week or longer, especially when you make arrangements in advance from the United States. (See "Renting a Car," later in this chapter, for more details.)

If, after reading the section that follows, you have additional questions or you want to confirm the current rules, call your nearest Mexican consulate or the Mexican Government Tourist Office. Although travel insurance companies are generally helpful, they may not have the most accurate information.

CAR DOCUMENTS

To drive your car into Mexico, you'll need a **temporary car-importation permit,** which is granted after you provide a required list of documents (see below). The permit can be obtained through Banco del Ejército (Banjercito) officials, who have a desk, booth, or office at the *aduana* (Mexican Customs) building after you cross the border into Mexico.

The following strict requirements for border crossing were accurate at press time:

- **A valid driver's license,** issued outside of Mexico.
- **Current, original car registration and a copy of the original car title.** If the registration or title is in more than one name and not all the named people are traveling with you, a notarized letter from the absent person(s) authorizing use of the vehicle for the trip is required; have it ready. The registration and your credit card (see below) must be in the same name.
- **A valid international major credit card.** With a credit card, you are required to pay only a $23 (£13) car-importation fee. The credit card must be in the same name as the car registration. If you do not have a major credit card (American Express, Diners Club, MasterCard, or Visa), you must post a bond or make a deposit equal to the value of the vehicle. Check cards are not accepted.
- **Original immigration documentation.** This is either your tourist permit (FMT) or the original immigration booklet, FM2 or FM3, if you hold more permanent status.
- **A signed declaration promising to return to your country of origin with the vehicle.** Obtain this form *(Carta Promesa de Retorno)* from AAA or Sanborn's before you go, or from Banjercito officials at the border. There's no charge. The form does not stipulate that you must return by the same border entry through which you entered.
- **Temporary Importation Application.** By signing this form, you state that you are only temporarily importing the car for

your personal use and will not be selling it. This is to help regulate the entry and restrict the resale of unauthorized cars and trucks. Make sure the permit is canceled when you return to the U.S.

If you receive your documentation at the border, Mexican officials will make two copies of everything and charge you for the copies. For up-to-the-minute information, a great source is the Customs office in Nuevo Laredo, or *Módulo de Importación Temporal de Automóviles, Aduana Nuevo Laredo* (© **867/712-2071**).

Important reminder: Someone else may drive, but the person (or relative of the person) whose name appears on the car-importation permit must *always* be in the car. (If stopped by police, a non-registered family member driving without the registered driver must be prepared to prove familial relationship to the registered driver—no joke.) Violation of this rule subjects the car to impoundment and the driver to imprisonment, a fine, or both. You can drive a car with foreign license plates only if you have a foreign (non-Mexican) driver's license.

MEXICAN AUTO INSURANCE

Liability auto insurance is legally required in Mexico. U.S. insurance is invalid; to be insured in Mexico, you must purchase Mexican insurance. Any party involved in an accident who has no insurance may be sent to jail and have his or her car impounded until all claims are settled. This is true even if you just drive across the border to spend the day. U.S. companies that broker Mexican insurance are commonly found at the border crossing, and several quote daily rates.

You can also buy car insurance through **Sanborn's Mexico Insurance,** P.O. Box 52840, 2009 S. 10th, McAllen, TX (© **800/222-0158;** www.sanbornsinsurance.com). The company has offices at all U.S. border crossings. Its policies cost the same as the competition's do, but you get legal coverage (attorney and bail bonds if needed) and a detailed mile-by-mile guide for your proposed route. Most of the Sanborn's border offices are open Monday through Friday, and a few are staffed on Saturday and Sunday. **AAA** auto club (www.aaa.com) also sells insurance.

RETURNING TO THE U.S. WITH YOUR CAR

You *must* return the car documents you obtained when you entered Mexico when you cross back with your car, or at some point within 180 days. (You can cross as many times as you wish within the 180 days.) If the documents aren't returned, heavy fines are imposed ($250/£139 for each 15 days late), your car may be impounded and confiscated, or you may be jailed if you return to Mexico. You can only return the car documents to a Banjercito official on duty at the Mexican *aduana* (Customs) building *before* you cross back into the United States. Some border cities have Banjercito officials on duty 24 hours a day, but others do not; some do not have Sunday hours.

BY BUS

Greyhound-Trailways (1-800-231-2222; www.greyhound.com), or its affiliates, offers service from around the United States to the Mexican border, where passengers disembark, cross the border, and buy a ticket for travel into Mexico. Many border crossings have scheduled buses from the U.S. bus station to the Mexican bus station.

6 Money & Costs

It's always advisable to bring money in a variety of forms on a vacation: a mix of cash, credit cards, and traveler's checks. You should also exchange enough petty cash to cover airport incidentals, tipping, and transportation to your hotel before you leave home, or withdraw money upon arrival at an airport ATM, though don't expect an ideal exchange rate. You can exchange money at your local American Express or Thomas Cook office or at your bank. American Express also dispenses traveler's checks and foreign currency via www.americanexpress.com or © 800/673-3782, but they'll charge a $15 order fee and additional shipping and handling costs.

CURRENCY

The currency in Mexico is the **peso.** Paper currency comes in denominations of 20, 50, 100, 200, and 500 pesos. Coins come in denominations of 1, 2, 5, 10, and 20 pesos, and 20 and 50 **centavos** (100 centavos = 1 peso). The current exchange rate for the U.S. dollar, and the one used in this book, is around 11 pesos; at that rate, an item that costs 11 pesos would be equivalent to US$1.

Getting **change** is a problem. Small-denomination bills and coins are hard to come by, so start collecting them early in your trip. Shopkeepers and taxi drivers everywhere always seem to be out of change and small bills; that's doubly true in markets.

Many establishments that deal with tourists, especially in coastal resort areas, quote prices in dollars. To avoid confusion, they use the abbreviations "Dlls." for dollars and "M.N." (*moneda nacional,* or national currency) for pesos.

Tips A Few Words about Prices

The peso's value continues to fluctuate—at press time, it was roughly 11 pesos to the dollar. Prices in this book (which are always given in U.S. dollars) have been converted to U.S. dollars at 11 pesos to the dollar. Most hotels in Mexico—with the exception of places that receive little foreign tourism—quote prices in U.S. dollars. Thus, currency fluctuations are unlikely to affect the prices most hotels charge.

Mexico has a **value-added tax** of 15% (*Impuesto de Valor Agregado,* or IVA; pronounced "*ee-bah*") on most everything, including restaurant meals, bus tickets, and souvenirs. (Exceptions are Cancún, Cozumel, and Los Cabos, where the IVA is 10%; as ports of entry, they receive a break on taxes.) Hotels charge the usual 15% IVA, plus a locally administered bed tax of 2% (in most areas), for a total of 17%. In Cancún, Los Cabos, and Cozumel, hotels charge the 10% IVA plus 2% room tax. The prices quoted by hotels and restaurants do not necessarily include IVA. You may find that upper-end properties (three or more stars) quote prices without IVA included, while lower-priced hotels include IVA. Always ask to see a printed price sheet and always ask if the tax is included.

Don't forget to have enough pesos to carry you over a weekend or Mexican holiday, when banks are closed. In general, avoid carrying the U.S. $100 bill, the bill most commonly counterfeited in Mexico and therefore the most difficult to exchange, especially in smaller towns. Because small bills and coins in pesos are hard to come by in Mexico, the $1 bill is very useful for tipping. A tip of U.S. coins, which cannot be exchanged into Mexican currency, is of no value to the service provider.

The bottom line on exchanging money: Ask first, and shop around. Banks generally pay the top rates.

Casas de cambio (exchange houses) are generally more convenient than banks because they have more locations and longer hours; the rate of exchange may be the same as at a bank or slightly lower. Before leaving a bank or exchange-house window, count your change in front of the teller before the next client steps up.

Large airports have currency-exchange counters that often stay open whenever flights are operating. Though convenient, they generally do not offer the most favorable rates.

A hotel's exchange desk commonly pays less favorable rates than banks; however, when the currency is in a state of flux, higher-priced hotels are known to pay higher rates than banks, in an effort to attract dollars. *Note:* In almost all cases, you receive a better rate by changing money first, then paying.

BANKS & ATMS

Banks in Mexico are rapidly expanding and improving services. They tend to be open weekdays from 9am until 5pm, and often for at least a half-day on Saturday. In larger resorts and cities, they can generally accommodate the exchange of dollars (which used to stop at noon) anytime during business hours. During times when the currency is in flux, a particular bank may not exchange dollars, so check before standing in line. Some, but not all, banks charge a service fee of about 1% to exchange traveler's checks. However, you can pay for most purchases directly with traveler's checks at the establishment's stated exchange rate. Don't even bother with personal checks drawn on a U.S. bank—the bank will wait for your check to clear, which can take weeks, before giving you your money.

The easiest and best way to get cash away from home is from an ATM (automated teller machine), sometimes referred to as a "cash machine," or a "cashpoint." The **Cirrus** (© **800/424-7787**; www.mastercard.com) and **PLUS** (© **800/843-7587**; www.visa.com) networks span the globe. Go to your bank card's website to find ATM locations at your destination. Be sure you know your daily withdrawal limit before you depart. *Note:* Many banks impose a fee every time you use a card at another bank's ATM, and that fee can be higher for international transactions (up to $5/£3 or more) than for domestic ones (where they're rarely more than $2/£1). In addition, the bank from which you withdraw cash may charge its own fee. For international withdrawal fees, ask your bank.

Money Matters

The universal currency sign **($)** is used to indicate pesos in Mexico. The use of this symbol in this book, however, denotes U.S. currency. Many establishments dealing with tourists, especially in coastal resort areas, quote prices in dollars. To avoid confusion, they use the abbreviations "Dlls." for dollars and "M.N." (*moneda nacional,* or national currency) for pesos. All dollar equivalencies in this book were based on an exchange rate of 11 pesos per dollar.

CREDIT CARDS

Credit cards are another safe way to carry money. They also provide a convenient record of all your expenses, and they generally offer relatively good exchange rates. You can withdraw cash advances from your credit cards at banks or ATMs but high fees make credit card cash advances a pricey way to get cash. Keep in mind that you'll pay interest from the moment of your withdrawal, even if you pay your monthly bills on time. Also, note that many banks now assess a 1% to 3% "transaction fee" on **all** charges you incur abroad (whether you're using the local currency or your native currency).

In Mexico, Visa, MasterCard, and American Express are the most commonly accepted cards. You'll be able to charge most hotel, restaurant, and store purchases, as well as almost all airline tickets, on your credit card. You generally can't charge gasoline purchases in Mexico. You can get cash advances of several hundred dollars on your card, but there may be a wait of 20 minutes to 2 hours.

Charges will be made in pesos, then converted into dollars by the bank issuing the credit card. Generally you receive the favorable bank rate when paying by credit card. However, be aware that some establishments in Mexico add a 5% to 7% surcharge when you pay with a credit card. This is especially true when using American Express. Many times, advertised discounts will not apply if you pay with a credit card.

TRAVELER'S CHECKS

You can buy traveler's checks at most banks. They are offered in denominations of $20, $50, $100, $500, and sometimes $1,000. Generally, you'll pay a service charge ranging from 1% to 4%.

Tips Dear Visa: I'm Off to the Mexican Riviera!

Some credit card companies recommend that you notify them of any impending trip abroad so that they don't become suspicious and block your charges when the card is used numerous times in a foreign destination. Even if you don't call your credit card company in advance, you can always call the toll-free emergency number (see "Fast Facts: Mexico," later in this chapter) if a charge is refused—a good reason to carry the phone number with you. But perhaps the most important lesson is to carry more than one card on your trip; if one card doesn't work for any number of reasons, you'll have a backup.

The most popular traveler's checks are offered by **American Express** (© **800/807-6233** or © 800/221-7282 for cardholders—this number accepts collect calls, offers service in several foreign languages, and exempts Amex gold and platinum cardholders from the 1% fee); **Visa** (© **800/732-1322**)—AAA members can obtain Visa checks for a $9.95 fee (for checks up to $1,500) at most AAA offices or by calling © **866/339-3378;** and **MasterCard** (© **800/223-9920**).

Be sure to keep a record of the traveler's checks' serial numbers separate from your checks in the event that they are stolen or lost. You'll get a refund faster if you know the numbers.

American Express, Thomas Cook, Visa, and **MasterCard** offer **foreign currency traveler's checks,** useful if you're traveling to one country or to the Euro zone; they're accepted at locations where dollar checks may not be.

Another option is the new prepaid traveler's check cards, reloadable cards that work much like debit cards but aren't linked to your checking account. The **American Express Travelers Cheque Card,** for example, requires a minimum deposit, sets a maximum balance, and has a one-time issuance fee of $14.95. You can withdraw money from an ATM (for a fee of $2.50 per transaction, not including bank fees), and the funds can be purchased in dollars, euros, or pounds. If you lose the card, your available funds will be refunded within 24 hours.

7 Travel Insurance

The cost of travel insurance varies widely, depending on the destination, the cost and length of your trip, your age and health, and the type of trip you're taking, but expect to pay between 5% and 8% of the vacation itself. You can get estimates from various providers through **InsureMyTrip.com**. Enter your trip cost and dates, your age, and other information, for prices from more than a dozen companies.

U.K. citizens and their families who make more than one trip abroad per year may find an annual travel insurance policy works out cheaper. Check **www.moneysupermarket.com**, which compares prices across a wide range of providers for single- and multi-trip policies.

Most big travel agents offer their own insurance and will probably try to sell you their package when you book a holiday. Think before you sign. **Britain's Consumers' Association** recommends that you insist on seeing the policy and reading the fine print before buying travel insurance. **The Association of British Insurers** (© 020/ 7600-3333; www.abi.org.uk) gives advice by phone and publishes *Holiday Insurance,* a free guide to policy provisions and prices. You might also shop around for better deals: Try **Columbus Direct** (© 0870/033-9988; www.columbusdirect.net).

If you'll be driving in Mexico, see "Getting Around: By Car," later in this chapter, for information on **collision, damage,** and **accident insurance.**

TRIP-CANCELLATION INSURANCE

Trip-cancellation insurance will help retrieve your money if you have to back out of a trip or depart early, or if your travel supplier goes bankrupt. Trip cancellation traditionally covers such events as sickness, natural disasters, and State Department advisories. The latest news in trip-cancellation insurance is the availability of **expanded hurricane coverage** and the **"any-reason"** cancellation coverage—which costs more but covers cancellations made for any reason. You won't get back 100% of your prepaid trip cost, but you'll be refunded a substantial portion. **TravelSafe** (© **888/885-7233;** www.travel safe.com) offers both types of coverage. Expedia also offers any-reason cancellation coverage for its air-hotel packages.

For details, contact one of the following recommended insurers: **Access America** (© 866/807-3982; www.accessamerica.com); **Travel Guard International** (© 800/826-4919; www.travelguard. com); **Travel Insured International** (© 800/243-3174; www.travel insured.com); and **Travelex Insurance Services** (© 888/457-4602; www.travelex-insurance.com).

MEDICAL INSURANCE

For travel overseas, most U.S. health plans (including Medicare and Medicaid) do not provide coverage, and the ones that do often require you to pay for services upfront and reimburse you only after you return home.

As a safety net, you may want to buy travel medical insurance, particularly if you're traveling to a remote or high-risk area where emergency evacuation might be necessary. If you require additional medical insurance, try **MEDEX Assistance** (© 410/453-6300; www.medexassist.com) or **Travel Assistance International** (© **800/ 821-2828;** www.travelassistance.com; for general information on services, call the company's **Worldwide Assistance Services, Inc.,** at © 800/777-8710).

Canadians should check with their provincial health plan offices or call **Health Canada** (✆ 866/225-0709; www.hc-sc.gc.ca) to find out the extent of their coverage and what documentation and receipts they must take home in case they are treated overseas.

LOST-LUGGAGE INSURANCE

On international flights (including U.S. portions of international trips), baggage coverage is limited to approximately US$9.10 (£4.60) per pound, up to approximately US$635 (£320) per checked bag. If you plan to check items more valuable than what's covered by the standard liability, see if your homeowner's policy covers your valuables, get baggage insurance as part of your comprehensive travel-insurance package, or buy Travel Guard's "BagTrak" product.

If your luggage is lost, immediately file a lost-luggage claim at the airport, detailing the luggage contents. Most airlines require that you report delayed, damaged, or lost baggage within 4 hours of arrival. The airlines are required to deliver luggage, once found, directly to your house or destination free of charge.

8 Health

GENERAL AVAILABILITY OF HEALTH CARE

In most of Mexico's resort destinations, health care meeting U.S. standards is now available. Mexico's major cities are also known for their excellent health care, although the facilities available may be fewer, and equipment older than what is available at home. Prescription medicine is broadly available at Mexico's pharmacies; however, be aware that you may need a copy of your prescription, or obtain a prescription from a local doctor. This is especially true in the border towns, such as in Tijuana, where many Americans have been crossing into Mexico specifically for the purpose of purchasing lower priced prescription medicines.

Contact the **International Association for Medical Assistance to Travelers** (IAMAT; ✆ 716/754-4883 or, in Canada, 416/652-0137; www.iamat.org) for tips on travel and health concerns in the countries you're visiting, and for lists of local, English-speaking doctors. The United States **Centers for Disease Control and Prevention** (✆ 800/311-3435; www.cdc.gov) provides up-to-date information on health hazards by region or country and offers tips on food safety. **Travel Health Online** (www.tripprep.com), sponsored by a consortium of travel medicine practitioners, may also

Healthy Travels to You

The following government websites offer up-to-date health-related travel advice.

- **U.S.:** www.cdc.gov/travel/
- **Canada:** www.hc-sc.gc.ca/index_e.html
- **U.K.:** www.dh.gov.uk Click on "Policy & Guidance", then "Health Advice for Travellers"
- **Australia:** www.dfat.gov.au/travel/

offer helpful advice on traveling abroad. You can find listings of reliable medical clinics overseas at the **International Society of Travel Medicine** (www.istm.org).

COMMON AILMENTS

BUGS & BITES   Mosquitoes and gnats are prevalent along the coast. Insect repellent *(repelente contra insectos)* is a must, and it's not always available in Mexico. If you'll be in these areas and are prone to bites, bring a repellent along that contains the active ingredient DEET. Avon's "Skin So Soft" also works well. If you're sensitive to bites, pick up some antihistamine cream from a drugstore at home. Another good remedy to keep the mosquitoes away is to mix citronella essential oil with basil, clove, and lavender essential oils. But remember, if you're traveling from the U.S. by air, you cannot carry any liquids (including creams and sprays) in containers larger than 3 oz. bottles in your carry-on. If you bring your own insect repellent, pack it in your checked baggage.

Most visitors won't ever see an *alacrán* (scorpion). But if one stings you, go immediately to a doctor. In Mexico you can buy scorpion toxin antidote at any drugstore. It is an injection and it costs around $25 (£14). This is a good idea if you plan to camp in a remote area where medical assistance can be several hours away.

MORE SERIOUS DISEASES   You shouldn't be overly concerned about tropical diseases if you stay on the normal tourist routes and don't eat street food. However, both dengue fever and cholera have appeared in Mexico in recent years. Talk to your doctor or to a medical specialist in tropical diseases about precautions you should take. You can also get medical bulletins from the U.S. State Department and the Centers for Disease Control and Prevention (see "Healthy Travels to You," above). Watch what you eat and drink; don't swim in stagnant water (ponds, slow-moving rivers, or wells); and avoid mosquito bites by covering up, using repellent, and sleeping under netting. The most dangerous areas seem to be on Mexico's west coast, away from the big resorts.

WHAT TO DO IF YOU GET SICK AWAY FROM HOME

For travel abroad, you may have to pay all medical costs upfront and be reimbursed later. Medicare and Medicaid do not provide coverage

---

 ### The Curse of Montezuma

"Montezuma's revenge" or "*turista*"—persistent diarrhea, often with fever, nausea, and vomiting—used to attack many travelers to Mexico. Improvements in infrastructure, sanitation, and education have practically eliminated this ailment, especially in well-developed resort areas. Most travelers drink only bottled water, which also helps to protect against unfamiliar bacteria. In resort areas, and generally throughout Mexico, only purified ice is used. If you do get sick, nothing beats Pepto Bismol, readily available in Mexico. Imodium is also available in Mexico and is used by many travelers for a quick fix. A good high-potency (or "therapeutic") vitamin supplement and even extra vitamin C can help; yogurt is good for healthy digestion.

Since dehydration can quickly become life-threatening, the Public Health Service advises that you be careful to replace fluids and electrolytes (potassium, sodium, and the like) during a bout of diarrhea. Drink Pedialyte, a rehydration solution available at most Mexican pharmacies, or natural fruit juice, such as guava or apple (stay away from orange juice, which has laxative properties), with a pinch of salt added.

Prevention: The U.S. Public Health Service recommends the following measures for preventing travelers' diarrhea: **Drink only purified water** (boiled water, canned or bottled beverages, beer, or wine). **Choose food carefully.** In general, avoid salads (except in first-class restaurants), uncooked vegetables, undercooked protein, and unpasteurized milk or milk products, including cheese. Choose food that is freshly cooked and still hot. In addition, something as simple as **clean hands** can go a long way toward preventing *turista*.

for medical costs outside the U.S. Before leaving home, find out what medical services your health insurance covers. To protect yourself, consider buying medical travel insurance (see "Medical Insurance," under "Travel Insurance," above).

Very few health insurance plans pay for medical evacuation back to the U.S. (which can cost $10,000 and up). A number of companies offer medical evacuation services anywhere in the world. If you're ever hospitalized more than 150 miles from home, **Medjet Assist** (© **800/527-7478;** www.medjetassistance.com) will pick you up and fly you to the hospital of your choice virtually anywhere in the world in a medically equipped and staffed aircraft 24 hours day, 7 days a week. Annual memberships are $225 individual, $350 family; you can also purchase short-term memberships.

Hospitals and **emergency numbers** are listed under the "Fast Facts" section in this chapter and in chapters 2, 5, and 6.

If you suffer from a chronic illness, consult your doctor before your departure. Pack **prescription medications** in your carry-on luggage, and carry them in their original containers, with pharmacy labels—otherwise they won't make it through airport security. Carry the generic name of prescription medicines, in case a local pharmacist is unfamiliar with the brand name.

EMERGENCY CARE   Puerto Vallarta has a modern, U.S.-standards health care facility that offers insured care. **Ameri-Med,** Plaza Neptuno, in Marina Vallarta (© **322/221-0023;** fax 322/221-0026; www.amerimed-hospitals.com), provides complete, 24-hour, emergency health care adhering to U.S. medical standards. Facilities include CAT scan, radiology, ultrasound, and emergency air-evacuation services. Prices are in line with the standard of care, meaning that it's more costly than other medical facilities in Mexico.

For extreme medical emergencies, a service from the United States will fly people to American hospitals: **Global Lifeline** (© **800/ 831-9307,** or 01-800/305-9400 in Mexico) is a 24-hour air ambulance. Several other companies offer air-evacuation service; for a list

---

Over-the-Counter Drugs

Antibiotics and other drugs that you'd need a prescription to buy in the States are available over the counter in Mexican pharmacies. Mexican pharmacies also carry a limited selection of common over-the-counter cold, sinus, and allergy remedies.

refer to the U.S. State Department website at http://travel.state.gov/medical.html.

9 Safety

You will probably feel physically safer in most Mexican cities and villages than in any comparable place at home. However, crime in Mexico has received attention in the North American press over the past several years. Many feel this unfairly exaggerates the real dangers, but note that crime rates, including taxi robberies, kidnappings, and highway carjackings, have risen. The most severe crime problems were concentrated in Mexico City, far away from the Mexican Riviera; however, Guadalajara has experienced an increase in street crime.

The crime rate is, on the whole, much lower in Mexico than in most parts of the United States, and the nature of crimes in general is less violent. Random, violent, or serial crime is essentially unheard of in Mexico. You are much more likely to meet kind and helpful Mexicans than you are to encounter those set on thievery and deceit. A good rule of thumb is that you can generally trust people whom you approach for help, assistance, or directions—but be wary of anyone who approaches you offering the same. The more insistent they are, the more cautious you should be.

BRIBES & SCAMS

As is the case around the world, there are the occasional bribes and scams in Mexico, targeted at people believed to be naive—such as the telltale tourist. For years Mexico was known as a place where bribes—called *mordidas* (bites)—were expected; however, the country is rapidly changing. Frequently, offering a bribe today, especially to a police officer, is considered an insult, and it can land you in deeper trouble.

If you believe a **bribe** is being requested, here are a few tips on dealing with the situation. Even if you speak Spanish, don't utter a word of it to Mexican officials. That way you'll appear innocent, all the while understanding every word.

When you are crossing the border, should the person who inspects your car ask for a tip, you can ignore the request—but understand that the official may decide to thoroughly search your belongings. If faced with a situation where you feel you're being asked for a *propina* (literally, "tip"; colloquially, "bribe"), how much should you offer? Usually $3 to $5 or the equivalent in pesos will do the trick. Many tourists have the impression that everything works better in Mexico if you "tip"; however, in reality, this only perpetuates the *mordida* attitude. If you are pleased with a service, feel free to tip, but you shouldn't tip simply to attempt to get away with something illegal or inappropriate, whether it is crossing the border without having your car inspected or not getting a ticket that's deserved.

Whatever you do, **avoid impoliteness;** under no circumstances should you insult a Latin American official. Extreme politeness, even in the face of adversity, rules Mexico. In Mexico, *gringos* have a reputation for being loud and demanding. By adopting the local custom of excessive courtesy, you'll have greater success in negotiations of any kind. Stand your ground, but do it politely.

In Mexico, you may encounter several types of **scams,** which are typical throughout the world. One involves some kind of a **distraction** or feigned commotion. While your attention is diverted, a pickpocket makes a grab for your wallet. In another common scam, an **unaccompanied child** pretends to be lost and frightened and takes your hand for safety. Meanwhile the child or an accomplice plunders your pockets. A third involves **confusing currency.** A shoeshine boy, street musician, guide, or other individual might offer you a service for a price that seems reasonable—in pesos. When it comes time to pay, he or she tells you the price is in dollars, not pesos. Be very clear on the price and currency when services are involved.

10 Specialized Travel Resources

FAMILY TRAVEL

Children are considered the national treasure of Mexico, and Mexicans will welcome and cater to them. Many parents were reluctant to bring young children into Mexico in the past, primarily due to health concerns, but there can hardly be a better place to introduce children to the adventure of exploring a different culture than Mexico. Puerto Vallarta is among the best destinations for traveling with little ones.

Hotels can often arrange for a babysitter. Some hotels in the moderate-to-luxury range even have small playgrounds and pools for children, and hire caretakers with special activity programs during the day. Few budget hotels offer these amenities.

Before leaving, ask your doctor which medications to take along. Disposable diapers cost about the same in Mexico but are of poorer quality. You can get high-quality brands, but at a higher price. Many stores sell Gerber's baby foods. Dry cereals, powdered formulas, baby bottles, and purified water are easily available in midsize and large cities or resorts.

Only the largest, most luxurious hotels provide cribs, but roll-away beds are often available. Child seats or high chairs at restaurants are common, but bring your own car seat; they are not readily available for rent in Mexico.

Children traveling abroad should have plenty of documentation on hand, particularly if they're traveling with someone other than their own parents (in which case a notarized form letter from a parent is often required). For details on entry requirements for children traveling to Mexico, see p. 5.

Throughout this book, the "Kids" icon distinguishes attractions, hotels, restaurants, and other destinations that are particularly attractive and accommodating to children and families.

Familyhostel (© **800/733-9753**; www.familytravelnetwork. com) takes the whole family, including kids ages 8 to 15, on moderately priced domestic and international learning vacations. Lectures, field trips, and sightseeing are guided by a team of academics.

Recommended family travel websites include **Family Travel Forum** (www.familytravelforum.com), a comprehensive site that offers customized trip planning; **Family Travel Network** (www.familytravelnetwork.com), an online magazine providing travel tips; **TravelWithYourKids.com** (www.travelwithyourkids.com), a comprehensive site written by parents for parents offering sound advice for long-distance and international travel with children.

GAY & LESBIAN TRAVELERS

Mexico is a conservative country, with deeply rooted Catholic religious traditions. As such, public displays of same-sex affection are rare and still considered shocking for men, especially outside of urban or resort areas. Women in Mexico frequently walk hand in hand, but anything more would cross the boundary of acceptability. However, gay and lesbian travelers are generally treated with respect and should not experience any harassment, assuming the appropriate regard is given to local culture and customs.

Puerto Vallarta is perhaps the most welcoming and accepting destination in Mexico. Susan Weisman's travel service **Bayside Properties** (© **322/223-4424**; www.baysidepropertiespv.com) rents gay-friendly condos, villas, and hotels for individuals and large groups.

Her services are customized to individual needs, and she can offer airport pickups and in-villa cooks.

The **International Gay and Lesbian Travel Association (IGLTA;** © **800/448-8550** or 954/776-2626; www.iglta.org) is the trade association for the gay and lesbian travel industry, and offers an online directory of gay- and lesbian-friendly travel businesses and tour operators.

Many agencies offer tours and travel itineraries specifically for gay and lesbian travelers. **Above and Beyond Tours** (© **800/397-2681;** www.abovebeyondtours.com) are gay Australia tour specialists. San Francisco–based **Now, Voyager** (© **800/255-6951;** www.nowvoyager. com) offers worldwide trips and cruises. **Olivia** (© **800/631-6277;** www.olivia.com) offers lesbian cruises and resort vacations.

Gay.com Travel (© **800/929-2268** or 415/644-8044; www.gay. com/travel or www.outandabout.com) is an excellent online successor to the popular *Out & About* print magazine. It provides regularly updated information about gay-owned, gay-oriented, and gay-friendly lodging, dining, sightseeing, nightlife, and shopping establishments in every important destination worldwide. British travelers should click on the "Travel" link at **www.uk.gay.com** for advice and gay-friendly trip ideas.

The Canadian website **GayTraveler** (www.gaytraveler.ca) offers ideas and advice for gay travel all over the world.

The following travel guides are available at many bookstores, or you can order them from any online bookseller: *Spartacus International Gay Guide, 35th Edition* (Bruno Gmünder Verlag; www.spartacusworld.com/gayguide) and *Odysseus: The International Gay Travel Planner, 17th Edition* (www.odyusa.com); and the *Damron* guides (www.damron.com), with separate, annual books for gay men and lesbians.

TRAVELERS WITH DISABILITIES

Mexico may seem like one giant obstacle course to travelers in wheelchairs or on crutches. At airports, you may encounter steep stairs before finding a well-hidden elevator or escalator—if one exists. Airlines will often arrange wheelchair assistance to the baggage area. Porters are generally available to help with luggage at airports and large bus stations, once you've cleared baggage claim.

Mexican airports are upgrading their services, but it is not uncommon to board from a remote position, meaning you either descend stairs to a bus that ferries you to the plane, which you board by climbing stairs, or you walk across the tarmac to your plane and ascend the stairs. Deplaning presents the same problem in reverse.

Escalators (and there aren't many in the country) are often out of order. Stairs without handrails abound. Few restrooms are equipped for travelers with disabilities; when one is available, access to it may be through a narrow passage that won't accommodate a wheelchair or a person on crutches. Many deluxe hotels (the most expensive) now have rooms with bathrooms for people with disabilities. Those traveling on a budget should stick with one-story hotels or hotels with elevators. Even so, there will probably still be obstacles somewhere. Generally speaking, no matter where you are, someone will lend a hand, although you may have to ask for it.

One exception is Puerto Vallarta, which has recently renovated the majority of its downtown sidewalks and plazas with ramps to accommodate wheelchairs (and baby strollers). Even the airport has ramps adjacent to stairways, and special wheelchair lifts. A local citizen with disabilities deserves the credit for this impressive task—setting the stage for greater accessibility in other towns and resorts.

Most disabilities shouldn't stop anyone from traveling. There are more options and resources out there than ever before.

Organizations offering a vast range of resources and assistance to travelers with disabilities include **MossRehab** (℅ **800/CALL-MOSS;** www.mossresourcenet.org); the **American Foundation for the Blind (AFB;** ℅ **800/232-5463;** www.afb.org); and **SATH (Society for Accessible Travel & Hospitality;** ℅ **212/447-7284;** www.sath.org). **AirAmbulanceCard.com** is now partnered with SATH and allows you to preselect top-notch hospitals in case of an emergency.

Access-Able Travel Source (℅ **303/232-2979;** www.access-able.com) offers a comprehensive database on travel agents from around the world with experience in accessible travel; destination-specific access information; and links to such resources as service animals, equipment rentals, and access guides.

Many travel agencies offer customized tours and itineraries for travelers with disabilities. Among them are **Flying Wheels Travel** (℅ **507/451-5005;** www.flyingwheelstravel.com); and **Accessible Journeys** (℅ **800/846-4537** or 610/521-0339; www.disability travel.com).

Flying with Disability (www.flying-with-disability.org) is a comprehensive information source on airplane travel. **Avis Rent a Car** (℅ **888/879-4273**) has an "Avis Access" program that offers services for customers with special travel needs. These include specially outfitted vehicles with swivel seats, spinner knobs, and hand controls; mobility scooter rentals; and accessible bus service. Be sure to reserve well in advance.

Also check out the quarterly magazine *Emerging Horizons* (www.emerginghorizons.com), available by subscription ($16.95 year U.S.; $21.95 outside U.S.).

The "Accessible Travel" link at **Mobility-Advisor.com** (www.mobility-advisor.com) offers a variety of travel resources to persons with disabilities.

British travelers should contact **Holiday Care** (② 0845-124-9971 in the U.K. only; www.holidaycare.org.uk) to access a wide range of travel information and resources for elderly people and those with disabilities.

SENIOR TRAVEL

Mexico is popular with retirees, and some of the most popular places for long-term stays are Puerto Vallarta and Guadalajara. For decades, North Americans have been living indefinitely in Mexico by returning to the border and recrossing with a new tourist permit every 6 months. Mexican immigration officials have caught on, and now limit the maximum time in the country to 6 months per year. This is to encourage even partial residents to acquire proper documentation.

AIM, Apdo Postal 31–70, 45050 Guadalajara, Jal., is a well-written, informative newsletter for prospective retirees. Issues have evaluated retirement in Aguascalientes, Puebla, San Cristóbal de las Casas, Puerto Ángel, Puerto Escondido and Huatulco, Oaxaca, Taxco, Tepic, Manzanillo, Melaque, and Barra de Navidad. Subscriptions are $18 to the United States and $21 to Canada. Back issues are three for $5.

Sanborn Tours, 2015 S. 10th St., Post Office Drawer 519, McAllen, TX 78505-0519 (② **800/395-8482;** www.sanborns.com), offers a "Retire in Mexico" orientation tour.

Mention that you're a senior when you make reservations. Most major U.S. airlines have canceled their senior discounts and coupon books, but many hotels still offer senior discounts.

Members of **AARP** (formerly known as the American Association of Retired Persons), 601 E St. NW, Washington, D.C. 20049 (② **888/687-2277;** www.aarp.org), get discounts on hotels, airfares, and car rentals. AARP offers members a wide range of benefits, including *AARP: The Magazine* and a monthly newsletter. Anyone over 50 can join.

Many reliable agencies and organizations target the 50-plus market. **Elderhostel** (② **800/454-5768;** www.elderhostel.org) arranges worldwide study programs for those age 55 and over. **ElderTreks** (② **800/741-7956** or 416/558-5000 outside North America; www. eldertreks.com) offers small-group tours to off-the-beaten-path or adventure-travel locations, restricted to travelers 50 and older.

Recommended publications offering travel resources and discounts for seniors include: the quarterly magazine *Travel 50 & Beyond* (www.travel50andbeyond.com) and the bestselling paperback *Unbelievably Good Deals and Great Adventures That You Absolutely Can't Get Unless You're Over 50 2005–2006, 16th Edition* (McGraw-Hill), by Joann Rattner Heilman.

SINGLE TRAVELERS

Mexico may be an old favorite for romantic honeymoons, but it's also a great place to travel on your own without really being or feeling alone. Although many Mexican hotels are starting to offer the same rates for single or double occupancies, many of the establishments in this book still offer singles at lower rates.

Mexicans are very friendly, and it's easy to meet other foreigners. But if you don't like the idea of traveling alone, then try **Travel Companion Exchange** (TCE; ② **631/454-0880;** www.travel companions.com), one of the nation's oldest roommate finders for single travelers. Register with them and find a travel mate who will split the cost of the room with you and be around as little, or as often, as you like during the day.

On package vacations, single travelers are often hit with a "single supplement" to the base price. To avoid it, you can agree to room with other single travelers or find a compatible roommate before you go, from one of the many roommate-locator agencies.

For more information, check out Eleanor Berman's classic *Traveling Solo: Advice and Ideas for More Than 250 Great Vacations, 5th Edition* (Globe Pequot), updated in 2005.

WOMEN TRAVELERS

Women traveling alone may find they feel safer traveling in Mexico than in some parts of the United States. However, *always* use the same common-sense precautions you would use anywhere else in the world and remain alert to what's going on around you.

Tips Special-Interest Trips

Culinary Adventures, 6023 Reid Dr. NW, Gig Harbor, WA 98335 (© **253/851-7676;** fax 253/851-9532; www.marilyn tausend.com), offers a short but special list of cooking tours of particular regions in Mexico known for excellent cuisine, and featuring well-known cooks. The owner, Marilyn Tausend, is the co-author of *Mexico the Beautiful Cookbook,* and *Cocinas de la Familia (Family Kitchens).*

Trek America, P.O. Box 189, Rockaway, NJ 07866 (© **800/ 221-0596** or 973/983-1144; fax 973/983-8551; www.trek america.com), organizes lengthy, active trips that combine trekking, hiking, van transportation, and camping in Mexico's Pacific coast, Guadalajara, and other destinations.

Mexicans in general, and men in particular, are nosy about single travelers, especially women. If a taxi driver or anyone else with whom you don't want to become friendly asks about your marital status, family, and so forth, some good advice is to make up a set of answers (regardless of the truth): "I'm married, traveling with friends, and I have three children." Saying you are single and traveling alone may send the wrong message. U.S. television—widely viewed now in Mexico—has given many Mexican men the image of American single women as being sexually promiscuous.

For more reading material, check out the award-winning website **Journeywoman** (www.journeywoman.com), a "real life" women's travel-information network where you can sign up for a free e-mail newsletter and get advice on everything from etiquette and dress to safety. The travel guide *Safety and Security for Women Who Travel* by Sheila Swan and Peter Laufer (Travelers' Tales Guides), offering common-sense tips on safe travel, was updated in 2004.

11 Sustainable Tourism/Ecotourism

The diverse geography of the Mexican Riviera and its wealth of eco- and adventure-tour options have made it a natural favorite of travelers interested in ecotourism.

For hands-on activities with local sealife while in Puerto Vallarta, consider **Open Air Expeditions** (p. 91), and **Dolphin Adventure** (p. 98). Hiking, boating, snorkeling, and scuba diving are all popular activities in Puerto Vallarta and the nearby resorts.

AMTAVE (Asociación Mexicana de Turismo de Aventura y Eco-turismo, A.C.) is an active association in Mexico of eco- and adventure-tour operators. They publish an annual catalog of participating firms and their offerings, all of which must meet certain criteria for security, and for quality and training of the guides, as well as for sustainability of natural and cultural environments. For more information, contact AMTAVE (℡ **800/509-7678; www.amtave.org**).

Each time you take a flight or drive a car CO_2 is released into the atmosphere. You can help neutralize this danger to our planet through "carbon offsetting"—paying someone to reduce your CO_2 emissions by the same amount you've added. Carbon offsets can be purchased in the U.S. from companies such as **Carbonfund.org** (www.carbonfund.org) and **TerraPass** (www.terrapass.org), and from **Climate Care** (www.climatecare.org) in the U.K.

Although one could argue that any vacation that includes an airplane flight can't be truly "green," you can go on holiday and still contribute positively to the environment. You can offset carbon emissions from your flight in other ways. Choose forward-looking companies that embrace responsible development practices, helping preserve destinations for the future by working alongside local people. An increasing number of sustainable tourism initiatives can help you plan a family trip and leave as small a "footprint" as possible on the places you visit.

Responsible Travel (www.responsibletravel.com) contains a great source of sustainable travel ideas run by a spokesperson for responsible tourism in the travel industry. **Sustainable Travel International** (www.sustainabletravelinternational.org) promotes responsible tourism practices and issues an annual Green Gear & Gift Guide.

You can find ecofriendly travel tips, statistics, and touring companies and associations—listed by destination under "Travel Choice"—at the TIES website, www.ecotourism.org. Also check out **Conservation International** (www.conservation.org)—which, with *National Geographic Traveler,* annually presents **World Legacy Awards** (www.wlaward.org) to those travel tour operators, businesses, organizations, and places that have made a significant contribution to sustainable tourism. **Ecotravel.com** is part online magazine and part ecodirectory that lets you search for touring companies in several categories (water-based, land-based, spiritually oriented, and so on).

In the U.K., **Tourism Concern** (www.tourismconcern.org.uk) works to reduce social and environmental problems connected to tourism and find ways of improving tourism so that local benefits are increased.

Frommers.com: The Complete Travel Resource

It should go without saying, but we highly recommend **Frommers.com**, voted Best Travel Site by *PC Magazine*. We think you'll find our expert advice and tips; independent reviews of hotels, restaurants, attractions, and preferred shopping and nightlife venues; vacation giveaways; and an online booking tool indispensable before, during, and after your travels. We publish the complete contents of over 128 travel guides in our **Destinations** section covering nearly 3,600 places worldwide to help you plan your trip. Each weekday, we publish original articles reporting on **Deals and News** via our free **Frommers.com Newsletter** to help you save time and money and travel smarter. We're betting you'll find our new **Events** listings (http://events.frommers.com) an invaluable resource; it's an up-to-the-minute roster of what's happening in cities everywhere—including concerts, festivals, lectures and more. We've also added weekly **Podcasts, interactive maps,** and hundreds of new images across the site. Check out our **Travel Talk** area featuring **Message Boards** where you can join in conversations with thousands of fellow Frommer's travelers and post your trip report once you return.

The **Association of British Travel Agents** (**ABTA;** www.abtamembers.org/responsibletourism) acts as a focal point for the U.K. travel industry and is one of the leading groups spearheading responsible tourism.

The **Association of Independent Tour Operators** (**AITO;** www.aito.co.uk) is a group of interesting specialist operators leading the field in making holidays sustainable.

For information about the ethics of swimming with dolphins and other outdoor activities, visit the **Whale and Dolphin Conservation Society** (www.wdcs.org) and **Tread Lightly** (www.treadlightly.org).

12 Staying Connected

TELEPHONES

Mexico's telephone system is slowly but surely catching up with modern times. All telephone numbers have 10 digits. Every city and town that has telephone access has a two-digit (Mexico City, Monterrey, and Guadalajara) or three-digit (everywhere else) area code. In Mexico City, Monterrey, and Guadalajara, local numbers have eight digits; elsewhere, local numbers have seven digits.

To place a local call, you do not need to dial the area code. Many fax numbers are also regular telephone numbers; ask whoever answers for the fax tone *("me da tono de fax, por favor")*.

Cellular phones are very popular for small businesses in resort areas and smaller communities. To call a cellular number inside the same area code, dial 044 and then the number. To dial the cellular phone from anywhere else in Mexico, dial 045, and then the three-digit area code and the seven-digit number.

To dial it from the U.S., dial 011-52-1, plus the three-digit area code and the seven-digit number.

To call Mexico:

1. Dial the international access code: 011 from the U.S.; 00 from the U.K., Ireland, or New Zealand; or 0011 from Australia.
2. Dial the country code 52.
3. Dial the two- or three-digit area code, then the eight- or nine-digit number. For example, to call the U.S. consulate in Acapulco, the whole number would be 011-52-744-469-0556. If you wanted to dial the U.S. embassy in Mexico City, the whole number would be 011-52-55-5209-9100.

To make international calls: To make international calls from Mexico, first dial 00 and then the country code (U.S. or Canada 1, U.K. 44, Ireland 353, Australia 61, New Zealand 64). Next dial the area code and number. For example, if you wanted to call the British Embassy in Washington, D.C., you would dial 00-1-202-588-7800.

For directory assistance: Dial 040 if you're looking for a number inside Mexico. *Note:* Often, listings of smaller businesses or restaurants appear under the owner's name, not the name of the business, and your chances of finding an English-speaking operator are slim to none.

For operator assistance: If you need operator assistance in making a call, dial 090 if you're trying to make an international call and 020 if you want to call a number in Mexico.

Toll-free numbers: Numbers beginning with 800 in Mexico are toll-free, but calling a U.S. toll-free number from Mexico costs the same as an overseas call. To call an 800 number in the U.S., dial 001-880 and the last seven digits of the toll-free number. To call an 888 number in the U.S., dial 001-881 and the last seven digits. For a number with an 887 prefix, dial 882; for 866, dial 883.

CELLPHONES

The three letters that define much of the world's wireless capabilities are **GSM** (Global System for Mobile Communications), a big, seamless network that makes for easy cross-border cellphone use throughout Europe and dozens of other countries worldwide. In the U.S., T-Mobile, AT&T Wireless, and Cingular use this quasi-universal system; in Canada, Microcell and some Rogers customers are GSM, and all Europeans and most Australians use GSM. GSM phones function with a removable plastic SIM card, encoded with your phone number and account information. If your cellphone is on a GSM system, and you have a world-capable multiband phone such as many Sony Ericsson, Motorola, or Samsung models, you can make and receive calls across civilized areas around much of the globe. Just call your wireless operator and ask for "international roaming" to be activated on your account, but be sure to ask about the applicable fees, as per-minute charges can be expensive.

For many, **renting** a phone is a good idea. While you can rent a phone from any number of overseas sites, including kiosks at airports and at car-rental agencies, we suggest renting the phone before you leave home. North Americans can rent one before leaving home from **InTouch USA** (© 800/872-7626; www.intouchglobal.com) or **RoadPost** (© 888/290-1606 or 905/272-5665; www.road post.com). InTouch will also, for free, advise you on whether your existing phone will work overseas; simply call © 703/222-7161 between 9am and 4pm EST, or go to **http://intouchglobal. com/travel.htm**.

Buying a phone can be economically attractive, as many nations have cheap prepaid phone systems. Once you arrive at your destination, stop by a local cellphone shop and get the cheapest package; you'll probably pay less than $100 (£56) for a phone and a starter calling card. Local calls may be as low as 10¢ per minute, and in many countries incoming calls are free.

VOICE-OVER INERNET PROTOCOL (VOIP)

If you have web access while traveling, you might consider a broadband-based telephone service (in technical terms, **Voice over Internet protocol,** or **VoIP**) such as Skype (www.skype.com) or Vonage (www.vonage.com), which allows you to make free international calls if you use their services from your laptop or in a cybercafe. Check the websites for details, restrictions, and fees.

INTERNET/E-MAIL
WITHOUT YOUR OWN COMPUTER

To find cybercafes in your destination check **www.cybercaptive. com** and **www.cybercafe.com**. In each of the specific destinations covered in this book, we list recommended Internet cafes, which are common in Mexico's Pacific coastal resorts.

Most major airports have **Internet kiosks** that provide Web access for a per-minute fee that's usually higher than cybercafe prices.

WITH YOUR OWN COMPUTER

More and more hotels, resorts, airports, cafes, and retailers are going **Wi-Fi** (wireless fidelity), becoming "hotspots" that offer free high-speed Wi-Fi access or charge a small fee for usage. Most laptops sold today have built-in wireless capability. To find public Wi-Fi hotspots at your destination, go to **www.jiwire.com**; its Hotspot Finder holds the world's largest directory of public wireless hotspots.

For dial-up access, many hotels in Mexico now offer high-speed Internet access for free, or a nominal daily charge.

Wherever you go, bring a **connection kit** of the right power and phone adapters, a spare phone cord, and a spare Ethernet network cable—or find out whether your hotel supplies them to guests.

Online Traveler's Toolbox

Veteran travelers usually carry some essential items to make their trips easier. Following is a selection of handy online tools to bookmark and use.

- **Airplane Food** (www.airlinemeals.net)
- **Airplane Seating** (www.seatguru.com; and www.airline quality.com)
- **Foreign Languages for Travelers** (www.travlang.com)
- **Maps** (www.mapquest.com)
- **Travel Warnings** (http://travel.state.gov, www.fco.gov. uk/travel, www.voyage.gc.ca, or www.dfat.gov.au/ consular/advice)
- **Universal Currency Converter** (www.xe.com/ucc)
- **Visa ATM Locator** (www.visa.com), **MasterCard ATM Locator** (www.mastercard.com)
- **Weather** (www.intellicast.com; and www.weather.com)

13 Packages for the Independent Traveler

Package tours are simply a way to buy the airfare, accommodations, and other elements of your trip (such as car rentals, airport transfers, and sometimes even activities) at the same time and often at discounted prices.

You can buy a package at any time of the year, but the best deals usually coincide with high season—from mid-December to April—when demand is at its peak, and companies are more confident about filling planes. You might think that package rates would be better during low season, when room rates and airfares plunge. But the key is air access, which is much easier during the winter. Packages vary widely, with some companies offering a better class of hotels than others. Some offer the same hotels for lower prices. Some offer flights on scheduled airlines, while others book charters. In some packages, your choices of accommodations and travel days may be limited. Each destination usually has some packagers that are better than the rest because they buy in even bigger bulk. Not only can that mean better prices, but it can also mean more choices.

One good source of package deals is the airlines themselves. Those offering packages to Mexico are listed below, in Recommended Packagers. Several big **online travel agencies**—Expedia, Travelocity, Orbitz, and Lastminute.com—also do a brisk business in packages.

Travel packages are also listed in the travel section of your local Sunday newspaper. Or check ads in national travel magazines such as *Arthur Frommer's Budget Travel Magazine, Travel & Leisure, National Geographic Traveler,* and *Condé Nast Traveler.*

WHERE TO BROWSE
- One specialist in Mexico vacation packages is **www.mexico travelnet.com**, an agency that offers most of the well-known travel packages to Mexico beach resorts, plus offers last-minute specials.
- Check out **www.2travel.com** and find the page with links to a number of the big-name Mexico packagers, including several of those listed here.
- For last-minute air-only or package bargains, check out **Vacation Hot Line** (www.vacationhotline.net). Once you find your deal, you'll need to call to make booking arrangements. This service offers packages from the popular Apple and Funjet vacation wholesalers.

RECOMMENDED PACKAGERS

- **Aeromexico Vacations** (℃ 800/245-8585; www.aeromexico. com) offers year-round packages to almost every destination it serves, including Puerto Vallarta. Aeromexico has a large (more than 100) selection of resorts in these destinations and more, in a variety of price ranges. The best deals are from Houston, Dallas, San Diego, Los Angeles, Miami, and New York, in that order.

- **Alaska Airlines Vacations** (℃ 800/468-2248; www.alaskaair. com) sells packages to Manzanillo/Costa Alegre and Puerto Vallarta. Alaska flies direct from Los Angeles, San Diego, San Jose, San Francisco, Seattle, Vancouver, Anchorage, and Fairbanks. The website publishes discounts that are not available through the phone operators.

- **American Airlines Vacations** (℃ 800/321-2121; www.aa vacations.com) has year-round deals to Guadalajara and Puerto Vallarta. You don't have to fly with American if you can get a better deal on another airline; land-only packages include hotel, hotel tax, and airport transfers. American's hubs to Mexico are Dallas/Fort Worth, Chicago, and Miami. The website offers unpublished discounts not available through the operators.

- **Apple Vacations** (℃ 800/517-2000; www.applevacations. com) offers inclusive packages to all the beach resorts, and has the largest choice of hotels in Manzanillo and Puerto Vallarta. Scheduled carriers for the air portion include American, United, Mexicana, Delta, US Airways, Reno Air, Alaska Airlines, Aero California, and Aeromexico. Apple perks include baggage handling and the services of a company representative at major hotels.

- **Classic Custom Vacations** (℃ 800/635-1333; www.classic customvacations.com) specializes in package vacations to Mexico's finest luxury resorts. It combines discounted first-class and economy airfare on American, Continental, Mexicana, Alaska, America West, and Delta with stays at the most exclusive hotels in Guadalajara, Puerto Vallarta, and Manzanillo. In many cases, packages also include meals, airport transfers, and upgrades. The prices are not for bargain hunters but for those who seek luxury, nicely packaged.

- **Continental Vacations** (℃ 800/301-3800; www.covacations. com) has year-round packages to Puerto Vallarta and Guadalajara. The best deals are from Houston; Newark, N.J.; and Cleveland. You must fly Continental. The Internet deals offer savings not available elsewhere.

- **Funjet Vacations** (book through any travel agent; www.fun jet.com for general information) is one of the largest vacation packagers in the United States. Funjet has packages to Puerto Vallarta. You can choose a charter or fly on American, Continental, Delta, Aeromexico, US Airways, Alaska Air, or United.
- **GOGO Worldwide Vacations** (© 888/636-3942; www.gogo wwv.com) has trips to all the major beach destinations, including Puerto Vallarta. It offers several exclusive deals from higher-end hotels. Book through any travel agent.
- **Mexicana Vacations,** or MexSeaSun Vacations (© 800/531-9321; www.mexicana.com) offers getaways to all the resorts. Mexicana operates daily direct flights from Los Angeles to Puerto Vallarta and Manzanillo.
- **Pleasant Mexico Holidays** (© 800/742-9244; www.pleasant holidays.com) is one of the largest vacation packagers in the United States, with hotels in Puerto Vallarta and other destinations.

REGIONAL PACKAGERS

From the East Coast: Liberty Travel (© 888/271-1584; www. libertytravel.com), one of the biggest packagers in the Northeast, often runs a full-page ad in the Sunday papers, with frequent Mexico specials. You won't get much in the way of service, but you will get a good deal.

From the West: Suntrips (© 800/514-5194 for departures within 14 days; www.suntrips.com) is one of the largest West Coast packagers for Mexico, with departures from San Francisco and Denver; regular charters to Puerto Vallarta and other destinations; and a large selection of hotels.

From the Southwest: Town and Country (book through travel agents) packages regular deals to Puerto Vallarta, Manzanillo, and other destinations with America West from the airline's Phoenix and Las Vegas gateways.

Resort Packages: The biggest hotel chains and resorts also sell packages. To take advantage of these offers, contact your travel agent or call the hotels directly.

14 Getting Around

If you decide to visit this region, you will have several choices about how to allot your time. Most people pick one coastal resort and stay there for the duration of their vacation, but, if you wish, you can easily enjoy more than one resort during your time in Mexico.

An important note: If your travel schedule depends on a vital connection—say, a plane trip or a ferry or bus connection—use the telephone numbers in this book or other resources to find out if the connection is still available. Don't assume that it is, even if you used it 2 years ago.

BY PLANE

To fly from point to point within Mexico, rely on Mexican airlines. Mexico has two large, privately owned national carriers: **Mexicana** (✆ **800/366-5400**) and **Aeromexico** (✆ **800/021-4000**), in addition to a new crop of low-cost regional carriers. Mexicana and Aeromexico both offer extensive connections to the United States as well as within Mexico.

New private and semi-private Mexican airlines include **Avolar** (✆ 866/370-4065; www.avolar.com.mx), **ABC Interjet** (✆ 01-800/011-2345; www.interjet.com.mx) and **Volaris** (✆ 01-800/7VOLARIS; www.volaris.com.mx), as well as Mexicana Airline's carrier **Click Mexicana** (✆ 01-800/112-5425; clickmx.com), which have all launched low-cost flights to different parts of Mexico. U.S.-based customers can also purchase tickets on Click through www.mexicana.com. **Aladia** (www.aladia.com), one of Mexico's newest airlines, offers flights between Cancún, Merida, Puebla and Vail, Colorado, and combines air service with special travel packages.

Of Mexico's low-fare airlines, Click serves the most cities, followed by Avolar (17), Interjet (7), and Volaris (5). For the most part, passengers are primarily Mexican nationals attracted by cheaper fares and better connections than those offered on the older carriers. So far, booking can be a challenge, as most websites are in Spanish only, and it is sometimes difficult to find an English-speaking agent. Also, prices are generally given only in pesos. Travelers accustomed to getting around on Mexican buses, however, may prefer this new travel option. In an effort to avoid the congestion at Mexico City Airport, three of the new low-cost carriers are based at Toluca Airport, which is about 40 minutes from Mexico City. Toluca Airport is in the process of a renovation and expansion to accommodate these additional flights.

Several of the new regional carriers are operated by or can be booked through Mexicana or Aeromexico. Regional carriers are **Aerocaribe** and **Aero Mar** (see Mexicana), or **Aerolitoral** (see Aeromexico), and are expensive, but they go to places that are difficult to reach. In each applicable section of this book, we mention regional carriers, with all pertinent telephone numbers.

Because major airlines can book some regional carriers, read your ticket carefully to see if your connecting flight is on one of these smaller carriers. They may leave from a different airport or check in at a different counter; this may be especially true in Guadalajara.

AIRPORT TAXES   Mexico charges an airport tax on all departures. Taxes on each domestic departure within Mexico are around $13 (£7), unless you're on a connecting flight and have already paid at the start of the flight.

Mexico charges an $18 (£10) "tourism tax," the proceeds of which go into a tourism promotional fund. Your ticket price may not include it, so be sure to have enough money to pay it at the airport upon departure.

RECONFIRMING FLIGHTS   Although Mexican airlines say it's not necessary to reconfirm a flight, it's still a good idea. To avoid getting bumped on popular, possibly overbooked flights, check in for an international flight 1½ hours in advance of travel.

BY CAR

Most Mexican roads are not up to U.S. standards of smoothness, hardness, width of curve, grade of hill, or safety markings. Driving at night is dangerous—the roads are rarely lit; trucks, carts, pedestrians, and bicycles usually have no lights; and you can hit potholes, animals, rocks, dead ends, or uncrossable bridges without warning.

The spirited style of Mexican driving sometimes requires super vision and reflexes. Be prepared for new customs, as when a truck driver flips on his left turn signal when there's not a crossroad for miles. He's probably telling you the road's clear ahead for you to pass. Another custom that's very important to respect is turning left. Never turn left by stopping in the middle of a highway with your left signal on. Instead, pull onto the right shoulder, wait for traffic to clear, then proceed across the road.

GASOLINE   There's one government-owned brand of gas and one gasoline station name throughout the country—**Pemex** (Petroleras Mexicanas). There are two types of gas in Mexico: *magna,* 87-octane unleaded gas, and *premium* 93 octane. In Mexico, fuel and oil are sold by the liter (which is slightly more than a quart: 40 liters equals about 11 gal.). Many franchise Pemex stations have bathroom facilities and convenience stores—a great improvement over the old ones. *Important note:* No credit cards are currently accepted for gas purchases.

TOLL ROADS   Mexico charges some of the highest tolls in the world for its network of new toll roads; as a result, they are rarely used. Generally speaking, though, using toll roads cuts travel time. Older toll-free roads are generally in good condition, but travel times tend to be longer.

BREAKDOWNS   If your car breaks down, help might already be on the way. Radio-equipped green repair trucks operated by uniformed English-speaking officers patrol major highways during daylight hours. These **"Green Angels"** perform minor repairs and adjustments free, but you pay for parts and materials.

Your best guide to repair shops is the Yellow Pages. For repairs, look under *Automóviles y Camiones: Talleres de Reparación y Servicio;* auto-parts stores are under *Refacciones y Accesorios para Automóviles.* To find a mechanic on the road, look for a sign that says TALLER MECANICO.

Places called *vulcanizadora* or *llantera* repair flat tires, and it is common to find them open 24 hours a day on the most traveled highways.

MINOR ACCIDENTS   When possible, many Mexicans drive away from minor accidents, or try to make an immediate settlement, to avoid involving the police. If the police arrive while the involved persons are still at the scene, everyone may be locked in jail until blame is assessed. In any case, you have to settle up immediately, which may take days. Foreigners who don't speak fluent Spanish are at a distinct disadvantage when trying to explain their version of the event. Three steps may help the foreigner who doesn't wish to do as the Mexicans do: If you were in your own car, notify your Mexican insurance company, whose job it is to intervene on your behalf. If you were in a rental car, notify the rental company immediately and ask how to contact the nearest adjuster. (You did buy insurance with the rental, right?) Finally, if all else fails, ask to contact the nearest Green Angel, who may be able to explain to officials that you are covered by insurance. See also "Mexican Auto Insurance" in "Getting There," earlier in this chapter.

RENTING A CAR

You'll get the best price if you reserve a car at least a week in advance in the United States. U.S. car-rental firms include **Advantage** (© 800/777-5500 in the U.S. and Canada; www.arac.com), **Avis** (© 800/331-1212 in the U.S., in Canada; www.avis.com), **Budget** (© 800/527-0700 in the U.S. and Canada; www.budget.com), **Hertz**

(℃ 800/654-3030 in the U.S. and Canada; www.hertz.com), **National** (℃ 800/CAR-RENT in the U.S. and Canada; www.nation alcar.com), and **Thrifty** (℃ 800/THRIFTY in the U.S. and Canada; www.thrifty.com), which often offers discounts for rentals in Mexico. For European travelers, **Kemwel Holiday Auto** (℃ 800/678-0678; www.kemwel.com) and **Auto Europe** (℃ 800/223-5555; www. autoeurope.com) can arrange Mexican rentals, sometimes through other agencies. These and some local firms have offices in Mexico City and most other large Mexican cities. You'll find rental desks at airports, all major hotels, and many travel agencies.

Cars are easy to rent if you are 25 years old or older and have a major credit card, valid driver's license, and passport with you. Without a credit card you must leave a cash deposit, usually a big one. One-way rentals are usually simple to arrange but more costly.

Car-rental costs are high in Mexico because cars are more expensive. The condition of rental cars has improved greatly over the years, and clean new cars are the norm. The basic cost of the 1-day rental of a Volkswagen Beetle at press time, with unlimited mileage (but before 15% tax and $15/£8 daily insurance), was $52 (£29) in Mexico City, and $44 (£24) in Puerto Vallarta. Renting by the week gives you a lower daily rate. Avis was offering a basic 7-day rate for a VW Beetle (before tax or insurance) of $220 (£122) in Puerto Vallarta, and $250 (£139) in Mexico City. Prices may be considerably higher if you rent around a major holiday. Also double-check charges for insurance—some companies will increase the insurance rate after several days. Always ask for detailed information about all charges you will be responsible for. Car-rental companies usually write credit card charges in U.S. dollars.

Deductibles   Be careful—these vary greatly; some are as high as $2,500 (£1,389), which comes out of your pocket immediately in case of damage. On a VW Beetle, Hertz's deductible is $1,000 (£556) and Avis's is $500 (£278).

Emergency Number   It's advisable to note the rental company's emergency number, as well as the direct number of the agency where you rented the car.

Insurance   Insurance is offered in two parts: **Collision and damage** insurance covers your car and others if the accident is your fault, and **personal accident** insurance covers you and anyone in your car. Read the fine print on the back of your rental agreement and note that insurance may be invalid if you have an accident while driving on an unpaved road.

Damage   Always inspect your car carefully and note every damaged or missing item, no matter how minute, on your rental agreement, or you may be charged.

BY TAXI

Taxis are the preferred way to get around almost all of the resort areas of Mexico, and also within Guadalajara. Short trips within towns are generally charged by preset zones, and are quite reasonable compared with U.S. rates. For longer trips or excursions to nearby cities, taxis can generally be hired for around $15 to $25 (£8–£14) per hour, or for a negotiated daily rate. Even drops to different destinations, say between Puerto Vallarta and Barra de Navidad, can be arranged. A negotiated one-way price is usually much less than the cost of a rental car for a day, and service is much faster than traveling by bus. For anyone who is uncomfortable driving in Mexico, this is a convenient, comfortable way to go. An added bonus is that you have a Spanish-speaking person with you in case you run into any car or road trouble. Many taxi drivers speak at least some English. Your hotel can assist you with the arrangements.

BY BUS

Mexican buses run frequently, are readily accessible, and can get you to almost anywhere you want to go. They're often the only way to get from large cities to other nearby cities and small villages. Don't hesitate to ask questions if you're confused about anything, but note that little English is spoken in bus stations.

Dozens of Mexican companies operate large, air-conditioned, Greyhound-type buses between most cities. Classes are *segunda* (second), *primera* (first), and *ejecutiva* (deluxe), which goes by a variety of names. Deluxe buses often have fewer seats than regular buses, show video movies, are air-conditioned, and make few stops. Many run express from point to point. They are well worth the few dollars more. In rural areas, buses are often of the school-bus variety, with lots of local color.

Whenever possible, it's best to buy your reserved-seat ticket, often using a computerized system, a day in advance on long-distance routes and especially before holidays. See the appendix for a list of helpful bus terms in Spanish.

15 Tips on Accommodations

MEXICO'S HOTEL RATING SYSTEM

The hotel rating system in Mexico is called "Stars and Diamonds." Hotels may qualify to earn one to five stars, or five diamonds. Many hotels that have excellent standards are not certified, but all rated hotels adhere to strict standards. The guidelines relate to service, facilities, and hygiene more than to prices.

Five-diamond hotels meet the highest requirements for rating: The beds are comfortable, bathrooms are in excellent working order, all facilities are renovated regularly, infrastructure is top-tier, and services and hygiene meet the highest international standards.

Five-star hotels usually offer similar quality, but with lower levels of service and detail in the rooms. For example, a five-star hotel may have less-luxurious linens, or perhaps room service during limited hours rather than 24 hours.

Four-star hotels are less expensive and more basic, but they still guarantee cleanliness and basic services such as hot water and purified drinking water. Three-, two-, and one-star hotels are at least working to adhere to certain standards: Bathrooms are cleaned and linens are washed daily, and you can expect a minimum standard of service. Two- and one-star hotels generally provide bottled water rather than purified water.

The nonprofit organization Calidad Mexicana Certificada, A.C., known as **Calmecac** (www.calmecac.com.mx), is responsible for hotel ratings.

HOTEL CHAINS

In addition to the major international chains, you'll run across a number of less-familiar brands in Mexico. They include:

- **Brisas Hotels & Resorts** (www.brisas.com.mx). These were the hotels that originally attracted jet-set travelers to Mexico. Spectacular in a retro way, these properties offer the laid-back luxury that makes a Mexican vacation so unique.
- **Fiesta Americana** and **Fiesta Inn** (www.posadas.com). Part of the Mexican-owned Grupo Posadas company, these hotels set the country's midrange standard for facilities and services. They generally offer comfortable, spacious rooms and traditional Mexican hospitality. Fiesta Americana hotels offer excellent beach-resort packages. Fiesta Inn hotels are usually more business oriented. Grupo Posadas also owns the more luxurious Caesar Park hotels and the eco-oriented Explorean hotels.

- **Hoteles Camino Real** (www.caminoreal.com). The premier Mexican hotel chain, Camino Real maintains a high standard of service at its properties, all of which carry five stars (see "Mexico's Hotel Rating System," above). Its beach hotels are traditionally located on the best beaches in the area. This chain also focuses on the business market. The hotels are famous for their vivid and contrasting colors.

- **Hoteles Krystal NH** (www.nh-krystal.mexico-hoteles.com). Grupo Chartwell recently acquired this family-owned chain. The hotels are noted for their family-friendly facilities and five-star standards. The beach properties' signature feature is a pool, framed by columns, overlooking the sea.

- **Quinta Real Grand Class Hotels and Resorts** (www. quintareal.com). These hotels, owned by Summit Hotels and Resorts, are noted for architectural and cultural details that reflect their individual regions. At these luxury properties, attention to detail and excellent service are the rule.

HOUSE & VILLAS RENTALS

House and villa rentals and swaps are becoming more common in Mexico, but no single recognized agency or business provides this service exclusively for Mexico. In the chapters that follow, we have provided information on independent services that we have found to be reputable.

With regard to general online services, the most extensive inventory of homes is found at **VRBO (Vacation Rentals by Owner;** www.vrbo.com). They have over 33,000 homes and condominiums worldwide, including a large selection in Mexico. Another good option is **VacationSpot** (www.vacationspot.com), owned by Expedia, and a part of its sister company, Hotels.com. It has fewer

---

Finds Out-of-the-Ordinary Places to Stay

Mexico lends itself beautifully to the concept of small, private hotels in idyllic settings. They vary in style from grandiose estates to palm-thatched bungalows. **Mexico Boutique Hotels** (www.MexicoBoutiqueHotels.com) specializes in smaller places to stay with a high level of personal attention and service. Most options have less than 50 rooms, and the accommodations consist of entire villas, *casitas,* bungalows, or a combination.

choices, but the company's criteria for adding inventory is much more selective, and often includes onsite inspections. They also offer toll-free phone support.

SURFING FOR HOTELS

In addition to the online travel booking sites **Travelocity, Expedia, Orbitz, Priceline,** and **Hotwire,** you can book hotels through **Hotels.com; Quikbook** (www.quikbook.com); and **Travelaxe** (www.travelaxe.net).

HotelChatter.com is a daily webzine offering smart coverage and critiques of hotels worldwide. Go to **TripAdvisor.com** or **Hotel Shark.com** for helpful independent consumer reviews of hotels and resort properties. It's a good idea to **get a confirmation number** and **make a printout** of any online booking transaction.

Booking a room online in Mexico is easy when dealing with the major hotel chains, but for independent and smaller hotels, it's likely you'll arrange your reservation via e-mail.

16 Tips on Dining

MEALTIMES

MORNING The morning meal, known as *el desayuno,* can be something light, such as coffee and sweet bread, or something more substantial: eggs, beans, tortillas, bread, fruit, and juice. It can be eaten early or late and is always a sure bet in Mexico. The variety and sweetness of the fruits is remarkable, and you can't go wrong with Mexican egg dishes.

MIDAFTERNOON The main meal of the day, known as *la comida* (or *el almuerzo*), is eaten between 2 and 4pm. Stores and businesses often close, and many people go home to eat and perhaps take a short afternoon siesta before going about their business. The first course is the *sopa,* which can be either *caldo* (soup) or *sopa de arroz* (rice) or both; then comes the main course, which ideally is a meat or fish dish prepared in some kind of sauce and served with beans, followed by dessert.

EVENING Between 8 and 10pm, most Mexicans have a light meal called *la cena.* If eaten at home, it is something like a sandwich, bread and jam, or perhaps tacos made from some of the day's leftovers. At restaurants, the most common thing to eat is *antojitos* (literally, "little cravings"), a general label for light fare. Antojitos include tostadas, tamales, tacos, and simple enchiladas, and are big hits with travelers. Large restaurants offer complete meals as well.

DINING OUT

Avoid eating at those inviting sidewalk restaurants that you see beneath the stone archways that border the main plazas. These places usually cater to tourists and don't need to count on getting any return business. But they are great for getting a coffee or beer.

For the main meal of the day many restaurants offer a multi-course blue-plate special called *comida corrida* or *menú del día.* This is the least expensive way to get a full dinner.

In Mexico, you need to ask for your check; it is generally considered inhospitable to present a check to someone who hasn't requested it. If you're in a hurry to get somewhere, ask for the check when your food arrives.

Tips are about the same as in the United States. You'll sometimes find a 15% **value-added tax** on restaurant meals, which shows up on the bill as "IVA." This is a boon to arithmetically challenged tippers, saving them from undue exertion.

To summon the waiter, wave or raise your hand, but don't motion with your index finger, which is a demeaning gesture that may even cause the waiter to ignore you. Or if it's the check you want, you can motion to the waiter from across the room using the universal pretend-you're-writing gesture.

Most restaurants do not have **nonsmoking sections;** when they do, we mention it in the reviews. But Mexico's wonderful climate allows for many open-air restaurants, usually set inside a courtyard of a colonial house, or in rooms with tall ceilings and open windows.

FAST FACTS: Mexico

Abbreviations Dept. (apartments); Apdo. (post office box); Av. (*avenida;* avenue); c/ (*calle;* street); Calz. (*calzada;* boulevard). "C" on faucets stands for *caliente* (hot), "F" for *fría* (cold). "PB" *(planta baja)* means ground floor; in most buildings the next floor up is the first floor (1).

Business Hours In general, businesses in larger cities are open between 9am and 7pm; in smaller towns many close between 2 and 4pm. Most close on Sunday. In resort areas it is common to find stores open at least in the mornings on Sunday, and for shops to stay open late, often until 8pm or even 10pm. Bank hours are Monday through Friday from 9 or

9:30am to anywhere between 3 and 7pm. Increasingly, banks open on Saturday for at least a half-day.

Cameras & Film Film costs about the same as in the United States. Tourists wishing to use a video or still camera at any archaeological site in Mexico or at many museums operated by the Instituto de Antropología e Historia (INAH) must pay $4 (£2) per camera at each site visited. (Listings for specific sites and museums note this fee.) Also, use of a tripod at any archaeological site requires a permit from INAH. It's courteous to ask permission before photographing anyone. It is never considered polite to take photos inside a church in Mexico. In some areas, there are other restrictions on photographing people and villages.

Car Rentals See "Getting Around," earlier in this chapter.

Climate See "When to Go," earlier in this chapter.

Currency See "Money," earlier in this chapter.

Customs **What You Can Bring Into Mexico**

When you enter Mexico, Customs officials will be tolerant as long as you have no illegal drugs or firearms. You're allowed to bring in two cartons of cigarettes or 50 cigars, plus 1 kilogram (2.2 lb.) of smoking tobacco; two 1-liter bottles of wine or hard liquor, and 12 rolls of film. A laptop computer, camera equipment, and sports equipment that could feasibly be used during your stay are also allowed. The underlying guideline is: Don't bring anything that looks as if it's meant to be resold in Mexico.

What You Can Take Home from Mexico

For specifics on what you can bring back to the U.S. and the corresponding fees, download the invaluable free pamphlet *Know Before You Go* online at **www.cbp.gov**. (Click on "Travel," and then click on "Know Before You Go! Online Brochure"). Or contact the **U.S. Customs & Border Protection (CBP),** 1300 Pennsylvania Ave., NW, Washington, DC 20229 (© **877/287-8667**) and request the pamphlet.

Returning **U.S. citizens** who have been away for at least 48 hours are allowed to bring back, once every 30 days, $800 worth of merchandise duty-free. You'll be charged a flat rate of 4% duty on the next $1,000 worth of purchases. Any dollar amount beyond that is dutiable at whatever rates apply. On mailed gifts, the duty-free limit is $200. Be sure to have your receipts or purchases handy to expedite the declaration process. *Note:* If you owe duty, you are required to pay on your arrival in the United States, by cash, personal check, government or traveler's check, or money order (and in some locations, a Visa or MasterCard).

To avoid having to pay duty on foreign-made personal items you owned before you left on your trip, bring along a bill of sale, insurance policy, jeweler's appraisal, or receipts of purchase. Or you can register items that can be readily identified by a permanently affixed serial number or marking—think laptop computers, cameras, and CD players—with Customs before you leave. Take the items to the nearest Customs office or register them with Customs at the airport from which you're departing. You'll receive, at no cost, a Certificate of Registration, which allows duty-free entry for the life of the item.

With some exceptions, you cannot bring fresh fruits and vegetables into the United States.

For a clear summary of **Canadian** rules, write for the booklet *I Declare,* issued by the **Canada Customs and Revenue Agency** (② **800/461-9999** in Canada, or 204/983-3500; www. cbsa-asfc.gc.ca). Canada allows its citizens a C$750 exemption, and you're allowed to bring back duty-free one carton of cigarettes, 1 can of tobacco, 40 imperial ounces of liquor, and 50 cigars. In addition, you're allowed to mail gifts to Canada valued at less than C$60 a day, provided they're unsolicited and don't contain alcohol or tobacco (write on the package "Unsolicited gift, under C$60 value"). All valuables should be declared on the Y-38 form before departure from Canada, including serial numbers of valuables you already own, such as expensive foreign cameras. *Note:* The C$750 exemption can only be used once a year and only after an absence of 7 days.

U.K. citizens returning from **a non-E.U. country** have a customs allowance of: 200 cigarettes; 50 cigars; 250 grams of smoking tobacco; 2 liters of still table wine; 1 liter of spirits or strong liqueurs (over 22% volume); 2 liters of fortified wine, sparkling wine, or other liqueurs; 60 cubic centimeters (ml) perfume; 250 cubic centimeters (ml) of toilet water; and £145 worth of all other goods, including gifts and souvenirs. People under 17 cannot have the tobacco or alcohol allowance. For more information, contact **HM Customs & Excise** at ② **0845/010-9000** (44-29/2050-1261 from outside the U.K.), or consult the website at www.hmce.gov.uk.

The duty-free allowance in **Australia** is A$900 or, for those under 18, A$ 450. Citizens can bring in 250 cigarettes or 250 grams of loose tobacco, and 2.25 liters of alcohol. If you're returning with valuables you already own, such as foreign-made cameras, you should file form B263. A helpful brochure available from Australian consulates or Customs offices is *Know Before You Go.* For more information, call the **Australian Customs Service** at (C) **1300/363-263,** or log on to www. customs.gov.au.

The duty-free allowance for **New Zealand** is NZ$700. Citizens over 17 can bring in 200 cigarettes, 50 cigars, or 250 grams of tobacco (or a mixture of all three if their combined weight doesn't exceed 250g); plus 4.5 liters of wine and beer, or 1.125 liters of liquor. New Zealand currency does not carry import or export restrictions. Fill out a certificate of export, listing the valuables you are taking out of the country; that way, you can bring them back without paying duty. Most questions are answered in a free pamphlet available at New Zealand consulates and Customs offices: *New Zealand Customs Guide for Travellers, Notice no. 4.* For more information, contact **New Zealand Customs,** The Customhouse, 17–21 Whitmore St., Box 2218, Wellington ((C) **04/473-6099** or 0800/428-786; www.customs.govt.nz).

Doctors & Dentists Every embassy and consulate can recommend local doctors and dentists with good training and modern equipment. See the list of embassies and consulates under "Embassies & Consulates," below. Hotels with a large foreign clientele can often recommend English-speaking doctors.

Drug Laws It may sound obvious, but don't use or possess illegal drugs in Mexico. Mexican officials have no tolerance for drug users, and jail is their solution, with very little chance of release until the sentence (usually a long one) is completed or heavy fines or bribes are paid. Remember, in Mexico the legal system assumes you are guilty until proven innocent. *Note:* It isn't uncommon to be befriended by a fellow user, only to be turned in by that "friend," who collects a bounty. Bring prescription drugs in their original containers. If possible, pack a copy of the original prescription with the generic name of the drug.

U.S. Customs officials are on the lookout for diet drugs that are sold in Mexico but illegal in the U.S. Possession could land you in a U.S. jail. If you buy antibiotics over the counter (which you can do in Mexico) and still have some left, U.S. Customs probably won't hassle you.

Drugstores Most pharmacies are open Monday through Saturday from 8am to 8pm. The major resort areas generally have one or two 24-hour pharmacies. Pharmacies take turns staying open during off hours; if you are in a smaller town and need to buy medicine during off hours, ask for the *farmacia de turno*.

Electricity The electrical system in Mexico is 110 volts AC (60 cycles), as in the United States and Canada. In reality, however, it may cycle more slowly and overheat your appliances. To compensate, select a medium or low speed on hair dryers. Many older hotels still have electrical outlets for flat two-prong plugs; you'll need an adapter for any plug with an enlarged end on one prong or with three prongs. Many better hotels have three-hole outlets *(trifásicos)*. Those that don't may have loan adapters, but to be sure, it's always better to carry your own.

Embassies & Consulates They provide valuable lists of doctors and lawyers, as well as regulations concerning marriages in Mexico. Contrary to popular belief, your embassy cannot get you out of jail, provide postal or banking services, or fly you home when you run out of money. Consular officers can provide advice on most matters and problems, however. Most countries have an embassy in Mexico City, and many have consular offices or representatives in the provinces.

The Embassy of the **United States** in Mexico City is at Paseo de la Reforma 305, next to the Hotel María Isabel Sheraton at the corner of Río Danubio (© **55/5080-2000** or 555/511-9980); hours are Monday through Friday from 8:30am to 5:30pm. Visit www.usembassy-mexico.gov for addresses of the U.S. consulates inside Mexico. There are U.S. Consulates General at López Mateos 924-N, Ciudad Juárez (© 656/611-3000); Progreso 175, Guadalajara (© 33/3268-2100); Av. Constitución 411 Pte., Monterrey (© 818/345-2120); and Tapachula 96, Tijuana (© 664/622-7400). In addition, there are consular agencies in Acapulco (© 744/469-0556); Cabo San Lucas (© 624/143-3566); Cancún (© 998/883-0272); Cozumel (© 987/872-4574); Hermosillo (© 662/289-3500); Ixtapa/Zihuatanejo (© 755/553-2100); Matamoros

(© 868/812-4402); Mazatlán (© 669/916-5889); Mérida (© 999/942-5700); Nogales (© 631/313-4820); Nuevo Laredo (© 867/714-0512); Oaxaca (© 951/514-3054); Puerto Vallarta (© 322/222-0069); San Luis Potosí (© 444/811-7802); and San Miguel de Allende (© 415/152-2357).

The Embassy of **Canada** in Mexico City is at Schiller 529, Col. Polanco (© **555/724-7900**); it's open Monday through Friday from 9am to 1pm. At other times, the name of a duty officer is posted on the door. Visit www.dfait-maeci.gc.ca for addresses of consular agencies in Mexico. There are Canadian consulates in Acapulco (© 744/484-1305); Cancún (© 998/883-3360); Guadalajara (© 333/615-6215); Mazatlán (© 669/913-7320); Monterrey (© 818/344-2753); Oaxaca (© 951/513-3777); Puerto Vallarta (© 322/293-0098); San José del Cabo (© 624/142-4333); and Tijuana (© 664/684-0461).

The Embassy of the **United Kingdom** in Mexico City is at Río Lerma 71, Col. Cuauhtémoc (© **55/5242-8500**; www.embajada britanica.com.mx). It's open Monday through Friday from 8:30am to 3:30pm.

The Embassy of **Ireland** in Mexico City is at Bulevar Cerrada, Avila Camacho 76, 3rd floor, Col. Lomas de Chapultepec (© **55/5520-5803**). It's open Monday through Friday from 9am to 5pm.

The Embassy of **Australia** in Mexico City is at Rubén Darío 55, Col. Polanco (© **55/51101-2200**). It's open Monday through Friday from 9am to 1pm.

The Embassy of **New Zealand** in Mexico City is at Jaime Balmes No.8, 4th floor, Col. Los Morales Polanco (© **55/5283-9460**; kiwimexico@compuserve.com.mx). It's open Monday through Friday from 8am to 3pm.

The **South African** Embassy in Mexico City is at Andrés Bello 10, 9th floor, Col. Polanco (© **55/5282-9260**). It's open Monday through Friday from 8am to 3:30pm.

Emergencies In case of emergency, dial © **065** from any phone within Mexico. For police emergency numbers, turn to "Fast Facts" in the chapters that follow. The 24-hour **Tourist Help Line** in Mexico City is © **01-800/903-9200** or 555/250-0151. The operators don't always speak English, but they are always willing to help. The tourist legal assistance office (Procuraduría del Turista) in Mexico City (© **555/625-8153** or 555/625-8154) always has an English speaker available. Though the phones are frequently busy, they operate 24 hours.

Language Spanish is the official language in Mexico. English is spoken and understood to some degree in most tourist areas. Mexicans are very accommodating with foreigners who try to speak Spanish, even in broken sentences. For basic vocabulary, refer to the appendix.

Legal Aid **International Legal Defense Counsel**, 111 S. 15th St., 24th floor, Packard Building, Philadelphia, PA 19102 (© **215/977-9982**), is a law firm specializing in legal difficulties of Americans abroad. See also "Embassies & Consulates," above.

Liquor Laws The legal drinking age in Mexico is 18; however, asking for ID or denying purchase is extremely rare. Grocery stores sell everything from beer and wine to national and imported liquors. You can buy liquor 24 hours a day, but during major elections, dry laws often are enacted for as much as 72 hours in advance of the election—and they apply to tourists as well as local residents. Mexico does not have laws that apply to transporting liquor in cars, but authorities are beginning to target drunk drivers more aggressively. It's a good idea to drive defensively.

It is not legal to drink in the street; however, many tourists do so. If you are getting drunk, you shouldn't drink in the street, because you are more likely to get stopped by the police.

Lost & Found To replace a **lost passport,** contact your embassy or nearest consular agent. You must establish a record of your citizenship and fill out a form requesting another FMT (tourist permit) if it, too, was lost. If your documents are stolen, get a police report from local authorities; having one *might* lessen the hassle of exiting the country without all your identification. Without the FMT, you can't leave the country, and without an affidavit affirming your passport request and citizenship, you may have problems at U.S. Customs when you get home. It's important to clear everything up *before* trying to leave. Mexican Customs may, however, accept the police report of the loss of the FMT and allow you to leave.

If you lose your **wallet** anywhere outside of Mexico City, before panicking, retrace your steps—you'll be surprised at how honest people are, and you'll likely find someone trying to find you to return your wallet.

If your wallet is stolen, the police probably won't be able to recover it. Be sure to notify all of your credit card companies right away, and file a report at the nearest police precinct. Your credit card company or insurer may require a police report number or record of the loss. Most credit card companies have an emergency toll-free number to call if your card is lost or stolen; these numbers are not toll-free within Mexico (see "Telephones" p. 32, for instructions on calling U.S. toll-free numbers). The company may be able to wire you a cash advance off your credit card immediately, and, in many places, can deliver an emergency credit card in a day or two. **Visa's** U.S. emergency number is ℂ **800/847-2911** or 410/581-9994. **American Express** cardholders and traveler's check holders should call ℂ **800/221-7282. MasterCard** holders should call ℂ **800/307-7309** or 636/722-7111. For other credit cards, call the toll-free number directory at ℂ **800/555-1212.**

If you need emergency cash over the weekend when all banks and American Express offices are closed, you can have money wired to you via **Western Union** (ℂ **800/325-6000;** www.westernunion.com).

Mail Postage for a postcard or letter is 1 peso; it may arrive anywhere from 1 to 6 weeks later. A registered letter costs $1.90 (£1). Sending a package can be quite expensive—the Mexican postal service charges $8 (£4) per kilo (2.2 lb.)—and is unreliable; it takes 2 to 6 weeks, if it arrives at all. The recommended way to send a package or important mail is through FedEx, DHL, UPS, or another reputable international mail service.

Passports **For Residents of the United States:** Whether you're applying in person or by mail, you can download passport applications from the U.S. State Department website at **www.travel.state.gov**. To find your regional passport office, either check the U.S. State Department website or call the **National Passport Information Center's** toll-free number (ℂ **877/487-2778**) for automated information.

For Residents of Canada: Passport applications are available at travel agencies throughout Canada or from the central Department of Foreign Affairs and International Trade, Ottawa, ON K1A 0G3 (ℂ **800/567-6868;** www.ppt.gc.ca).

For Residents of the United Kingdom: To pick up an application for a standard 10-year passport (5-year passport for children under 16), visit your nearest passport office, major post office, or travel agency or contact the **United Kingdom Passport Service** at ✆ **0870/521-0410** or search its website at www.ukpa.gov.uk.

For Residents of Ireland: You can apply for a 10-year passport at the **Passport Office,** Setanta Centre, Molesworth Street, Dublin 2 (✆ **01/671-1633;** www.irlgov.ie/iveagh). Those under age 18 and over 65 must apply for a €12 3-year passport. You can also apply at 1A South Mall, Cork (✆ **021/ 272-525)** or at most main post offices.

For Residents of Australia: You can pick up an application from your local post office or any branch of Passports Australia, but you must schedule an interview at the passport office to present your application materials. Call the **Australian Passport Information Service** at ✆ **131-232,** or visit the government website at www.passports.gov.au.

For Residents of New Zealand: You can pick up a passport application at any New Zealand Passports Office or download it from their website. Contact the **Passports Office** at ✆ **0800/ 225-050** in New Zealand or 04/474-8100, or log on to www. passports.govt.nz.

Pets Animals coming from the United States and Canada need to be checked for health within 30 days before arrival in Mexico. Most veterinarians in major cities have the appropriate paperwork—an official health certificate, to be presented to Mexican Customs officials, that ensures the pet's vaccinations are up-to-date. When you and your pet return from Mexico, U.S. Customs officials will require the same type of paperwork. If your stay extends beyond the 30-day time frame of your U.S.-issued certificate, you'll need an updated Certificate of Health issued by a veterinarian in Mexico. To check last-minute changes in requirements, consult the Mexican Government Tourist Office nearest you (see "Visitor Information," earlier in this chapter).

Police In Mexico City, police are to be suspected as frequently as they are to be trusted; however, you'll find many who are quite honest and helpful. In the rest of the country, especially in the tourist areas, most are very protective of international visitors. Several cities, including Puerto Vallarta, Mazatlán, Cancún, and Acapulco, have a special corps of English-speaking Tourist Police to assist with directions, guidance, and more.

Restrooms See "Toilets," below.

Smoking Smoking is permitted and generally accepted in most public places, including restaurants, bars, and hotel lobbies. Nonsmoking areas and hotel rooms for nonsmokers are becoming more common in higher-end establishments, but they tend to be the exception rather than the rule.

Taxes The 15% IVA (value-added) tax applies on goods and services in most of Mexico, and it's supposed to be included in the posted price. There is a 5% tax on food and drinks consumed in restaurants that sell alcoholic beverages with an alcohol content of more than 10%; this tax applies whether you drink alcohol or not. Tequila is subject to a 25% tax. Mexico imposes an exit tax of around $18 (£10) on every foreigner leaving the country.

Time Zone Central Time prevails throughout most of Mexico. The states of Sonora, Sinaloa, and parts of Nayarit are on Mountain Time. The state of Baja California Norte is on Pacific Time, but Baja California Sur is on Mountain Time. All of Mexico observes **daylight saving time.**

Tipping Most service employees in Mexico count on tips for the majority of their income, and this is especially true for bellboys and waiters. Bellboys should receive the equivalent of 50¢ to $1 per bag; waiters generally receive 10% to 20%, depending on the level of service. It is not customary to tip taxi drivers, unless they are hired by the hour or provide touring or other special services.

Toilets Public toilets are not common in Mexico, but an increasing number are available, especially at fast-food restaurants and Pemex gas stations. These facilities and restaurant and club restrooms commonly have attendants, who expect a small tip (about 50¢).

Water Most hotels have decanters or bottles of purified water in the rooms, and the better hotels have either purified water from regular taps or special taps marked *agua purificada.* Some hotels charge for in-room bottled water. Virtually any hotel, restaurant, or bar will bring you purified water if you request it but will usually charge you for it. Drugstores and grocery stores sell bottled purified water. Some popular brands are Santa María, Ciel, and Bonafont. Evian and other imported brands are also widely available.

2

Settling into Puerto Vallarta

By Lynne Bairstow

No matter how extensively I travel in Mexico, Puerto Vallarta remains my favorite part of this colorful country, for its unrivaled combination of simple pleasures and sophisticated charms. No other place in Mexico offers both the best of the country's natural beauty and an authentic dose of its vibrant culture.

Puerto Vallarta's seductive innocence captivates visitors, beckoning them to return—and to bring friends. Beyond the cobblestone streets, graceful cathedral, and welcoming atmosphere, Puerto Vallarta offers a wealth of natural beauty and man-made pleasures. Hotels of all classes and prices, over 250 restaurants, a sizzling nightlife, and enough shops and galleries to tempt even jaded consumers make this town a perennial favorite.

Vallarta (as locals refer to it) was never the "sleepy little fishing village" that many proclaim. It began life as a port for processing silver brought down from mines in the Sierra Madre—then was forever transformed by a movie director and two star-crossed lovers. In 1963, John Huston brought stars Ava Gardner and Richard Burton here to film the Tennessee Williams play *Night of the Iguaña.* Burton's new love, Elizabeth Taylor, came along to ensure the romance remained in full bloom—even though both were married to others at the time. Titillated, the international paparazzi arrived, and when they weren't shooting photos of the famous couple—or of Gardner water-skiing back from the set, surrounded by a bevy of beach boys—they photographed the beauty of Puerto Vallarta.

Luxury hotels and shopping centers have sprung up north and south of the original town, allowing Vallarta to grow into a city of 350,000 without sacrificing its considerable charms. It boasts the services and infrastructure—and, unfortunately now the traffic—of a modern city, while still retaining the authenticity of a colonial Mexican village.

Cool breezes flow down from the mountains along the Río Cuale, which runs through the center of town. Fanciful public sculptures grace the *malecón* (boardwalk), which is bordered by lively restaurants, shops, and nightclubs. The *malecón* is a magnet for both residents and visitors, who stroll the main walkway to take in an ocean breeze, a multihued sunset, or a moonlit, perfect wave.

If I sound partial, it's not just because Puerto Vallarta is my favorite of Mexico's sunny resorts; this has been my home for the past 16 years. I live here in good company—there's a considerable colony of American, Canadian, and European residents. Perhaps they feel as I do: that the surrounding mountains offer the equivalent of a continual, comforting embrace, adding to that sense of welcome that so many visitors feel as well.

1 Puerto Vallarta Essentials

885km (549 miles) NW of Mexico City; 339km (210 miles) W of Guadalajara; 285km (177 miles) NW of Manzanillo; 447km (277 miles) SE of Mazatlán; 239km (148 miles) SW of Tepic

GETTING THERE AND DEPARTING

BY PLANE　For a list of international carriers serving Mexico, see chapter 1. Local numbers of some international carriers serving Puerto Vallarta are **Alaska Airlines** (© 322/221-1350 or -1353), **American Airlines** (© 322/221-1799 or -1927), **America West** (© 322/221-1333,** or 001-880/235-9292 inside Mexico), **Continental** (© 322/221-1025 or -2212), **Frontier** (© 800/432-1359), and **Ted** (United's lower-cost carrier offers direct service from San Francisco and Denver; © 800/225-5833 in the U.S.).

AeroMéxico (© 322/221-1204 or -1030) flies from Los Angeles, San Diego, Aguascalientes, Guadalajara, La Paz, León, Mexico City, Morelia, and Tijuana. **Mexicana** (© 322/224-8900 or 221-1266) has direct or nonstop flights from Chicago, Los Angeles, Guadalajara, Mazatlán, and Mexico City.

Major car rental agencies have counters at the airport, including **Budget** (© 800/472-3325 in the U.S., or 322/221-1730), **Hertz** (© 322/221-1473 or -1399), **National** (© 322/221-1226), and **Alamo** (© 322/221-1228), open during flight arrivals; they generally can also deliver a car to your hotel. Daily rates run $58 to $78 (£32–£43). You need a car only if you plan to explore surrounding cities or are staying either along the southern coast, or north of Nuevo Vallarta.

Puerto Vallarta: Hotel Zone & Beaches

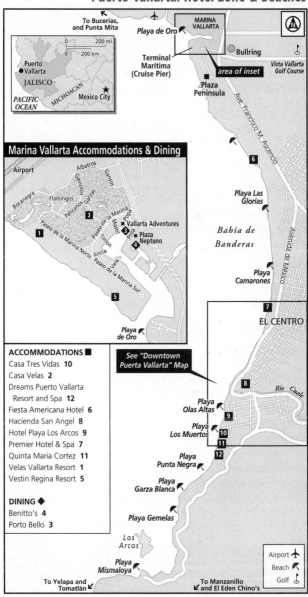

To Bucerias, and Punta Mita

Playa de Oro

MARINA VALLARTA

Terminal Marítima (Cruise Pier)

Bullring

area of inset

Vista Vallarta Golf Course

Plaza Peninsula

Ave. Francisco M. Ascencio

Marina Vallarta Accommodations & Dining

Airport

Albatros

Gaviotas

Gansos

Bocanegra

Pelicanos

Garzas

Flamingos

Paseo de la Marina

Paseo de la Marina Norte

Mastil

Popa

Proa

Timon

Ancla

Vela

Paseo de la Marina Sur

Vallarta Adventures

Plaza Neptuno

Playa de Oro

6

Playa Las Glorias

Bahía de Banderas

Avenida de México

Playa Camarones

7

EL CENTRO

See "Downtown Puerta Vallarta" Map

8

Rio Cuale

Playa Olas Altas

9

Playa Los Muertos

10

11

12

Playa Punta Negra

Playa Garza Blanca

Playa Gemelas

Los Arcos

Playa Mismaloya

To Yelapa and Tomatlán

To Manzanillo and El Eden Chino's

ACCOMMODATIONS ■
Casa Tres Vidas **10**
Casa Velas **2**
Dreams Puerto Vallarta
  Resort and Spa **12**
Fiesta Americana Hotel **6**
Hacienda San Angel **8**
Hotel Playa Los Arcos **9**
Premier Hotel & Spa **7**
Quinta Maria Cortez **11**
Velas Vallarta Resort **1**
Vestin Regina Resort **5**

DINING ◆
Benitto's **4**
Porto Bello **3**

Inset map (Mexico)
200 mi.
200 km.
Puerto Vallarta
JALISCO
MICHOACAN
PACIFIC OCEAN
Mexico City

Airport ✈
Beach
Golf

BY CAR   The coastal Highway 200 is the only choice from Mazatlán (6 hr. north) or Manzanillo (3½–4 hr. south). Highway 15 from Guadalajara to Tepic takes 6 hours; to save as much as 2 hours, take Highway 15A from Chapalilla to Compostela, bypassing Tepic, then continue south on Highway 200 to Puerto Vallarta.

BY BUS   The bus station, **Central Camionera de Puerto Vallarta,** is just north of the airport, approximately 11km (7 miles) from downtown. It offers overnight guarded parking and baggage storage. Most major first-class bus lines operate from here, with transportation to points throughout Mexico, including Mazatlán, Tepic, Manzanillo, Guadalajara, and Mexico City. Taxis into town cost approximately $7.50 (£4.15) and are readily available; public buses operate from 7am to 11pm and regularly stop in front of the arrivals hall.

ORIENTATION
ARRIVING BY PLANE   The airport is close to the north end of town near the Marina Vallarta, about 10km (6¼ miles) from downtown. **Transportes Terrestres** minivans and **Aeromovil** taxis make the trip. They use a zone pricing system, with fares clearly posted at the ticket booths. Fares start at $10 (£5.50) for a ride to Marina Vallarta and go up to $35 (£19) for the south shore hotels. Federally licensed airport taxis exclusively provide transportation from the airport, and their fares are more than three times as high as city (yellow) taxi fares. A trip to downtown Puerto Vallarta costs $22 (£12), whereas a return trip using a city taxi costs only $8 (£4.40). Only airport cabs may pick up passengers leaving the airport. However, if you don't have too much baggage, you can cross the highway using the overpass, where you'll find yellow cabs lined up. Note that when you arrive at the International Arrivals gate, after you collect your baggage, you enter into an enclosed area with colorful wall displays and an aggressive group of seemingly helpful greeters; beware— these are timeshare hustlers, and their goal, often in the guise of offering you free or discounted transportation, is to get you to attend a timeshare presentation. Keep walking—just outside this booth are the bona fide taxi and transportation alternatives.

VISITOR INFORMATION   Prior to arrival, a great source of general information is the **Puerto Vallarta Tourism Board** (© 888/ 384-6822 in the U.S.; www.visitpuertovallarta.com). If you have questions after you arrive, visit the **Municipal Tourism Office** at Juárez and Independencia (© 322/223-2500, ext. 230) in a corner of the white Presidencia Municipal building (city hall) on the northwest end of the main square. In addition to offering a listing of current events and promotional brochures for local activities and services, the employees can also assist with specific questions—there's usually an English speaker on staff. This is also the office of the tourist police. It's open Monday through Friday from 8am to 9pm. During low season it may close for lunch between 2 and 4pm.

The **State Tourism Office,** Plaza Marina L 144, second floor (© **322/221-2676,** -2677, or -2678; fax 322/221-2680), also offers brochures and can assist with specific questions about Puerto Vallarta and other points in the state of Jalisco, including Guadalajara, Costa Alegre, the town of Tequila, and the program that promotes stays in authentic rural haciendas. It's open Monday through Friday from 9am to 5pm.

CITY LAYOUT   The seaside promenade, the *malecón,* is a common reference point for giving directions. It's next to **Paseo Díaz Ordaz** and runs north-south through the central downtown area. From the waterfront, the town stretches back into the hills a half-dozen blocks. The areas bordering the **Río Cuale** are the oldest parts of town—the original Puerto Vallarta. The area immediately south of the river, called **Olas Altas** after its main street (and sometimes Los Muertos after the beach of the same name), is home to a growing selection of sidewalk cafes, fine restaurants, espresso bars, and hip nightclubs. In the center of town, nearly everything is within walking distance both north and south of the river. **Bridges** on Insurgentes (northbound traffic) and Ignacio Vallarta (southbound traffic) link the two sections of downtown.

AREA LAYOUT   Beyond downtown, Puerto Vallarta has grown along the beach to the north and south. Linking downtown to the airport is **Avenida Francisco Medina Ascencio.** Along this main thoroughfare are many high-rise hotels (in an area called the **Zona Hotelera,** or Hotel Zone), plus several shopping centers with a variety of dining options.

Marina Vallarta, a resort city within a city, is at the northern edge of the Hotel Zone not far from the airport. It boasts modern luxury hotels, condominiums, and homes; a huge marina with 450 yacht slips; a golf course; restaurants and bars; and several shopping plazas. Because it was originally a swamp, the beaches are the least desirable in the area, with darker sand and seasonal inflows of cobblestones. The Marina Vallarta peninsula faces the bay and looks south to the town of Puerto Vallarta.

Nuevo Vallarta is a booming planned resort north of the airport, across the Ameca River in the state of Nayarit (about 13km/8 miles north of downtown). It also has hotels, condominiums, and a yacht marina, with a growing selection of restaurants and shopping, including the new Paradise Plaza mall. Most hotels there are all-inclusive, with some of the finest beaches in the bay, but guests usually travel into Puerto Vallarta (about $15/£8.25 a cab ride) for anything other than poolside or beach action. Regularly scheduled public bus service costs about $1.50 (85p) and runs until 10pm.

Bucerías, a small beachside village of cobblestone streets, villas, and small hotels, is farther north along Banderas Bay, 30km (19 miles) beyond the airport. Past Bucerías, following the curved coastline of Banderas Bay you'll find La Cruz de Huanaxcle, site of a new mega-marina project currently under construction, but still a charming seaside town with *mucho* local color. Continue on to the end of the road and you'll reach **Punta Mita.** Once a rustic fishing village, it has been artfully developed as a luxury destination. In the works are a total of three exclusive luxury boutique resorts, private villas, and two golf courses. The site of an ancient celestial observatory, it is an exquisite setting, with white-sand beaches and clear waters. The northern shore of Banderas Bay is emerging as the area's most exclusive address for luxury villas and accommodations.

In the other direction from downtown is the southern coastal highway, home to more luxury hotels. Immediately south of town lies the exclusive residential and rental district of **Conchas Chinas.** Ten kilometers (6 miles) south, on **Playa Mismaloya** (where *Night of the Iguana* was filmed), lies the Barceló La Jolla de Mismaloya resort. There's no road on the southern shoreline of Banderas Bay, but three small coastal villages are popular attractions for visitors to Puerto Vallarta: **Las Animas, Quimixto,** and **Yelapa,** all accessible only by boat. The tiny, pristine cove of **Caletas,** site of John Huston's former home, is a popular day- or nighttime excursion (see "Boat Tours," in chapter 3).

GETTING AROUND

BY TAXI   Taxis are plentiful and relatively inexpensive. Most trips from downtown to the northern Hotel Zone and Marina Vallarta cost $4 to $9 (£4.40–£4.95); to or from Marina Vallarta to Mismaloya Beach (to the south) costs $12 to $15 (£6.60–£8.25). Rates are charged by zone and are generally posted in the lobbies of hotels. Taxis can also be hired by the hour or day for longer trips. Rates run

Tips Don't Let Taxi Drivers Steer You Wrong

Beware of restaurant recommendations offered by taxi drivers—many receive a commission from restaurants where they discharge passengers. Be especially wary if a driver tries to talk you out of a restaurant you've already selected.

$15 to $18 (£8.25–£9.90) per hour, with discounts available for full-day rates—consider this an alternative to renting a car.

BY CAR   Rental cars are readily available at the airport, through travel agencies, and through the most popular U.S. car rental services, but unless you're planning a distant side trip, don't bother. Car rentals are expensive, averaging $66 (£36) per day, and parking around town is very challenging, unless you opt for one of the two new parking garages constructed on either end of the *malecón* zone (at Park Hidalgo to the north, and adjacent to the northern border of the Cuale River to the south). If you see a sign for a $10 (£5.50) Jeep rental or $20 (£11) car rental, be aware that these are lures to get people to attend timeshare presentations. Unless you are interested in a timeshare, stopping to inquire will be a waste of your time.

BY BUS   City buses, easy to navigate and inexpensive, will serve just about all your transportation needs. They run from the airport through the Hotel Zone along Morelos Street (1 block inland from the *malecón*), across the Río Cuale, and inland on Vallarta, looping back through the downtown hotel and restaurant districts on Insurgentes and several other downtown streets. To get to the northern hotel strip from old Puerto Vallarta, take the ZONA HOTELES, IXTAPA, or LAS JUNTAS bus. These buses may also post the names of hotels they pass, such as Krystal, Fiesta Americana, Sheraton, and others. Buses marked MARINA VALLARTA travel inside this area, stopping at the major hotels there.

Other buses operate every 10 to 15 minutes south to either Mismaloya Beach or Boca de Tomatlán (a sign in the front window indicates the destination) from Constitución and Basilio Badillo, a few blocks south of the river.

Buses run generally from 6am to 11pm, and it's rare to wait more than a few minutes for one. The fare is about 50¢ (30p). You do not have to have exact change; the driver will make change.

Tips **Steer Clear of the Rambo Bus!**

Buses in Vallarta tend to be rather aggressive, and some even sport names—including "Terminator," "Rambo," and "Tornado." Don't tempt fate by assuming these buses will stop for pedestrians. Although Vallarta has an extremely low crime rate, bus accidents are frequent—and frequently fatal.

BY BOAT   The *muelle* (cruise-ship pier), also called Terminal Marítima, is where **excursion boats** to Yelapa, Las Animas, Quimixto, and the Marietas Islands depart. It's north of town near the airport, an inexpensive taxi or bus ride from town. Just take any bus marked IXTAPA, LAS JUNTAS, PITILLAL, or AURORA and tell the driver to let you off at the Terminal Marítima. *Note:* Odd though it may seem, you must pay a $1.50 (85p) fee (this is a federal tax) to gain access to the pier—and your departing excursion boat.

Water taxis to Yelapa, Las Animas, and Quimixto leave at 10:30 and 11am from the pier at Los Muertos Beach (south of downtown), on Rodolfo Rodríguez next to the Hotel Marsol. Another water taxi departs at 11am from the beachside pier at the northern edge of the *malecón*. A round-trip ticket to Yelapa (the farthest point) costs $25 (£14). Return trips usually depart between 3 and 4pm, but confirm the pickup time with your water taxi captain. Other water taxis depart from Boca de Tomatlán, about 30 minutes south of town by public bus. These water taxis are the better option if you want more flexible departure and return times from the southern beaches. Generally, they leave on the hour for the southern shore destinations, or more frequently if traffic is heavy. Prices run about $12 (£6.60) round-trip, with rates now clearly posted on a sign on the beach. A private water taxi costs $55 to $100 (£30–£55), depending on your destination, and allows you to choose your own return time. They'll take up to eight people for that price, so often people band together at the beach to hire one.

FAST FACTS: Puerto Vallarta

American Express The local office is at Morelos 660, at the corner of Abasolo (𝄍 **01-800/504-0400** and 01-800/333-3211 in Mexico, or 322/223-2955). It's open Monday through Friday from 9am to 6pm, Saturday from 9am to 1pm. It offers excellent, efficient travel agency services in addition to money exchange and traveler's checks.

Area Code The telephone area code is **322**.

Climate For information on the climate and weather, see chapter 1, "When to Go."

Consumer Assistance Tourists with complaints about taxis, stores, abusive timeshare presentations, or other matters should contact **PROFECO,** the consumer protection office (*©* 322/225-0000; fax 322/225-0018). The office is open Monday through Friday from 8:30am to 3:30pm and may not have fluent English-speaking staff.

Currency Exchange Banks are found throughout downtown and in the other prime shopping areas. Most banks are open Monday through Friday from 9am to 5pm, with shorter hours on Saturday. ATMs are common throughout Vallarta, including the central plaza downtown. They are becoming the most favorable way to exchange currency, with bank rates plus 24-hour convenience. *Casas de cambio* (money exchange houses), located throughout town, offer longer hours than the banks with only slightly lower exchange rates.

Drugstores **CMQ Farmacia,** Basilio Badillo 365 (*©* 22/222-1330), is open 24 hours and makes free deliveries to hotels between 11am and 10pm with a minimum purchase of $20 (£11). **Farmacias Guadalajara,** Emiliano Zapata 232 (*©* 322/224-1811), is also open 24 hours.

Embassies & Consulates The **U.S. Consular Agency** office (*©* 322/222-0069; fax 322/223-0074; 24 hr. a day for emergencies) is located in Nuevo Vallarta, in the Paradise Plaza, Local 1, on the street level between the plaza and the Paradise Village Yacht Club. It's open Monday through Friday from 10am to 2pm. The **Canadian Consulate** (*©* 322/293-0099 or -0098; 24-hr. emergency line 01-800/706-2900 in Mexico) is located in Plaza Las Glorias, 1951 Blvd. Francisco Medina Ascencio, Edificio Obelisco, Loc. 108 (you'll see the Canadian flag hanging from the balcony). It's open Monday through Friday from 9am to 3pm.

Emergencies **Police** emergency, *©* **060**; local police, *©* 322/290-0513 or -0512; intensive care **ambulance,** *©* 322/225-0386 (*Note:* English-speaking assistance is not always available at this number); **Cruz Roja (Red Cross),** ℂ **322/222-1533; Global Life Ambulance Service** (provides both ground and air ambulance service), ℂ **322/226-1010,** ext. 304.

Hospitals The following offer U.S.-standards service and are available 24 hours: **Ameri-Med Urgent Care,** Avenida Francisco Medina Ascencio at Plaza Neptuno, Loc. D-1, Marina Vallarta (ℂ **322/221-0023;** fax 322/221-0026; www.amerimed-hospitals. com); **San Javier Marina Hospital,** Av. Francisco Medina Ascencio 2760, Zona Hotelera (ℂ **322/226-1010**), and **Cornerstone Hospital,** Av. los Tules 136 (behind Plaza Caracol; ℂ **322/ 224-9400**).

Internet Access Puerto Vallarta is probably the most wired destination in Mexico. Recommended is **Café.com** (ℂ **322/ 222-0092**), Olas Altas 250, at the corner of Basilio Badillo; it charges $2 (£1.10) for 30 minutes. It offers complete computer services, a full bar, and food service. It's open daily from 8am to 2am. Some hotels have lobby e-mail kiosks, but they're more expensive than the Net cafes.

Newspapers & Magazines *Vallarta Today,* a daily English-language newspaper (ℂ **322/225-3323** or 224-2829), is a good source for local information and upcoming events. The bilingual quarterly city magazine *Vallarta Lifestyles* (ℂ **322/221-0106**) is also very popular. Both are for sale at area newsstands and hotel gift shops. The weekly English-language *P.V. Tribune* (ℂ **322/223-0585**) is distributed free throughout town and offers an objective local viewpoint.

Post Office The *correo* is at Colombia Street, behind Hidalgo park, and is open Monday through Friday from 9am to 6pm, Saturday from 9am to 1pm.

Safety Puerto Vallarta enjoys a very low crime rate. Public transportation is safe to use, and Tourist Police (dressed in white safari uniforms with white hats) are available to answer questions, give directions, and offer assistance. Most encounters with the police are linked to using or purchasing drugs—so don't (see "Fast Facts," chapter 1). *Note:* The tourist police conduct random personal searches for drugs. Although there is some question about their right to do this, the best course of action if they want to frisk you is to comply—objecting will likely result in a free tour of the local jail. However, you are within your rights to request the name of the officer. Report any unusual incidents to the local consular office.

2 Where to Stay

Beyond a varied selection of hotels and resorts, Puerto Vallarta offers many alternative accommodations. Oceanfront or marina-view condominiums and elegant private villas can offer families and small groups a better value and more ample space than a hotel. For more information on short-term rentals, check out **www.costavallarta boutiquevillas.com**. Prices start at $99 (£54) a night for non-beachside condos and go to $3,000 (£1,650) for penthouse condos or private villas. Susan Weisman's **Bayside Properties,** Francisco Rodríguez 160, corner of Olas Altas (© **322/223-4424** and 222-8148; www.baysidepropertiespv.com), rents condos, villas, and hotels for individuals and large groups, including gay-friendly accommodations. She can arrange airport pickup and in-villa cooks. Another reputable option is the full-service travel agency, **Holland's** (© **415/841-1194** or 888/8672723; www.puertovallartavillas. com). For the ultimate, indulge in a Punta Mita Villa rental within this exclusive resort. Contact **Mita Residential** (© **877/561-2893** in the U.S., or 329/291-5300; www.mitaresidential.com).

This section lists hotels in directional order, moving south along Banderas Bay from the airport.

MARINA VALLARTA

Marina Vallarta is the most modern and deluxe area of hotel development in Puerto Vallarta. Located immediately south of the airport and just north of the cruise-ship terminal, it's a planned development whose centerpiece is a 450-slip modern marina.

The hotels reviewed below are on the beachfront of the peninsula. The beaches here are much less attractive than beaches in other parts of the bay; the sand is darker, firmly packed, and, during certain times of the year, quite rocky. These hotels compensate with oversize pool areas and exotic landscaping. This area suits families and those looking for lots of centralized activity. Marina Vallarta is also home to an 18-hole **golf course** designed by Joe Finger.

In addition to the hotels below, an excellent choice is **Casa Velas,** on the golf course at Pelícanos 311 (© **866/612-1097** in the U.S., or 322/226-6688; www.hotelcasavelas.com). The elegant, boutique-style hotel has extra large rooms, an on-site spa, and a lovely pool. Although not located on the beach, it has a stunning beach club with food and beverage service, a pool, and sun chairs, with shuttle service for guests. High-season rates average $650 (£358), all inclusive.

Due to traffic (rather than distance), a taxi from the Marina to downtown takes 20 to 30 minutes.

Velas Vallarta Grand Suite Resort ✿✿✿ *Kids*   The beachside Velas Vallarta is an excellent choice for families. Each suite offers a full-size, fully equipped kitchen, ample living and dining areas, separate bedroom or bedrooms, and a large balcony with seating. The suites are decorated in a sophisticated, modern design featuring jewel-tone colors, Huichol art and Mexican textiles, feather beds with goose down comforters, 27-inch flatscreen TVs, modern kitchen appliances, and teak-wood furniture on balconies and terraces. Special extras include a pillow menu and luxury bathroom amenities. This property is part hotel, part full-ownership condominiums, which means each suite is the size of a residential unit. The suites all have partial ocean views; they face a central area where three freeform swimming pools, complete with bridges and waterfalls, meander through tropical gardens. A full range of services means you'd never need to leave the place if you don't want to. The Marina Vallarta Golf Club is across the street, and special packages are available for Velas guests. Guests may pay an extra fee for the Gold Crown All-Inclusive option, which is one of the most premium all-inclusive programs in Mexico.

Paseo de la Marina 485, Marina Vallarta, 48354 Puerto Vallarta, Jal. © **800/ VELAS-PV (835-2778)** in the U.S. and Canada, or 322/221-0091. Fax 322/ 221-0755. www.velasvallarta.com. 361 units. $390 (£215) double; $740–$1,110 (£407–£611) suite. All inclusive prices. AE, DC, MC, V. Free indoor parking. **Amenities:** 2 restaurants; poolside snack bar; lobby bar; 3 outdoor pools; golf privileges at Marina Vallarta Golf Club; 3 lighted tennis courts; fitness center w/spa and massage; beach w/water-sports equipment; complimentary bikes; activities program for children and adults; concierge; travel agency; car rental; minimarket; deli; salon; room service; laundry service. *In room:* A/C, TV, kitchen, coffeemaker, hair dryer, iron, safe.

Westin Resort & Spa Puerto Vallarta ✿✿   Stunning architecture and vibrant colors are the hallmark of this award-winning property, considered Puerto Vallarta's finest. Although the grounds are large—over 8 hectares (20 acres) with 260m (853 ft.) of beachfront—the warm service and gracious hospitality create the feeling of an intimate resort. Hundreds of tall palms surround the spectacular central freeform pool. You'll find hammocks strung between the palms closest to the beach, where there are also private beach cabañas. Rooms are contemporary in style, with oversize wood furnishings, tile floors, original art, and tub/shower combinations. Balconies have panoramic views. Eight junior suites and some double rooms have Jacuzzis, and the five grand suites and presidential suite are two-level, with ample living areas. Two floors of rooms make up the Royal Beach Club, with VIP services, including private concierge. The fitness center is one of Vallarta's most well-equipped facilities, with regularly scheduled spinning and yoga classes. **Nikki Beach** (www.nikkibeach.com), a renowned haven for the hip, is the on-site, beachfront restaurant and club, complete with big, white bed-size lounges for taking in the sun, or enjoying libations anytime from noon until the early morning hours. Their Sunday champagne brunch is especially popular.

Paseo de la Marina Sur 205, Marina Vallarta, 48354 Puerto Vallarta, Jal. ⓒ **800/ 228-3000** in the U.S., or 322/226-1100. Fax 322/226-1144. www.starwoodhotels. com/westin. 280 units. High season $265–$529 (£146–£291) double, $559–$725 (£307–£399) suite; low season $119–$389 (£65–£214) double, $429–$659 (£236–£362) suite. AE, DC, MC, V. Free parking. **Amenities:** 2 restaurants; Nikki Beach Club; 2 poolside bars; lobby bar; oceanside pool; golf privileges at Marina Vallarta Golf Club; 3 lighted grass tennis courts; state-of-the-art health club, sauna, steam room, solarium, whirlpool, massage, and salon; Kids' Club; travel agency; car rental; shopping arcade; room service; laundry service. *In room:* A/C, TV, minibar, coffeemaker, hair dryer, iron, safe.

THE HOTEL ZONE

The main street running between the airport and town is Avenida Francisco Medina Ascencio. The hotels here offer excellent, wide beachfronts with generally tranquil waters for swimming. From here it's a quick taxi or bus ride to downtown.

Fiesta Americana Puerto Vallarta ✦   The Fiesta Americana's towering, three-story, thatched *palapa* lobby is a landmark in the Hotel Zone, and the hotel is known for its excellent beach and friendly service. An abundance of plants, splashing fountains, constant breezes, and comfortable seating areas in the lobby create a casual South Seas ambience. The nine-story terra-cotta building embraces a large plaza with a pool facing the beach. Marble-trimmed rooms in neutral tones with pastel accents contain carved headboards and comfortable rattan and wicker furniture. All have private balconies with ocean and pool views.

Av. Francisco Medina Ascencio Km 2.5, 48300 Puerto Vallarta, Jal. ⓒ **322/226-2100.** Fax 322/224-2108. www.fiestaamericana.com. 291 units. High season $209–$400 (£116–£222) double; low season $120–$196 (£66–£108) double; year-round $256–$819 (£141–£450) suite. AE, DC, MC, V. Limited free parking. **Amenities:** 3 restaurants; lobby bar w/live music nightly; large pool w/activities and children's activities in high season; travel agency; salon; room service; laundry service. *In room:* A/C, TV, minibar, hair dryer, safe.

Premier Hotel & Spa ★★ You couldn't ask for a better location to be close to all that Vallarta's vibrant *centro* has to offer. Located on a wide swathe of golden sand beach—and just a few blocks north of the start of the *malecón*—the Premier is easy walking distance or a quick taxi ride to downtown restaurants, shops, galleries, and clubs. With a first-rate spa and a policy that restricts guests to ages 16 and older, it's a place that caters to relaxation. Four types of rooms are available, but all are decorated in warm colors with tile floors and light wood furnishings. Deluxe rooms have ocean views, a respectable seating area with comfortable chairs, plus a sizable private balcony—request one of several that has an outdoor whirlpool. Seven suites have a separate living room plus a dining area with private bar, and a spacious terrace. These rooms also have a double whirlpool tub, and separate glass-enclosed shower. The top-of-the-line master suites have all that the above suites offer, plus an outdoor whirlpool on the spacious balcony. The stunning bi-level spa is the real attraction of this hotel—scented with aromatherapy and glowing with candlelight, it uses top-notch, 100% natural products, most based on Mexico's natural treasures like coconut, aloe, and papaya. If you're not tempted by the nearby and accessible dining choices in downtown Vallarta, the Premier also offers an all-inclusive option, with all meals and drinks included.

San Salvador 117, behind the Buenaventura Hotel, Col. 5 de Diciembre, 48350 Puerto Vallarta, Jal. ⓒ **877/886-9176** in the U.S., or 322/226-7001 and 322/226-7040. Fax 322/226-7043. www.premiereonline.com.mx. 83 units. Room only: high season $135–$430 (£74–£237) double; low season $135–$370 (£74–£204) double. All-inclusive: high season $295–$545 (£162–£300) per person, based on double occupancy; low season $185–$360 (£102–£198) per person, double. AE, MC, V. Limited street parking. No children younger than 16 accepted. **Amenities:** 3 restaurants; 2 outdoor pools; fitness center; full spa; travel agency; salon; room service; laundry service. *In room:* A/C, TV, minibar, coffeemaker, hair dryer, safe.

DOWNTOWN TO LOS MUERTOS BEACH

This part of town has recently undergone a renaissance; economical hotels and good-value guesthouses dominate. Several blocks off the beach, you can find numerous budget inns offering clean, simply furnished rooms; most offer discounts for long-term stays. Much of Vallarta's nightlife activity now centers in the areas south of the Río Cuale and along Olas Altas.

Hacienda San Angel ★★★ *Finds* This enchanting boutique hotel may not be on the beach, but you'll hardly miss it, you'll be so pampered in the stunning suites, or satisfied enjoying the view from the rooftop heated pool or Jacuzzi and sun deck. It's my top choice for a luxury stay in Puerto Vallarta. Once Richard Burton's home in Puerto Vallarta, it's located just behind Puerto Vallarta's famed church, making it easy walking distance to all of the restaurants, shopping, and galleries of downtown. The Hacienda consists of five villas; the first two are joined to the third villa by a path that winds through a lovely terraced garden filled with tropical plants, flowers, statuary, and a charming fountain, while the Las Campañas private one-bedroom villa is located on the northern border of the garden. The newest villa offers four suites, each with sweeping views. A large, heated pool and deck offer panoramic views of the city and Bay of Banderas, while a second sun deck with Jacuzzi literally overlooks the church's crown, across to the water beyond. Each of the Hacienda's 10 elegant suites is individually decorated, accented with exquisite antiques and original art. Bed linens and coverings are of the finest quality, with touches like Venetian lace and goose-down pillows. Each morning, you'll wake to continental breakfast served outside your suite at your requested hour. Sophisticated style, coupled with casual Vallarta charm, make Hacienda San Angel the top "find" in Mexico for the discriminating traveler. Hacienda is now open for dinner for nonguests to enjoy (p. 77).

Miramar 336, Col. Centro, 48300 Puerto Vallarta, Jal. © **415/738-8220** or 322/222-2692. www.haciendasanangel.com. 10 units. High season $265–$565 (£146–£311) double; low season $235–$495 (£146–£272) double. All rates include daily continental breakfast. Rates for the entire Hacienda or separate villas consisting of 3 suites each are also available. MC, V. Very limited street parking available. **Amenities:** Menu of full breakfast, lunch, and dinner, or private chef available; 2 outdoor pools; rooftop sun deck w/Jacuzzi; concierge; tour services; complimentary Internet access. *In room:* A/C, TV/DVD, hair dryer, safe, CD player.

Hotel Playa Los Arcos ☆☆   This is one of Vallarta's perennially popular hotels and a favorite of mine, with a stellar location in the heart of Los Muertos Beach, central to the Olas Altas sidewalk-cafe action and close to downtown. The four-story structure is U-shaped, facing the ocean, with a small swimming pool in the courtyard. Rooms with private balconies overlook the pool. The 10 suites have ocean views; 5 of these have kitchenettes. The standard rooms are small but pleasantly decorated and immaculate, with carved wooden furniture painted pale pink. On the premises are a *palapa* beachside bar with occasional live entertainment, a gourmet coffee shop, and the popular Kaiser Maximilian's gourmet restaurant. It's 7 blocks south of the river.

Olas Altas 380, 48380 Puerto Vallarta, Jal. © **800/648-2403** in the U.S., or 322/222-1583 and 322/226-7100. Fax 322/226-7104. www.playalosarcos.com. 175 units. High season $105–$145 (£58–£80) double, $155–$175 (£85–£96) suite; low season $85–$120 (£47–£66) double, $118–$152 (£65–£84) suite. AE, MC, V. Limited street parking. **Amenities:** 2 restaurants; lobby bar; outdoor pool; tour desk; car-rental desk; babysitting; laundry; safe. *In room:* A/C, TV.

SOUTH TO MISMALOYA

Casa Tres Vidas 🌴🌴 *Value*   Terraced down a hillside to Conchas Chinas Beach, Casa Tres Vidas is three individual villas that make great, affordable lodgings for families or groups of friends. Set on a stunning private cove, Tres Vidas gives you the experience of your own private villa, complete with service staff. It offers outstanding value for the location—close to town, with panoramic views from every room—as well as for the excellent service. Each villa has at least two levels and over 460 sq. m (nearly 5,000 sq. ft.) of mostly open living areas, plus a private swimming pool, heated whirlpool, and air-conditioned bedrooms. The Vida Alta penthouse villa has three bedrooms, plus a rooftop deck with pool and bar. Vida Sol villa's three bedrooms sleep 10 (two rooms have two king-size beds each). Directly on the ocean, Vida Mar is a four-bedroom villa, accommodating eight. The staff prepares gourmet meals in your villa twice a day—you choose the menu and pay only for the food. If you're planning a wedding, Tres Vidas and its adjacent sister property, Quinta María Cortez, do a stunning job.

Sagitario 132, Playa Conchas Chinas, 48300 Puerto Vallarta, Jal. © **888/640-8100** or 801/531-8100 in the U.S., or 322/221-5317. Fax 322/221-53-27. www.casatres vidas.com. 3 villas. High season $700 (£385) villa; low season $500 (£275) villa. Rates include services such as housekeeping and meal preparation. Special summer 1- or 2-bedroom rates available; minimum 3 nights. AE, MC, V. Very limited street parking. **Amenities:** 2 prepared daily meals; private outdoor pool; concierge; tour desk; car rental. *In room:* A/C (in bedrooms), safe.

Dreams Puerto Vallarta Resort & Spa 🌴🌴   Formerly the Camino Real, this original luxury hotel in Puerto Vallarta was taken over by AMResorts in 2004 and turned into the premium all-inclusive Dreams Resort. It has the nicest beach of any Vallarta hotel, with soft white sand in a private cove. Set apart from other properties, with a lush mountain backdrop, it retains the exclusivity that made it popular from the beginning—yet it's only a 5- to 10-minute ride to town. The hotel consists of two buildings: the 250-room main hotel, which curves gently with the shape of the Playa Las Estacas, and the newer 11-story Club Tower, also facing the beach and ocean. An ample pool fronts the main building, facing the beach. Standard rooms in the main building are large; some have sliding doors opening onto the beach, and others have balconies. Club Tower rooms (from the sixth floor up) feature balconies with whirlpool tubs. The top floor consists of six two-bedroom suites, each with a private swimming pool, and with special concierge services. All rooms feature ocean views, and are decorated in vibrant colors, with marble floors and artwork by local renowned artist Manuel Lepe. In 2004, all rooms were completely renovated, with additions including two new swimming pools (including an adults-only tranquillity pool), a wedding gazebo, and upgraded health club and spa.

Carretera Barra de Navidad Km 3.5, Playa Las Estacas, 48300 Puerto Vallarta, Jal. © 866/237-3267 in the U.S. and Canada, or 322/226-5000. Fax 322/221-6000. www.dreamsresorts.com. 337 units. All-inclusive rates include all meals, premium drinks, activities, airport transfers, tips, and taxes. $360 (£198) double; $440 (£242) junior suite; $520 (£286) suite. AE, DC, MC, V. Free secured parking. **Amenities:** 5 restaurants; lobby bar; pool bar; 3 outdoor pools; 2 lighted grass tennis courts; fully equipped health club; spa; children's program (Easter and Christmas vacations only); travel agency; car rental; convenience store; room service; laundry service. *In room:* A/C, TV, minibar, hair dryer, iron, safe.

Quinta María Cortez ⭐⭐⭐ *Finds* A sophisticated, imaginative B&B on the beach, this is Puerto Vallarta's most original place to stay—and one of Mexico's most memorable inns. Most of the seven large suites, uniquely decorated with antiques, whimsical curios, and original art, have a kitchenette and balcony. Sunny terraces, a small pool, and a central gathering area with fireplace and *palapa*-topped dining area (where an excellent full breakfast is served) occupy different levels of the seven-story house. A rooftop terrace offers another sunbathing alternative—and is among the best sunset-watching spots in town. The quinta is on a beautiful cove on Conchas Chinas beach. A terrace fronting the beach accommodates chairs for taking in the sunset.

The Quinta María wins my highest recommendation (in fact, I enjoyed living here for a few years when it still accepted long-term stays), but admittedly it's not for everyone. Air-conditioned areas are limited, due to the open nature of the suites and common areas. Those who love it return year after year, charmed by this remarkable place and by the consistently gracious service.

A specialty of QMC and its adjacent sister property Casa Tres Vidas (see above) is planning and hosting weddings.

Sagitario 126, Playa Conchas Chinas, 48300 Puerto Vallarta, Jal. © 888/640-8100 or 801/536-5850 in the U.S., or 322/221-5317. Fax 322/221-53-27. www.quinta-maria.com. 7 units. High season $105–$235 (£58–£129) double; low season $95–$175 (£52–£96) double. Rates include breakfast. AE, MC, V. Very limited street parking. Children younger than 18 not accepted. **Amenities:** Small outdoor pool; concierge. *In room:* Fridge, coffeemaker, hair dryer, safe.

YELAPA

Verana ★★★ *(Moments)*   The magical Verana is my current favorite place to stay in Mexico. It has an unparalleled ability to inspire immediate relaxation and a deep connection with the natural beauty of the spectacular coast. Although Yelapa is 30 minutes by water taxi from town, even those unfamiliar with the village should consider it. Verana has eight rustic yet sophisticated suites located among seven bungalows, set into a hillside with sweeping views of the mountains and ocean. Each is a work of art, hand-crafted with care and creativity by owners Heinz Leger, a former film production designer, and prop stylist Veronique Lieve. Each has a private terrace and two beds—but you won't find TVs, telephones, or other distractions. My favorite suite is the Studio; it's the most contemporary, with a wall of floor-to-ceiling windows that perfectly frame the spectacular view. The European-trained chef prepares scrumptious creations—global cuisine with a touch of Mexico. Verana also has a magically crafted spa, and a yoga hut where daily classes take place. Compare this to the prices of the other rustic-chic resorts along Mexico's Pacific coast, and you'll find it's a true value. Adventurous travelers should not miss a stay at this unique place.

Domicilio Conocido, 48300 Yelapa, Jal. ℭ **800/530-7176** or 310/360-0155 in the U.S., or 322/222-2360. www.verana.com. 7 villas. Winter/high season $280–$470 (£154–£259) villa per night with 5-night minimum; $700 (£385) 3-bedroom Casa Grande per night; extra person $60 (£33) per night. Mandatory daily breakfast and dinner charge $70 (£39) per person; lunch and beverages extra. Shorter stays based on availability. Closed during summer months. AE, MC, V. Management helps arrange transportation from Puerto Vallarta to Boca, where a private boat runs to Yelapa; from there, Verana is a gentle hike or mule ride away. **Amenities:** Restaurant/bar; 2 prepared daily meals; outdoor pool; morning yoga classes; spa w/massage services; tours and excursions; library. *In room:* No phone.

3 Where to Dine

Puerto Vallarta has the most exceptional dining scene of any resort town in Mexico. Over 250 restaurants serve cuisines from around the world, in addition to fresh seafood and regional dishes. Chefs from France, Switzerland, Germany, Italy, and Argentina have come for visits and stayed to open restaurants. In celebration of this diversity, Vallarta's culinary community hosts a 2-week-long gourmet dining festival each November (p. 9).

Dining is not limited to high-end options—there are plenty of small, family-owned restaurants, local Mexican kitchens, and vegetarian cafes. Vallarta also has branches of the world food-and-fun chains: Hard Rock Cafe, Outback Steakhouse, and even Hooters. I won't bother to review these restaurants, where the quality and decor are so familiar.

Of the inexpensive local spots, one favorite is **El Planeta Vegetariano,** Iturbide 270, just down from the main church (© **322/ 222-3073**), serving an inexpensive, bountiful, and delicious vegetarian buffet, which changes for breakfast and lunch/dinner. It's open daily. Breakfast ($4.50/£2.50) is served from 8am till noon; the lunch and dinner buffets ($6.50/£3.60) are served from noon to 10pm; no credit cards are accepted.

MARINA VALLARTA

Contrary to conventional travel wisdom, most of the best restaurants in the Marina are in hotels. Especially notable are **Andrea** (fine Italian cuisine), at Velas Vallarta, and **Nikki Beach** (fusion), on the beachfront of the Westin Resort & Spa. (See "Where to Stay," earlier in this chapter, for more information.) Other choices are along the boardwalk bordering the marina yacht harbor.

Benitto's ⁂ CAFE   Wow! What a sandwich! Benitto's food would be reason enough to come to this tiny, terrific cafe inside the Plaza Neptuno—but added to that are the original array of sauces and the very personable service. This place is popular with locals for light breakfasts, filling lunches, and fondue and wine in the evenings. It's the best place in town for pastrami, corned beef, or other traditional (gringo) sandwich fare, all served on gourmet bread. Draft beer and wine are available, as are the cafe's specialty infused waters.

Inside Plaza Neptuno. © **322/209-0287.** benittoscafe@prodigy.net.mx. Breakfast $3–$6 (£1.65–£3.30); main courses $5–$7 (£2.75–£3.85). No credit cards. Mon–Sat 8:30am–9:30pm.

Porto Bello ⁂⁂ ITALIAN   One of the first restaurants in the marina, Porto Bello remains a favorite for its flavorful Italian dishes and exceptional service. For starters, the fried calamari is delicately seasoned, and the grilled vegetable antipasto could easily serve as a full meal. Signature dishes include fusilli with artichokes, black olives, lemon juice, basil, olive oil, and Parmesan cheese, and sautéed fish filet with shrimp and clams in saffron tomato sauce. The indoor dining room is air-conditioned, and there's also marina-front seating. The restaurant occasionally schedules live music in the evening.

Marina Sol, Loc. 7 (Marina Vallarta *malecón*). © **322/221-0003.** Reservations recommended for dinner. Main courses $8–$24 (£4.40–£13). AE, MC, V. Daily noon–11pm.

DOWNTOWN
EXPENSIVE
Café des Artistes/Thierry Blouet Cocina de Autor ⭑⭑⭑
FRENCH/INTERNATIONAL   This sophisticated restaurant is known as the place in town for that very special evening. Creative in its menu and innovative in design, the dinner-only restaurant rivals those in any major metropolitan city for its culinary sophistication. The award-winning chef and owner, Thierry Blouet, is both a member of the French Academie Culinaire and a Maitre Cuisinier de France. Along with the Café are two other special places: the upscale Bar Constantini lounge, and separate, but connected Thierry Blouet Cocina de Autor dining area. All are located in a restored house that resembles a castle. The interior of the original Café des Artistes combines murals, lush fabrics, and an array of original works of art, with both an interior dining area as well as a lushly landscaped terraced garden area. The menu of this section is a changing delight of French gourmet bistro fare, which draws heavily on Chef Blouet's French training, yet uses regional specialty ingredients. Noteworthy entrees include sea bass filet served with a lentil, bacon, and coriander stew; and the renowned roasted duck glazed with honey, soy, ginger, and lime sauce, and served with a pumpkin risotto. At the sleek and stylish Cocina de Autor, the fixed-priced tasting menu (prices depend on the number of plates you select, from three to six) offers you a choice of the chef's most creative and sumptuous creations, with each dish creatively combining ingredients to present one memorable "flavor"—choose any combination of starters, entrees, or desserts. After dining, you're invited to the cognac and cigar room, an exquisite blend of old adobe walls, flickering candles, and elegant leather chairs. Or, move on to the adjacent Bar Constantini, with its live jazz music and plush sofas, for a fitting close to a memorable meal. It's without a doubt worth the splurge.

Chef Thierry has also opened a new venue, **Thierry's Prime Steakhouse** in the Plaza Peninsula mall (Blvd. Francisco Medina Ascencio 2485, local Ancla Sub. A; ✆ **322/331-1212**). It features aged prime steaks, plus a limited selection of fish and chicken dishes. It's open for lunch and dinner daily.

Guadalupe Sánchez 740. ✆ **322/222-3228**, -3229, or -3230. www.cafe desartistes.com. Reservations recommended. Main courses $9–$31 (£4.95–£17). Cocinade Autor tasting menu $25–$68 (£14–£37). AE, MC, V. Daily 6–11:30pm (lounge until 2am).

MODERATE

Daiquiri Dick's 𝄐𝄐 MODERN AMERICAN   A Vallarta dining institution, Daiquiri Dick's has been around for over 22 years, evolving its winning combination of decor, service, and scrumptious cuisine. The menu is among Vallarta's most sophisticated, and the genuinely warm staff and open-air location fronting Los Muertos Beach add to the feeling of casual comfort. As lovely as the restaurant is, though, and as notorious as the fresh-fruit daiquiris are, the food is the main attraction. It incorporates touches of Tuscan, Thai, and Mexican. Start with grilled asparagus wrapped in prosciutto and topped with shaved Asiago cheese, then try an entree such as sesame-crusted tuna, grilled rare and served with wild greens; pistachio chicken served with polenta; or my favorite, simple yet indulgent lobster tacos. Chocolate banana bread pudding makes a perfect finish. Daiquiri Dick's is a great place for groups as well as for a romantic dinner. It's one of the few places that are equally enjoyable for breakfast, lunch, or dinner.

Olas Altas 314. ℂ **322/222-0566.** www.ddpv.com. Main courses $6.50–$25 (£3.60–£14). AE, MC, V. Daily 9am–10:30pm. Closed Sept.

de Santos 𝄐 MEDITERRANEAN   After it opened a few years ago, de Santos quickly became the hot spot in town for late-night dining and bar action. Unfortunately, the food doesn't live up to the atmosphere and music, but it's still a worthwhile place to go, if the scene is as important in a dining experience as the substance. The menu is Mediterranean-inspired; best bets include lightly breaded calamari, paella Valenciana, and thin-crust pizza. The cool, refined interior feels more urban than resort, and it boasts the most sophisticated sound system in town—including a DJ who spins to match the mood of the crowd. It probably helps that one of the partners is also a member of the wildly popular Latin group Maná. Open-air terrace dining is in the back. Prices are extremely reasonable for the quality and overall experience of an evening here. Be sure to stay and check out the adjacent club—still the hottest nightspot in town (see "Puerto Vallarta after Dark," chapter 3).

Morelos 771, Centro. ℂ **322/223-3052.** www.desantos.com.mx. Reservations recommended during high season. Main courses $5–$20 (£2.75–£5.50). AE, MC, V. Daily 5pm–1am; bar closes at 4am on weekends.

Hacienda San Angel 𝄐𝄐 MEXICAN   Meals at Hacienda San Angel were so popular with its guests, the owner decided to share the experience with other visitors to Puerto Vallarta as well. In addition to experiencing the exquisite beauty of the Hacienda itself, diners are treated to one of the most stunning views of town, overlooking the night lights of the city to the bay beyond. The very limited seating each night—by prior reservation only—is on the upper terrace of the Hacienda, near its main rooftop pool. Tables are elegantly set with linens and antique silverware. The menu changes periodically, but features classic Mexican fare, along with international favorites. Starters include crispy fried calamari with a selection of sauces, grilled seasonal vegetables in a tomato, olive oil, and basil balsamic vinaigrette, or a seafood soup flavored with mescal and thyme. The specialty is the grilled *Cabreria,* a tender bone-in steak, served with black beans, garlic-stuffed portobello mushroom, and a three-chile sauce. Other standouts include their chicken *mole,* and the herb-encrusted rack of lamb in a green-pepper sauce. They offer full bar service, and an ample selection of wines to accompany your meal. Service is understated and attentive. Start the evening by arriving at 6pm for a cocktail hour with live music—you may also enjoy strolling the grounds of the Hacienda.

In the Hacienda San Angel hotel (p. 70), Miramar 336, Centro. (C) **322/222-2692.** Reservations required. Main courses $17–$30 (£9.35–£17), with 20% gratuity added to all checks. MC, V. Mon–Sat 7pm–last guest (guests may arrive at 6pm for cocktail hour, but no later than 9pm to be served).

Las Palomas ✻ MEXICAN   One of Puerto Vallarta's first restaurants, this is the power-breakfast place of choice—and a popular hangout for everyone else throughout the day. Authentic in atmosphere and menu, it's one of Puerto Vallarta's few genuine Mexican restaurants. Breakfast is the best value. The staff pours mugs of steaming coffee spiced with cinnamon as soon as you're seated. Try classic *huevos rancheros* or *chilaquiles* (tortilla strips, fried and topped with red or green spicy sauce, cream, cheese, and fried eggs). Lunch and dinner offer traditional Mexican specialties, plus a selection of stuffed crepes. The best places for checking out the *malecón* and watching the sunset while sipping an icy margarita are the spacious bar and the upstairs terrace.

Paseo Díaz Ordaz 610. (C) **322/222-3675.** www.laspalomaspvr.com. Breakfast $3.50–$10 (£1.95–£5.50); lunch $8.50–$20 (£4.70–£11); main courses $8.50–$22 (£4.70–£12). AE, MC, V. Daily 8am–11pm.

Trio ✻✻✻ *Finds* INTERNATIONAL   Trio is the darling of Vallarta restaurants, where chef-owners Bernhard Güth and Ulf Henricksson's undeniable passion for food imbues each dish. Trío is noted for its perfected melding of Mexican and Mediterranean flavors; memorable entrees include San Blas shrimp in a fennel-tomato vinaigrette served over broiled *nopal* cactus, herb risotto with toasted sunflower seeds and quail, and pan-roasted sea bass with glazed grapes, mashed potatoes, and sauerkraut in a white-pepper sauce. These dishes may not be on the menu when you arrive, though—it's a constantly changing work of art. The atmosphere is always comfortable and welcoming, modest yet stylish. The rooftop bar area allows for a more comfortable wait for a table or for after-dinner coffee. A real treat!

Guerrero 264. (✆) 322/222-2196. www.triopv.com. Reservations recommended. Main courses $14–$26 (£7.70–£14). AE, MC, V. Year-round daily 6pm–midnight; high season Mon–Fri noon–3:30pm.

Xitomates 🐱🐱 MEXICAN   Located in the heart of downtown, this creative Mexican restaurant has earned raves for its intimate atmosphere and chef/owner Luis Fitch's exceptionally creative versions of the country's culinary treasures. It's named for one of Mexico's contributions to gastronomy—the tomato (*xitomatl,* in the ancient Aztec language of Náhuatl). The menu mixes Mexican with Caribbean, Asian, and Mediterranean influences, and the presentation is as creative as the preparation. Starters include their signature coconut shrimp in a tangy tamarind sauce, thinly sliced scallops with cucumber and jicama julienne, or mushrooms stuffed with shrimp or *huitlacoche* (a mushroom that grows on corn stalks). Main courses range from grilled salmon filet in a poblano chile sauce, to a tender rib-eye steak with mushrooms, delicately flavored with the

---

Tapas, Anyone?

Certainly, much of modern Mexico's culture draws on the important influence of Spain, so it only makes sense that Spanish culinary traditions would be evident as well. Within the last several years, dining on tapas has soared in popularity here. Of the many options, these are my favorites: the long-standing **Barcelona Tapas,** Matamoros and 31 de Octubre streets ((✆) **322/222-0510**), a large and lovely restaurant on a terrace built high on a hillside, with sweeping views of the bay. They serve tapas and a selection of Spanish entrees, including paella, from 5pm to midnight. **La Esquina de los Caprichos,** Miramar 402, corner of Iturbide ((✆) **322/222-0911**) is a tiny place, known as having the most reasonably priced ($2.50–$6/£1.40–£3.30) tapas in town, and perhaps the tastiest. Hours are Monday to Saturday from 1 to 10pm. It closes from mid-July to the end of August.

Mexican herb, epazote. The house specialty dessert is a Toluca ice-cream cake. The warmly decorated dining room is accented with tin star lamps and flickering candles. An excellent wine list and full bar complement the exquisite dining.

Morelos 570, across from Galería Uno. ⓒ 322/222-1695. www.losxitomates.com. Main courses $8–$22 (£4.40–£12). AE, MC, V. Daily 6pm–midnight.

INEXPENSIVE

Agave Grill ⚛ MEXICAN   Agave Grill occupies most of the space at the Casa de Tequila in central downtown. It's located in a beautiful garden setting in the back, within a classic hacienda-style building. The space has been put to excellent use: This cafe serves modern, casual Mexican cuisine and is an ideal spot to stop for a snack or a margarita while shopping. Start with an order of chiles anchos, stuffed with cream cheese and raisins, or the *antojitos mexicanos,* a sampler of Mexican snacks including sopes, quesadillas, a *tamal,* and guacamole. Favorite main courses include *chichilo negro,* a bone-in filet of beef with Oaxaca smoked mole, or the duck tacos in a *pipián* chile sauce. For a sweet finish, don't miss their tequila foam with chocolate sauce served with churros. All tortillas are handmade, as are the savory salsas. An elegant bar borders the room, serving undoubtedly Vallarta's most original selection of fine tequilas, many from small distilleries. In addition to the tequilas and fresh fruit margaritas, Agave Grill also serves a selection of fine Mexican wines.

Morelos 589. ⓒ 322/222-2000. Main courses $6–$17 (£3.30–£9.35). MC, V. Mon–Sat noon–11pm.

El Arrayán ⚛⚛⚛ *Finds* MEXICAN   The traditional but original Arrayán is the pot of gold at the end of the rainbow for anyone in search of authentic Mexican cuisine. Owner Carmen Porras enlisted Mexico City chef Carmen Titita (praised by James Beard for her culinary work) to assist in the design of the kitchen and creation of the restaurant's concise menu, which features genuine regional dishes. The open-air dining area surrounds a cozy courtyard, while its exposed brick walls and funky-chic decor showcase a modern view of Mexican classics—tin tubs serve as sinks in the bathrooms, while colorful plastic tablecloths and primitive art enliven the dining room. Start with an order of plantain fritters filled with black beans, or an unusual salad of diced *nopal* cactus paddles with fresh cheese. Main courses include their tacos filled with prime beef filet, or Mexican duck *carnitas,* served in an *arrayán*-orange sauce. (*Arrayán,* the namesake of the place, is a small bittersweet fruit native to the region.) Homemade, fresh-fruit ice creams are an especially tasty finish to your meal. The full bar offers an extensive selection of tequilas and regional liquors, while nonalcoholic beverages center on *aguas frescas*, a blended drink of fresh fruit and water. Don't miss sampling their signature *raicilla* martini—made with the potent local spirit (raicilla) and infused with herbs. The excellent service is a plus to this can't-miss dining experience—you can't miss the pink facade with the large bell at the entry.

Allende 344, just past Matamoros, on the corner with Miramar. ℂ **322/222-7195.** www.elarrayan.com.mx. Main courses $11–$14 (£6.05–£7.70). AE, MC, V. Wed–Mon 6–11pm. Closed Aug.

Vitea ☆☆☆ *Finds* INTERNATIONAL This beachfront bistro is run by the chef/owners of Trío, and their recipe for success means the place is bustling at any hour, and has become a favorite among locals. Due to strategically placed mirrors on the back wall, every seat has a view of the ocean, while the eclectic interior is cheerful and inviting. Seating is at small bistro-style tables, along a banquette that runs the length of the back wall, or at the small but beautiful bar. The long, narrow bistro faces the waterfront between the central plaza and river. But enough about looks—what counts here is the exceptional fare, which is both classic and original. Starters include a tomato and Roquefort salad with pecans, foie gras with Spanish plum sauce, and an exquisite bistro salad with bacon. Quiche is always on the menu, with changing selections, and main courses include chickpea ravioli with portobello mushrooms, Wiener schnitzel with salad, or a traditional steak frites. Lunch offers lighter fare, including heavenly deli sandwiches. You won't be disappointed here, no matter what you order! The full bar has an excellent selection of wines, and the service is exceptional.

Malecón no. 2, at Libertad. ℂ **322/222-8703** or **-8695.** Reservations recommended during peak dining hours. Main courses $7–$19 (£3.85–£10). MC, V. Daily noon–midnight.

SOUTH OF THE RIO CUALE TO OLAS ALTAS

South of the river is the densest restaurant area, where you'll find Basilio Badillo, the street nicknamed "Restaurant Row." A second main dining drag has emerged along Calle Olas Altas, with a variety of cuisines and price categories. Cafes and espresso bars, generally open from 7am to midnight, line its wide sidewalks.

EXPENSIVE

Café Kaiser Maximilian ☆☆ INTERNATIONAL This is the prime place to go if you want to combine exceptional food with great people-watching. It's a bistro-style cafe with a casually elegant atmosphere with a genuine European feel. Austrian-born owner Andreas Rupprechter is always on hand to ensure that the service is as impeccable as the food is delicious. Indoor, air-conditioned dining is at cozy tables; sidewalk tables are larger and great for groups of friends. The cuisine merges old-world European preparations with regional fresh ingredients. My favorite is filet of trout with spinach, tomato, and almond ragout; but also notable is their mustard chicken with mashed potatoes, and the rack of lamb with polenta, endives, and lima beans. Desserts are especially tempting, as are gourmet coffees—Maximilian has an Austrian cafe and pastry shop next door.

Olas Altas 380-B (at Basilio Badillo, in front of the Hotel Playa Los Arcos), Zona Romántica. ℭ **322/223-0760**. Reservations recommended in high season. Main courses $16–$26 (£8.80–£14). AE, MC, V. Mon–Sat 6–11pm.

Le Bistro MEXICAN/INTERNATIONAL   A long-standing favorite, Le Bistro is recommended for their breakfast, though I would personally pass on it for dinner. I consider a morning meal here one of Vallarta's best values. Le Bistro is known for its elegant decor, great recorded jazz music, and open-air setting on the island in the midst of the Río Cuale—all creating a singular experience that blends sophistication with a typical Vallarta atmosphere. The specialty is crepes, which come in a variety of flavors for breakfast, lunch, or dinner. The lunch and dinner menu also features a selection of Mexican cuisine, including duck in Oaxacan black *mole,* and rock Cornish hen stuffed with herbed rice, dried tropical fruits, and nuts, finished in mango cilantro sauce. The vegetarian offerings are more creative than most. An extensive wine list and ample selection of specialty coffees complement the menu.

Isla Río Cuale 16-A (just east of northbound bridge). ℭ **322/222-0283**. www.lebistro. com.mx. Reservations recommended for dinner in high season. Breakfast $5–$8 (£2.75–£4.40); main courses $19–$25 (£10–£14). AE, MC, V. Mon–Sat 9am–midnight.

MODERATE

Archie's Wok ⭐⭐⭐ *(Finds* ASIAN/SEAFOOD   Since 1986, Archie's has been legendary in Puerto Vallarta for serving original cuisine influenced by the intriguing flavors of Thailand, China, and the Philippines. Archie was Hollywood director John Huston's private chef during the years he spent in the area. Today his wife Cindy upholds his legacy at this tranquil retreat. The Thai mai tai and other tropical drinks, made from only fresh fruit and juices, are a good way to kick off a meal, as are the consistently crispy and delicious Filipino spring rolls. The popular Singapore fish filet features lightly battered filet strips in sweet-and-sour sauce; Thai garlic shrimp are prepared with fresh garlic, ginger, cilantro, and black pepper. Vegetarians have plenty of options, including broccoli, tofu, mushroom, and cashew stir-fry in black-bean-and-sherry sauce. Thursday through Saturday from 8 to 11pm, there's live classical harp and flute in Archie's Oriental garden.

Francisca Rodríguez 130 (a half block from the Los Muertos pier). © **322/222-0411.** Main courses $6–$21 (£3.30–£12). MC, V. Mon–Sat 2–11pm. Closed Sept–Oct.

Espresso ⋐⋐ ITALIAN   This popular eatery is Vallarta's best late-night dining option. The two-level restaurant is on one of the town's busiest streets—across from El Torito's sports bar, and cater-cornered from the lively Señor Frog's—meaning that traffic noise is a factor, though not a deterrent. The food is superb, the service attentive, and the prices more than reasonable. Owned by a part-nership of lively Italians, it serves food authentic in preparation and flavor, from thin-crust, brick-oven pizzas to savory homemade pas-tas. My favorite pizza is the Quattro Stagioni, topped with arti-chokes, black olives, ham, and mushrooms. Excellent calzones and panini (sandwiches) are also options. I prefer the rooftop garden, but many patrons gravitate to the pool table in the air-conditioned downstairs, which features major sports and entertainment events on satellite TV. Espresso also has full bar service and draft beer and is especially popular with *vallartenses* (locals).

Ignacio L. Vallarta 279. © **322/222-3272.** Main courses $6.50–$18 (£3.60–£9.90). MC, V. Daily 9am–2am.

La Palapa ⋐⋐ SEAFOOD/MEXICAN   This colorful, open-air, *palapa*-roofed restaurant on the beach is a decades-old local favorite, and with each visit, I have found the quality of the food and the service keeps improving. It's an exceptional dining experience, day or night. Enjoy a tropical breakfast by the sea, lunch on the beach, cocktails at sunset, or a romantic dinner (on a cloth-covered table in the sand). For lunch and dinner, seafood is the specialty; featured dishes include macadamia-and-coconut-crusted prawns, and poached red snapper with fresh cilantro sauce. Its location in the heart of Los Muertos Beach makes it an excellent place to start or end the day; I favor it for breakfast or, even better, a late-night sweet temptation and specialty coffee, while watching the moon over the bay. A particular draw is the all-you-can-eat Sunday brunch, which entitles you to a spot on popular Los Muertos Beach for the day. You can enjoy the extra-comfortable beach chairs for postbrunch sun-bathing. A new bar area features acoustic guitars and vocals nightly from 8 to 11pm, generally performed by the owner, Alberto.

Pulpito 103. © **322/222-5225.** www.lapalapapv.com. Reservations recommended for dinner in high season. Breakfast $2.50–$12 (£1.40–£6.60); main courses $7–$28 (£3.85–£15); salad or sandwiches $5–$12 (£2.75–£6.60). AE, MC, V. Daily 9am–11pm.

INEXPENSIVE

Café San Angel CAFE   This comfortable, classic sidewalk cafe is a local gathering place from sunrise to sunset. For breakfast, choose a burrito stuffed with eggs and chorizo sausage, a three-egg Western omelet, crepes filled with mushrooms, Mexican classics like *huevos rancheros* and *chilaquiles,* or a tropical fruit plate. Deli sandwiches, crepes, and pastries round out the small but ample menu. The cafe also serves exceptional fruit smoothies and perfectly made espresso drinks. Note that the service is reliably slow and frequently frustrating, so choose this place if you have time on your side—and keep in mind that it offers the best people-watching in the area. Bar service and Internet access are available.

Olas Altas 449 (at Francisco Rodríguez). ℂ 322/223-1273. Breakfast $3.50–$6 (£1.95–£3.30); main courses $3.50 (£1.95). No credit cards. Daily 8am–1am.

Fajita Republic 🅐 MEXICAN/SEAFOOD/STEAKS   Fajita Republic is consistently popular—and deservedly so. It has hit on a winning recipe: delicious food, ample portions, welcoming atmosphere, and low prices. The specialty is, of course, fajitas, grilled to perfection in every variety: steak, chicken, shrimp, combo, and vegetarian. All come with a generous tray of salsas and toppings. This "tropical grill" also serves sumptuous barbecued ribs, Mexican *molcajetes* with incredibly tender strips of marinated beef filet, and grilled shrimp. Starters include fresh guacamole served in a giant spoon and the ever-popular Mayan cheese sticks (breaded and deep-fried). Try an oversize mug or pitcher of Fajita Rita Mango Margaritas—or any another spirited temptation. This is a casual, fun, festive place in a garden of mango and palm trees. A second location in Nuevo Vallarta, across from the Grand Velas Resort, is drawing equal raves with the same menu and prices.

Pino Suárez 321 (at Basilio Badillo), 1 block north of Olas Altas. ℂ 322/222-3131. Main courses $9–$17 (£4.95–£9.35). MC, V. Daily 5pm–midnight.

Red Cabbage Café (El Repollo Rojo) 🅐🅐 *Finds* MEXICAN   The tiny, hard-to-find cafe is worth the effort—a visit here will reward you with exceptional traditional Mexican cuisine and a whimsical crash course in contemporary culture. The small room is covered wall-to-wall and table-to-table with photographs, paintings, movie posters, and news clippings about the cultural icons of Mexico. Frida Kahlo figures prominently in the decor, and a special menu duplicates dishes she and husband Diego Rivera prepared for guests.

Specialties from all over Mexico include divine *chiles en nogada* (poblanos stuffed with ground beef, pine nuts, and raisins, topped with sweet cream sauce and served cold), intricate chicken *mole* from Puebla, and hearty *carne en su jugo* (steak in its juice). In addition, the vegetarian menu is probably the most diverse and tasty in town. This is not the place for an intimate conversation, however—the poor acoustics cause everyone's conversations to blend together, although generally what you're hearing from adjacent tables are raves about the food. Also, this is a nonsmoking restaurant—the only one I'm aware of in town.

Calle Rivera del Río 204A (across from Río Cuale). ℭ 322/223-0411. Main courses $9–$20 (£4.95–£11). No credit cards. Daily 5–10:30pm.

JUNGLE RESTAURANTS

One of the unique attractions of Puerto Vallarta is its "jungle restaurants," south of town toward Mismaloya. They offer open-air dining in a tropical setting by the sea or beside a mountain river. The many varieties of "jungle" and "tropical" tours (see "Organized Tours," in the next chapter) include a stop for swimming and lunch. If you travel on your own, a taxi is the best transportation—the restaurants are quite a distance from the main highway. Taxis are usually waiting for return patrons.

The most recommendable of the jungle restaurants is the ecologically sensitive **El Nogalito** ℱ (ℭ/fax **322/221-5225**). Located beside a clear jungle stream, the exceptionally clean, beautifully landscaped ranch serves lunch, beverages, and snacks on a shady, relaxing terrace. Several hiking routes depart from the grounds, and the restaurant provides a guide (whom you tip) to point out the native plants, birds, and wildlife. It's much closer to town than the other jungle restaurants: To find it, travel to Punta Negra, about 8km (5 miles) south of downtown Puerto Vallarta. A well-marked sign points up Calzada del Cedro, a dirt road, to the ranch. It's open daily from noon to 5:30pm. No credit cards are accepted.

Just past Boca de Tomatlán, at Highway 200 Km 20, is **Chico's Paradise** (ℭ **322/223-6005**). It offers spectacular views of massive rocks—some marked with petroglyphs—and the surrounding jungle and mountains. There are natural pools and waterfalls for swimming, plus a small market selling pricey trinkets. The menu features excellent seafood as well as Mexican dishes. The quality is quite good, and the portions are generous, although prices are higher than in town—remember, you're paying for the setting. It's open daily from 10am to 6pm. No credit cards are accepted.

3

Exploring Puerto Vallarta & Beyond

By Lynne Bairstow

Beyond its cobblestone streets, graceful cathedral, and welcoming atmosphere, Puerto Vallarta offers a wealth of natural beauty and manufactured pleasures.

Ecotourism activities are gaining ground here—from mountain biking the Sierra foothills to whale-watching, ocean kayaking, and diving with giant mantas in Banderas Bay. Forty-two kilometers (26 miles) of beaches, many in pristine coves accessible only by boat, extend around the bay. High in the Sierra Madres, the mystical Huichol Indians still live in relative isolation in an effort to protect their centuries-old culture from outside influences. Known for sustaining one of the stronger art communities in Latin America, Puerto Vallarta also has an impressive selection of art galleries featuring unique original works by Mexican artists and craftsmen.

Villages such as Rincon de Guayabitos, Barra de Navidad, and Melaque are laid-back and almost undiscovered. Starkly different from the spirited resort towns, they offer travelers a glimpse into local culture. Excursions to these smaller villages make easy day trips or extended stays.

1 Beaches, Activities & Excursions

Travel agencies can provide information on what to see and do in Puerto Vallarta and can arrange tours, fishing trips, and other activities. Most hotels have a tour desk on-site. Of the many travel agencies in town, I highly recommend **Tukari Servicios Turísticos,** Av. España 316 (© **322/224-7177;** fax 322/224-2350; www.tukari. com), which specializes in ecological and cultural tours. Another source is **Xplora Adventours** (© **322/223-0661**), in the Huichol Collection shop on the *malecón.* It has listings of all locally available tours, with photos, explanations, and costs; however, be aware that a timeshare resort owns the company, so part of the information you

Downtown Puerto Vallarta

ATTRACTIONS ●

Gringo Gulch
(neighborhood) **18**
Isla del Río Cuale **23**
Main Square **13**
Municipal Market **22**
Parish of Nuestra Señora
de Guadalupe **14**
Terra Noble Art & Healing
Center **1**

ACCOMMODATIONS ■

Hacienda San Angel **17**
Hotel Playa Los Arcos **27**

Dining ◆

Agave Grill **12**
Archie's Wok **29**
Azul 96 **5**
Barcelona Tapas **6**
Café des Artistes/Thierry
Blouet Cocina de Autor **8**
Café Kaiser Maximilian **27**
Café San Angel **28**
Carlos O'Brian's **3**
Daiquiri Dick's **26**
De Santos **4**
El Arrayán **7**
El Planeta Vegetariano **15**
Espresso **24**

Fajita Republic **25**
La Bodeguita
del Medio **2**
La Esquina de los
Capricios **16**
La Palapa **30**
Las Palomas **10**
Le Bistro **21**
Red Cabbage Café **31**
Trio **19**
Vitea **20**
Xitomates **11**
Z'Tai **9**

receive will be an invitation to a presentation, which you may decline. **American Express Travel Services,** Morelos 660 (© **322/ 223-2955**), also has a varied selection of high-quality, popular tours. One of the tour companies with the largest—and best quality—selection of boat cruises and land tours is **Vallarta Adventures** 𝕮𝕮𝕮 (© **888/303-2653** in the U.S., or 322/297-1212, ext. 3; www.vallarta-adventures.com). I can highly recommend any of their offerings. Book with them directly and get a 10% discount when you mention Frommer's.

THE BEACHES

For years, beaches were Puerto Vallarta's main attraction. Although visitors today are exploring more of the surrounding geography, the sands are still a powerful draw. Over 42km (26 miles) of beaches extend around the broad Bay of Banderas, ranging from action-packed party spots to secluded coves accessible only by boat.

IN TOWN   The easiest to reach is **Playa Los Muertos** (also known as Playa Olas Altas or Playa del Sol), just off Calle Olas Altas, south of the Río Cuale. The water can be rough, but the wide beach is home to a diverse array of *palapa* restaurants that offer food, beverage, and beach-chair service. The most popular are the adjacent El Dorado and La Palapa, at the end of Pulpito Street. On the southern end of this beach is a section known as "Blue Chairs"—the most popular gay beach. Vendors stroll Los Muertos, and beach volleyball, parasailing, and jet-skiing are all popular pastimes. The **Hotel Zone** is also known for its broad, smooth beaches, accessible primarily through the hotel lobbies.

SOUTH OF TOWN   **Playa Mismaloya** is in a beautiful sheltered cove about 10km (6 miles) south of town along Highway 200. The water is clear and beautiful, ideal for snorkeling off the beach. Entrance to the public beach is just to the left of the **Barceló La Jolla de Mismaloya** (© **322/226-0600**). The movie *Night of the Iguana* was filmed at Mismaloya, and the resort has a restaurant on the restored film set—**La Noche de la Iguana Set Restaurant,** open daily from noon to 11pm. The movie runs continuously in a room below the restaurant, and still photos from the filming hang in the restaurant. The restaurant is accessible by land on the point framing the south side of the cove. Just below the restaurant is **John Huston's Bar & Grill,** serving drinks and light snacks daily from 11am to 6pm.

The beach at **Boca de Tomatlán,** just down the road, has numerous *palapa* restaurants where you can relax for the day—you buy drinks, snacks, or lunch, and you can use their chairs and *palapa* shade.

The two beaches are accessible by public buses, which depart from the corner of Basilio Badillo and Insurgentes every 15 minutes from 5:30am to 10pm and cost just 50¢ (30p).

Las Animas, Quimixto, and **Yelapa** beaches offer a true sense of seclusion; they are accessible only by boat (see "Getting Around," in chapter 2, for information about water-taxi service). They are larger than Mismaloya, offer intriguing hikes to jungle waterfalls, and are similarly set up, with restaurants fronting a wide beach. Overnight stays are available at Yelapa (see "Side Trips from Puerto Vallarta," later in this chapter).

NORTH OF TOWN   The beaches at **Marina Vallarta** are the least desirable, with darker sand and seasonal inflows of stones.

The entire northern coastline from Bucerías to Punta Mita is a succession of sandy coves alternating with rocky inlets. For years the beaches to the north, with their long, clean breaks, have been the favored locale for surfers. The broad, sandy stretches at **Playa Anclote, Playa Piedras Blancas,** and **Playa Destiladeras,** which all have *palapa* restaurants, have made them favorites with local residents looking for a quick getaway—but come soon, because this area is slated for luxury development, easy access to these shores is likely to be limited in the coming years. At Playa Anclote you'll find a broad, sandy beach with protected swimming areas and a few great *palapa* restaurants. Of the restaurants, El Anclote and El Dorado have been the long-standing favorites, but **Mañana** (© **329/291-6374**), has raised the culinary bar of this casual dining area. It's open Tuesday through Sunday from 10am to 9pm, in summer 1 to 9pm. All have beach chairs available for your postmargarita nap in the sun. If you're seeking solace from the sun, head to the **Pink Bonsai** (© **329/291-6468**), which serves creative sushi, tempting tempuras, and the delectable changing specials of Chef/Owner Karl, who enjoys fusing Asian with Mexican flavors. It's located in the Plaza of Shops, second level, on the left-hand side of the short main road entering Playa Anclote (Av. de las Redes 75, Punta de Mita). It's open Monday through Saturday, 1pm to 6pm.

You can also hire a *panga* (small motorized boat) at Playa Anclote from the fisherman's cooperative on the beach and have the captain take you to the **Marietas Islands** ⟨★★★ just offshore. These uninhabited islands are a great place for bird-watching, diving, snorkeling, or just exploring. Blue-footed booby birds (found only here, and in the Galapagos) can be spotted all along the islands' rocky coast, and giant mantas, sea turtles, and colorful tropical fish swim among the coral cliffs. The islands are honeycombed with caves and hidden beaches—including the stunning Playa de Amor (Beach of Love) that only appears at low tide. You enter a shallow passageway to access this semicircular stretch of sand. There's also a cave 12m (40 ft.) below the surface with an air pocket where divers can remove their regulators and have an underwater conversation! Humpback whales congregate around these islands during the winter months, and *pangas* can be rented for a do-it-yourself whale-watching excursion. Trips cost about $30 (£17) per hour. You can also visit these islands aboard one of the numerous day cruises that depart from the cruise-ship terminal in Puerto Vallarta.

The stellar white-sand beach at **Punta Mita,** home of the Four Seasons, is closed to road access, except for owners in and guests of this residential resort development.

ORGANIZED TOURS

BOAT TOURS Puerto Vallarta offers a number of boat trips, including sunset cruises and snorkeling, swimming, and diving excursions. They generally travel one of two routes: to the **Marietas Islands,** a 30- to 45-minute boat ride off the northern shore of Banderas Bay, or to **Yelapa, Las Animas,** or **Quimixto** along the southern shore. The trips to the southern beaches make a stop at **Los Arcos,** an island rock formation south of Puerto Vallarta, for snorkeling. Don't base your opinion of underwater Puerto Vallarta on this, though—dozens of tour boats dump quantities of snorkelers overboard at the same time each day, exactly when the fish know *not* to be there. It is, however, an excellent site for night diving. When comparing boat cruises, note that some include lunch, while most provide music and an open bar on board. Most leave around 9:30am, stop for 45 minutes of snorkeling, and arrive at the beach destination around noon for a 21/2-hour stay before returning around 3pm. At Quimixto and Yelapa, visitors can take a half-hour hike to a jungle waterfall or rent a horse for the ride. Prices range from $45 (£25) for a sunset cruise or a trip to one of the beaches with open bar, to $85 (£47) for an all-day outing with open bar and meals.

One boat, the *Marigalante* (© **322/223-0309;** www.marigalante. com.mx), is an exact replica of Columbus's ship the *Santa María,* built in honor of the 500th anniversary of his voyage to the Americas. It features a daytime "Pirate Land" Morning Cruise daily from 8am until 3:30pm ($70/£39 per person), complete with breakfast, picnic barbecue and treasure hunt, as well as a sunset dinner (adult oriented) cruise from 6 to 10pm ($80/£44 per person) with fireworks and dance party. Children 3 to 11 are half price (children 2 and under are free).

One of the best outings is a day trip to **Caletas** ☆☆, the cove where John Huston made his home for years. **Vallarta Adventures** (ⓒ **888/ 303-2653** in the U.S., or 322/297-1212, ext. 3; www.vallarta-adventures.com) holds the exclusive lease on the private cove and has done an excellent job of restoring Huston's former home, adding exceptional day-spa facilities, and landscaping the beach, which is wonderful for snorkeling. They also have a colony of sea lions that play with the visiting divers! You'll have a hard time deciding whether to kayak, take a yoga class, hike through surrounding trails, or simply relax in the hammocks strung between palms on the beach. One of their most popular excursions to Caletas is $80 (£44) per person; $40 (£22) for children 4 to 11. The evening cruise includes dinner and a spectacular contemporary dance show, "Rhythms of the Night" (see "Puerto Vallarta after Dark," later in this chapter).

Travel agencies sell tickets and distribute information on all cruises. If you prefer to spend more time at Yelapa or Las Animas without snorkeling and cruise entertainment, see the information about travel by water taxis, in chapter 2, under "Getting Around."

Whale-watching tours become more popular each year. Viewing humpback whales is almost a certainty from mid- to late November to March. The majestic whales have migrated to this bay for centuries (in the 17th c. it was called "Humpback Bay") to bear their calves. The noted local authority is **Open Air Expeditions,** Guerrero 339 (ⓒ/fax **322/222-3310;** www.vallartawhales.com). It offers ecologically oriented, oceanologist-guided 4-hour tours on the soft boat *Prince of Whales,* the only boat in Vallarta specifically designed for whale-watching. Cost is $83 (£46) for adults, $50 (£28) for children 5 to 10, and travel is in a group of up to 12. Twice-daily departures (8:30am and 1:30pm) include a healthful snack. **Vallarta Adventures** (see above) offers a variety of whale-watching excursions that may combine time for snorkeling, or simply focus on photographing these exquisite mammals. Prices range from $68 to $80 (£37–£44), and offer a choice of boat, ranging from small boats to bring you closest for photos, to graceful sailboats. All trips include a predeparture briefing on whale behavior.

LAND TOURS   Tukari Servicios Turísticos (see "Beaches, Activities & Excursions," above) can arrange trips to the fertile birding grounds near **San Blas,** 3 to 4 hours north of Puerto Vallarta in the state of Nayarit, and shopping trips to **Tlaquepaque** and **Tonalá**

(6 hr. inland, near Guadalajara). A day trip to **Rancho Altamira,** a 20-hectare (50-acre) working ranch, includes a barbecue lunch and horseback riding, then a stroll through **El Tuito,** a small nearby colonial-era village. The company can also arrange an unforgettable morning at **Terra Noble Art & Healing Center** ☆☆ (© **322/223-3530** or 222-5400; www.terranoble.com), a mountaintop day spa and center for the arts where participants can get a massage, *temazcal* (ancient, indigenous sweat lodge), or treatment; work in clay and paint; and have lunch in a heavenly setting overlooking the bay. Call ahead for reservations, and make sure to advise if you want to have lunch there.

Hotel travel desks and travel agencies, including Tukari and American Express, can also book the popular **Tropical Tour** or **Jungle Tour** ($30/£17), a basic orientation to the area. These excursions are expanded city tours that include a drive through the workers' village of Pitillal, the affluent neighborhood of Conchas Chinas, the cathedral, the market, the Taylor-Burton houses, and lunch at a jungle restaurant. Any stop for shopping usually means the driver picks up a commission for what you buy.

The **Sierra Madre Expedition** is another excellent tour offered by **Vallarta Adventures** (see "Boat Tours," above). The daily excursion travels in Mercedes all-terrain vehicles north of Puerto Vallarta through jungle trails, stops at a small town, ventures into a forest for a brief nature walk, and winds up on a pristine secluded beach for lunch and swimming. The $75 (£41) outing is worthwhile because it takes tourists on exclusive trails into scenery that would otherwise be off-limits.

AIR TOURS   Speaking of off-limits, you can explore some of the most remote and undiscovered reaches of the Sierra Madre mountains in Vallarta Adventures' **San Sebastián Air Expedition** (© **888/303-2653** in the U.S., or 322/297-1212, ext. 3; www. vallarta-adventures.com). A 15-minute flight aboard a 14-seat turboprop Cessna Caravan takes you into the heart of the Sierra Madre. The plane is equipped with raised wings, which allow you to admire—and photograph—the mountain scenery. The plane arrives on a gravel landing strip in the old mining town of San Sebastián, a beautiful village that dates from 1603. One of the oldest mining towns in Mexico, it reached its prosperous peak in the 1800s, with over 30,000 inhabitants. Today, San Sebastián remains an outstanding example of how people lived and worked in a remote mountain town—it's a living museum. The half-day adventure costs $155 (£85), which covers the flight, a walking tour of the town (including a stop at the old Hacienda Jalisco, a favored getaway of John Huston, Liz and Dick, and their friends), and brunch in town. Other excursions include overnight stays and return trips by bike or horseback. If you prefer more leisurely travel, they offer a similar tour taking you by land in air-conditioned minivans for the 90-minute drive up the mountains, for $75 (£41) per person. Another **bus tour** to San Sebastián, which costs $75 (£41) per person, and includes a guide, departs at 9am and returns at 5pm. Call Pacific Travel (© **322/225-2270**) to make reservations.

Vallarta Adventures (see "Boat Tours," above) also offers a similar—yet different—air tour to the mountain villages of **Mascota** and **Talpa de Allende** ☝☝, where you'll learn about the religious significance of these traditional towns. In Mascota, stroll the cobblestone streets lined with adobe houses and colonial haciendas, stopping at the majestic town church, dedicated to the Virgen de los Dolores (Virgin of Sorrows), which was completed in 1880 and took more than 100 years to construct. You'll stop for lunch and tour a local *raicilla* distillery to sample this locally popular beverage before traveling on to Talpa. Talpa is known for being home to one of Mexico's most revered icons, the Virgen Rosario de Talpa, believed to grant miracles with her healing powers. Ask for one yourself, as you visit the Gothic church that bears her name, or simply wander around this pastoral village, set in a valley surrounded by pine-covered mountains. The 6-hour adventure includes airfare and lunch, for $175 (£96) per person. Departures are Mondays and Wednesdays at 10:30am, from the Aerotron private airport (adjacent to the Puerto Vallarta International Airport).

Vallarta Adventures also offers air tours to remote mountain villages where the **Huichol Indians** live (Fri departures, at a cost of $210/£116), as well as to the **Copper Canyon,** and the mystical village of **Mexcaltitan** (Mon departures, at a cost of $255/£140), all departing from Puerto Vallarta. Details and online booking options are available at www.vallarta-adventures.com.

TOURS IN TOWN   Every Wednesday and Thursday in high season (late Nov–Easter), the **International Friendship Club** (© **322/222-5466**) offers a **private home tour** of four villas in town. It costs $35 (£19) per person, with proceeds donated to local charities. Arrive early, because this tour sells out quickly. It starts at the Hotel Posada Río Cuale, adjacent to the southbound bridge over the Río Cuale. Get there at 10am, and you can buy breakfast while you wait for the group to gather. The tour departs at 10:30am and lasts approximately

3½ hours. Also ask them about a new tour of the exquisite villas on the north shore planned to be inaugurated in late 2007.

A tour of the **Public Sculptures** of the *malecón* is hosted by Galería Pacífico owner Gary Thompson, each Tuesday at 9:30am, from December through April. Lasting a couple of hours, you'll stroll the *malecón* learning about the artists who created Vallarta's most visible art, and their inspirations. Frequently, Gary is joined by one or more of the artists on this tour. For more details, contact the gallery at © **322/221-1982.**

STAYING ACTIVE

DIVING & SNORKELING   Underwater enthusiasts from beginner to expert can arrange scuba diving or snorkeling through **Vallarta Adventures** (© **888/303-2653** in the U.S., or 322/297-1212, ext. 3; www.vallarta-adventures.com), a five-star PADI dive center. You may snorkel or dive at Los Arcos, a company-owned site at Caletas Cove (where you'll dive in the company of sea lions), Quimixto Coves, the Marietas Islands, or the offshore La Corbeteña, Morro, and Chimo reefs. The company also offers a full range of certification courses (up to Instructor). **Chico's Dive Shop,** Díaz Ordaz 772–5, near Carlos O'Brian's (© **322/222-1895;** www.chicos-diveshop.com), offers similar diving and snorkeling trips and is also a PADI five-star dive center. Chico's is open daily from 8am to 10pm and has branches at the Marriott, Las Palmas, Holiday Inn, Fiesta Americana, Krystal, San Marino, Villa del Palmar, Paradise Village, and Playa Los Arcos hotels. You can also snorkel off the beaches at Mismaloya and Boca de Tomatlán; elsewhere, there's not much to see other than a sandy bottom.

ECOTOURS & ACTIVITIES   **Open Air Expeditions** (©/fax 322/222-3310;** www.vallartawhales.com) offers nature-oriented trips, including birding and ocean kayaking in Punta Mita. **Ecotours de México,** Ignacio L. Vallarta 243 (©/fax **322/222-6606**), has eco-oriented tours, including seasonal (Aug–Dec) trips to a turtle preservation camp where you can witness hatching baby Olive Ridley turtles.

A popular Vallarta adventure activity is **canopy tours.** You glide from treetop to treetop, getting an up-close-and-personal look at a tropical rainforest canopy and the trails far below. Expert guides assist you to the special platforms, and you move from one to another using pulleys on horizontal traverse cables, while the guides explain the tropical flora surrounding you. They also offer assistance—and moral support—as you rappel back down to the forest floor. Tours depart from the **Vallarta Adventures** (see "Diving &

Snorkeling," above) offices in both Marina Vallarta and Nuevo Vallarta at 8am, returning at 2pm. The price ($79/£43 for adults, $58/£32 for children 8–12) includes the tour, unlimited nonalcoholic beverages, and light snacks. Their newest offering is the **Outdoor Adventure,** which combines a ride on the canopy line with a day of adventure activities. You'll learn wilderness survival techniques while hiking through the Sierra Madre foothills, splashing through streams, rappelling down waterfalls, then taking a 300m (984-ft.) zip line over jungle landscape. The 6½ hour tour costs $110 (£61), for those who are physically fit, ages 12 and older.

A second option is available in the southern jungles of Vallarta, over the Orquidias River, through **Canopy Tours de Los Veranos** (© 322/223-6060; www.canopytours-vallarta.com). This tour will pick you up at the Canopy office, near the south side Pemex station, to transport you to their facilities upriver from Mismaloya. Departures are on the hour, from 9am to 2pm. In addition to the 13 cables—the longest being a full 350m (1,148 ft.)—it also offers climbing walls, waterslides, and horseback riding. The guides here are noted for helping even the faintest of heart propel through the treetops. Price is $80 (£44) for adults, or $50 (£28) for children ages 6 and older. Use of the natural-granite climbing wall (helmets and climbing-shoe use included) is $18 (£9.90); the 1½-hour jungle horseback riding tour costs $35 (£19).

FISHING Arrange fishing trips through travel agencies or through the **Cooperativa de Pescadores (Fishing Cooperative),** on the *malecón* north of the Río Cuale, next door to the Rosita Hotel (© 322/222-1202). Fishing charters cost $100 (£55) per person, for one to eight people; or select from other options where the price varies with the size of the boat; a boat can be rented for 8 hours for $450 (£248). Although the posted price at the fishing cooperative is the same as you'll find through travel agencies, you may be able to negotiate a lower price at the cooperative, which does not accept credit cards. It's open Monday through Sunday from 7am to 10pm, but make arrangements a day ahead. You can also arrange fishing trips at the Marina Vallarta docks, or by calling **Fishing with Carolina** (© 322/224-7250; cell 044-322/292-2953; fishingwith carolina@hotmail.com), which uses a 9m (30-ft.) Uniflite sportsfisher, fully equipped with an English-speaking crew. Fishing trips cost $350 (£193) for up to four people for 4 hours and include equipment and bait, but drinks, snacks, and lunch are optional, at $12 (£6.60) per person. If you mention Frommer's when you make your reservation, they'll offer a free lunch with your booking. All boats have brand new engines.

GOLF Puerto Vallarta is an increasingly popular golf destination; five courses have opened in the past 6 years, bringing the total in the region to nine. The Joe Finger-designed private course at the **Marina Vallarta Golf Club** (© 322/221-0073) is an 18-hole, par-74 course that winds through the Marina Vallarta peninsula and affords ocean views. It's for members only, but most luxury hotels in Puerto Vallarta have memberships for their guests. Greens fees are $90 to $136 (£50–£75) in high season, $115 (£63) in low season. Fees include golf cart, range balls, and tax. Hiring a caddy costs $10 (£5.50). Club rentals, lessons, and special packages are available.

North of town in the state of Nayarit, about 15km (9⅓ miles) beyond Puerto Vallarta, is the 18-hole, par-72 **Los Flamingos Club de Golf** (© 329/296-5006; www.flamingosgolf.com.mx). It features beautiful jungle vegetation and underwent a renovation and upgrade of the course in 2005. It's open from 7am to 7pm daily, with a snack bar (but no restaurant) and full pro shop. The daylight greens fee is $140 (£77), which drops to $90 (£50) after 2:30pm. It includes the use of a golf cart; hiring a caddy costs $20 (£11) plus tip, and club rental is $30 to $40 (£17–£22). A free shuttle runs from downtown Puerto Vallarta; call for pickup times and locations.

The breathtaking Jack Nicklaus Signature course at the **Punta Mita Golf Club** 🏆🏆🏆 (© 329/291-6000; fax 329/291-6060) has 8 oceanfront holes and an ocean view from every hole. Its hallmark is the optional Hole 3B, the "Tail of the Whale," with a long drive to a green on a natural island—the only natural-island green in the Americas. It requires an amphibious cart to take you over when the tide is high, and there's an alternate hole for when the ocean or tides are not accommodating. The course is open only to guests staying in the Punta Mita resort or Four Seasons, or to members of other golf clubs with a letter of introduction from their pro. Other selected area hotels also have guest privileges—ask your concierge. Greens fees for hotel guests are $185 (£102) for 18 holes and $110 (£61) for 9 holes, and for nonguests are $230 (£127), including cart, with (Calloway) club rentals for $60 (£33). Lessons are also available. In early 2008, a second Jack Nicklaus Signature course will open in Punta Mita, adjacent to the new St. Regis Resort slated to open at the same time.

Another Jack Nicklaus course is at the **Vista Vallarta Golf Club** (© 322/290-0030; www.vistavallartagolf.com), along with one designed by Tom Weiskopf. These courses were the site of the 2002 PGA World Cup Golf Championships. The club is in the foothills of the Sierra Madre, behind the bullring in Puerto Vallarta. A round costs $174 (£96) per person. Cart fee is an extra $46 (£25), with club rentals available for $49 (£27) per set/per round.

The Robert von Hagge–designed **El Tigre** course at Paradise Village (© **866/843-5951** in the U.S., or **322/297-0773;** www.paradisevillage.com; www.eltigregolf.com), in Nuevo Vallarta, opened in March 2002. The 7,239-yard course is on relatively flat land, but the design incorporates challenging bunkers, undulating fairways, and water features on several holes. El Tigre also offers lessons and has an expansive clubhouse. This seems to be the favored course of local pros. Greens fees are $185 (£102) a round, or $85 (£47) if you play after 2pm. Club rentals are $45 (£25).

HORSEBACK-RIDING TOURS Travel agents and local ranches can arrange guided horseback rides. **Rancho Palma Real,** Carretera Vallarta, Tepic 4766 (© **322/222-0501**), has an office 5 minutes north of the airport; the ranch is in Las Palmas, approximately 40 minutes northeast of Vallarta. It is by far the nicest horseback riding tour in the area. The horses are in excellent condition, and you enjoy a tour of local farms on your way to the ranch. The price ($62/£34; American Express or cash only) includes breakfast and lunch.

Another excellent option is **Rancho El Charro,** Av. Francisco Villa 895 (© **322/224-0114;** cell 044-322/294-1689; www.rancho elcharro.com), which has beautiful, well-cared for horses, and a variety of rides for all levels, departing from their ranch at the base of the Sierra Madre Mountains. Rides range in length from 3 to 8 hours, and in price from $56 to $100 (£31–£55). There's even the $69 (£38) Wild Ride, where you gallop along a ridge to a jungle waterfall—too often, riders are disappointed with only trotting along well-marked trails on these excursions, and this ride allows experienced riders much more freedom. Rancho El Charro also has multiple-day rides—check their website for details. **Rancho Ojo de Agua,** Cerrada de Cardenal 227, Fracc. Las Aralias (©/fax **322/ 224-0607;** www.mexonline.com), also offers high-quality tours, from its ranch located 10 minutes by taxi north of downtown toward the Sierra Madre foothills. The rides last 3 hours (10am–1pm, 3–6pm, or 4–7pm) and take you up into the mountains overlooking the ocean and town. The cost is $59 (£32). Both ranches have other tours available as well as their own comfortable base camp for serious riders who want to stay out overnight.

PARASAILING Parasailing and other watersports are available at many beaches along the Bay of Banderas. The most popular spot is at Los Muertos Beach. WaveRunners, banana boats, and parasailing are available by the hour, half-day, or full day. Be forewarned, however, that the swiftly shifting winds in Banderas Bay can make this a dangerous proposition. Fly at your own risk!

SAILING I personally believe that a trip to the Vallarta area is not complete without a journey out on the water—there's no better way to see the entirety of the area, the beauty of the surrounding mountains, and get a sense of the area than from the perspective of a sailboat. Banderas Bay is increasingly being used at the site of national and international regatta competitions.

A recent (2005) and welcome addition to Vallarta's sailing scene is most impressive—**Coming About** ⟨⟨⟨ (© 322/222-4119; www.coming-about.com) is a women-only sailing school that provides hands-on sailing instruction for day-sailing excursions, as well as week-long sailing classes at a variety of skill levels. Owned and operated by Pat Henry, who spent 8 years sailing around the globe, then wrote about it in her book *By the Grace of the Sea: A Woman's Solo Odyssey Around the World,* the classes are challenging, inspiring, and entertaining, as Pat shares her adventures with participants. Dubbed "any woman's sailing school," the goal is to take away the fear and the mystery, and make the skill of sailing accessible to everyone. Courses range from a 1-day introductory course to a 9-day bareboat charter captain course. Fees for the 1-day course are $475 (£261) for four people; $2,800 to $3,600 (£1,540–£1,980) per person, based on double occupancy, for the 9-day course, including hotel.

SWIMMING WITH DOLPHINS Ever been kissed by a dolphin? Take advantage of a unique opportunity to swim with Pacific bottlenose dolphins in one of two facilities—a clear lagoon or a special swim facility that's part of the Vallarta Adventures' offices. **Dolphin Adventure** ⟨⟨⟨ (© 888/303-2653 in the U.S., or 322/297-1212, ext. 3; www.vallarta-adventures.com) operates an interactive dolphin-research facility—considered the finest in Latin America—that allows limited numbers of people to swim with dolphins Monday through Saturday at scheduled times. Cost for the swim is $135 (£74). Reservations are required, and they generally sell out at least a week in advance. You may prefer the **Dolphin Encounter** ($69/£38), which allows you to touch and learn about the dolphins in smaller pools, so you're ensured up-close-and-personal time with

---

> **(Tips A Spectator Sport**
>
> **Bullfights** are held December through April beginning at 5pm on Wednesday at the La Paloma bullring, across the highway from the town pier. Travel agencies can arrange tickets, which cost around $25 (£14).

---

them. You can even be a **Trainer for a Day,** a special 7-hour program of working alongside the more experienced trainers and the dolphins, for a cost of $250 (£138). The **Dolphin Kids** program, for children ages 4 to 8, is a gentle introduction to dolphins, featuring the Dolphin Adventure baby dolphins and their mothers interacting with the children participants ($60/£33). I give this my highest recommendation. Not only does the experience leave you with an indescribable sensation, but it's also a joy to see these dolphins—they are well cared for, happy, and spirited. The program is about education and interaction, not entertainment or amusement, and is especially popular with children ages 10 and older.

TENNIS   Many hotels in Puerto Vallarta offer excellent tennis facilities; they often have clay courts. The full-service **Canto del Sol Tennis Club** (© **322/224-0123** and 322/226-0123; www.canto delsol.com) is at the Canto del Sol hotel in the Hotel Zone. It offers indoor and outdoor courts (including a clay court), full pro shop, lessons, clinics, and partner matches.

A STROLL THROUGH TOWN

Puerto Vallarta's cobblestone streets are a pleasure to explore; they're full of tiny shops, rows of windows edged with curling wrought iron, and vistas of red-tile roofs and the sea. Start with a walk up and down the *malecón.*

Among the sights you shouldn't miss is the **municipal building** on the main square (next to the tourism office), which has a large Manuel Lepe mural inside in its stairwell. Nearby, right up Independencia, sits the picturesque **Parish of Nuestra Señora de Guadalupe church,** Hidalgo 370 (© **322/222-1326**), topped with a curious crown held in place by angels—a replica of the one worn by Empress Carlota during her brief time in Mexico as Emperor Maximilian's wife. On its steps, women sell religious mementos; across the narrow street, stalls sell native herbs for curing common ailments. Services in English are held each Saturday at 5pm, and Sunday at 10am. Regular hours are Monday through Saturday from 7:30am to 8:30pm,

---

Moments   A Spectacular Sight

Performances of the **Voladores de Papantla (Papantla Flyers)** take place every day at 10 and 11am; and in the evenings, Friday to Wednesday at 7:30, 8:30, and 9:30pm on the *malecón,* adjacent to the "Boy on a Seahorse" statue. In this pre-Columbian religious ritual, four men are suspended from the top of a tall pole, circling around it (as if in flight), while another beats a drum and plays a flute while balanced at the top. It signifies the four cardinal points, and the mystic "center" of the self, a sacred direction for ancient Mexican cultures.

Sunday from 6:30am to 8:30pm. Note that entrance is restricted to those properly dressed—no shorts or sleeveless shirts allowed.

Three blocks south of the church, head east on Libertad, lined with small shops and pretty upper windows, to the **municipal market** by the river. (It's the Río Cuale Mercado, but I once overheard a tourist ask for the "real quality" market.) After exploring the market, cross the bridge to the island in the river; sometimes a painter is at work on its banks. Walk down the center of the island toward the sea, and you'll come to the tiny **Museo Río Cuale** (no phone; Mon–Sat 10am–5pm; free admission), which has a small but impressive permanent exhibit of pre-Columbian figurines.

Retrace your steps to the market and Libertad, and follow Calle Miramar to the brightly colored steps up to Zaragoza. Up Zaragoza to the right 1 block is the famous **pink arched bridge** that once connected Richard Burton's and Elizabeth Taylor's houses. In this area, known as **"Gringo Gulch,"** many Americans have houses.

2 Shopping

Shopping in Puerto Vallarta is generally concentrated in small, eclectic, independent shops rather than impersonal malls. You can find excellent **folk art,** original **clothing** designs, fine jewelry, and creative home accessories at great prices. Vallarta is known for having the most diverse and impressive selection of **contemporary Mexican fine art** outside Mexico City. It also has an abundance of tacky T-shirts and the ubiquitous **silver jewelry.**

THE SHOPPING SCENE

There are a few key shopping areas: central downtown, the Marina Vallarta *malecón,* the popular *mercados,* and on the beach—where the merchandise comes to you. Some of the more attractive shops are 1 to 2 blocks in **back of the *malecón.*** Start at the intersection of Corona and Morelos streets—interesting shops spread out in all directions from here. **Marina Vallarta** has two shopping plazas, Plaza Marina and Neptuno Plaza, on the main highway from the airport into town, which offer a limited selection of shops, with Plaza Neptuno primarily featuring home decor shops. Although still home to a few interesting stores, the *marina malecón* (marina boardwalk) is dominated by real estate companies, timeshare vendors, restaurants, and boating services. A new (September 2006) addition to Vallarta's shopping and dining scene is the modern **Plaza Peninsula** (located on Av. Francisco Medina Ascencio 2485, just south of the cruise ship terminal and north of the Ameca River bridge; no phone number or website), in front of a large waterfront condominium development of the same name. It's home to more than 30 businesses including Vallarta's first **Starbucks,** as well as art galleries, boutiques, and a varied selection of restaurants. There is underground parking, plus public sculptures and comfy outdoor seating. It has quickly emerged as Vallarta's current hotspot for hanging out in the evenings, especially with teens.

Puerto Vallarta's **municipal market** is just north of the Río Cuale, where Libertad and A. Rodríguez meet. The *mercado* sells clothes, jewelry, serapes, leather accessories and suitcases, papier-mâché parrots, stuffed frogs and armadillos, and, of course, T-shirts. Be sure to comparison-shop, and bargain before buying. The market is open daily from 9am to 7pm. Upstairs, a **food market** serves inexpensive Mexican meals—for more adventurous diners, it's probably the best value and most authentic dining experience in Vallarta. An **outdoor market** is along Río Cuale Island, between the two bridges. Stalls sell crafts, gifts, folk art, and clothing. New to downtown is the **Small Vallarta** (© **322/222-7530**) on Paseo Díaz Ordaz 928, on the eastern side, just before the start of the *malecón.*

Tips Beware of the Silver Scam

Much of the silver sold on the beach is actually alpaca, a lower-quality silver metal (even though many pieces are stamped with the designation ".925," supposedly indicating true silver). Prices for silver on the beach are much lower, as is the quality. If you're looking for a more lasting piece of jewelry, you're better off in a silver shop.

It is a "small mall" featuring tourist-friendly shops and dining options, including Carl's Jr.'s burgers, Häagen-Dazs ice cream, a Swatch watch shop, El Mundo de Tequila, and a Diamonds International jewelry store.

In most of the better shops and galleries, shipping, packing, and delivery to Puerto Vallarta hotels are available. Some will also ship to your home address. Note that while bargaining is expected in the *mercados* and with beach vendors, stores generally charge fixed—and fair—prices for their wares.

THE LOWDOWN ON HUICHOL INDIAN ART

Puerto Vallarta offers the best selection of Huichol art in Mexico. Descendants of the Aztec, the Huichol are one of the last remaining indigenous cultures in the world that has remained true to its ancient traditions, customs, language, and habitat. The Huichol live in adobe structures in the high Sierras (at an elevation of 1,400m/4,592 ft.) north and east of Puerto Vallarta. Due to the decreasing fertility (and therefore productivity) of the land surrounding their villages, they have come to depend on the sale of their artwork for sustenance.

Huichol art has always been cloaked in a veil of mysticism—probably one of the reasons serious collectors seek out this form of *artesanía*. Colorful, symbolic yarn "paintings," inspired by visions experienced during spiritual ceremonies, characterize Huichol art. In the ceremonies, artists ingest peyote, a hallucinogenic cactus, which induces brightly colored visions; these are considered messages from their ancestors. The visions' symbolic and mythological imagery influences the art, which encompasses not only yarn paintings but also fascinating masks and bowls decorated with tiny colored beads.

The Huichol might be geographically isolated, but they are learning the importance of good business and have adapted their art to meet consumer demand. Original Huichol art, therefore, is not necessarily traditional. Iguanas, jaguars, sea turtles, frogs, eclipses, and eggs appear in response to consumer demand. More traditional works depict deer, scorpions, wolves, or snakes.

The Huichol have also had to modify their techniques to create more pieces in less time and meet increased demand. Patterned fill-work, which is faster to produce, sometimes replaces the detailed designs that are used to fill the pieces. The same principle applies to yarn paintings. While some are beautiful depictions of landscapes and even abstract pieces, they are not traditional themes.

Fun Fact   A Huichol Art Primer: Shopping Tips

Huichol art falls into two main categories: yarn paintings and beaded pieces. All other items you might find in Huichol art galleries are either ceremonial objects or items used in everyday life.

Yarn paintings are made on a wood base covered with wax and meticulously overlaid with colored yarn. Designs represent the magical vision of the underworld, and each symbol gives meaning to the piece. Paintings made with wool yarn are more authentic than those made with acrylic; however, acrylic yarn paintings are usually brighter and have more detail because the threads are thinner. It is normal to find empty spaces where the wax base shows. Usually the artist starts with a central motif and works around it, but it's common to have several independent motifs that, when combined, take on a different meaning. A painting with many small designs tells a more complicated story than one with only one design and fill-work on the background. Look for the story of the piece on the back of the painting. Most Huichol artists write in pencil in Huichol and Spanish.

Beaded pieces are made on carved wooden shapes depicting different animals, wooden eggs, or small bowls made from gourds. The pieces are covered with wax and tiny *chaquira* beads are applied one by one to form designs. Usually the beaded designs represent animals; plants; the elements of fire, water, or air; and certain symbols that give a special meaning to the whole. Deer, snakes, wolves, and scorpions are traditional elements; other figures, such as iguanas, frogs, and any animals not indigenous to Huichol territory, are incorporated by popular demand. Beadwork with many small designs that do not exactly fit into one another is more time-consuming and has a more complex symbolic meaning. This kind of work has empty spaces where the wax shows.

You may see Huichol Indians on the streets of Vallarta—they are easy to spot, dressed in white clothing embroidered with colorful designs. A number of fine Huichol galleries are in downtown Puerto Vallarta (see individual listings under "Crafts & Gifts" and "Decorative & Folk Art," below).

One place to learn more about the Huichol is **Huichol Collection,** Morelos 490, across from the sea-horse statue on the *malecón* (© **322/223-2141**). Not only does this shop offer an extensive selection of Huichol art in all price ranges, but it also has a replica of a Huichol adobe hut, informational displays explaining more about their fascinating way of life and beliefs, and usually a Huichol artist at work. However, note that this is a timeshare sales location, so don't be surprised if you're hit with a pitch for a "free" breakfast and property tour. **Peyote People,** Juarez 222 (© **322/222-2302,** and 222-6268; www.peyotepeople.com), is a more authentic shop specializing in Huichol yarn paintings and bead art from San Andres Cohamiata, one of the main villages of this indigenous group, up in the high Sierra. The shop is open Monday through Friday from 10am until 9pm and Saturday and Sunday 10am to 6pm.

CIGARS & TEQUILA

La Casa del Habano   This fine tobacco shop has certified quality cigars from Cuba, along with humidors, cutters, elegant lighters, and other smoking accessories. It's also a local cigar club, with a walk-in humidor for regular clients. In the back, you'll find comfy leather couches, TV sports, and full bar service—in other words, a manly place to take a break from shopping. Open Monday through Saturday from noon to 9pm. Aldama 170. © **322/223-2758.**

La Casa del Tequila 🍸   Here you'll find an extensive selection of premium tequilas, plus information and tastings. Also available are books, tequila glassware, and other tequila-drinking accessories. The shop has recently (2005) been downsized to accommodate the **Agave Grill** (see "Where to Dine," in chapter 2) in the back, but now you can enjoy tasty Mexican fare and margaritas while you shop! Open Monday through Saturday from noon to 11pm. Morelos 589. © **322/222-2000.**

CLOTHING

Vallarta's single true department store is **LANS,** with branches at Juárez 867 (© **322/226-9100;** www.lans.com.mx), and in Plaza Caracol, next door to the supermarket Gigante, in the Hotel Zone (© **322/226-0204**). Both offer a wide selection of name-brand clothing, accessories, footwear, cosmetics, and home furnishings. Along with the nationally popular **LOB, Carlos 'n' Charlie's,** and **Bye-Bye** brands, Vallarta offers a few distinctive shops.

Laura López Labra Designs   The most comfortable clothing you'll ever enjoy. LLL is renowned for her trademark all-white (or natural) designs in 100% cotton or lace. Laura's fine gauze fabrics float in her designs of seductive skirts, romantic dresses, blouses, beachwear, and baby dolls. Men's offerings include cotton drawstring pants and lightweight shirts. Other designs include a line of precious children's clothing and some pieces with elaborate embroidery based on Huichol Indian designs. Personalized wedding dresses are also available. Open Monday through Saturday from 10am to 3:30pm and from 5 to 9pm. Basilio Badillo 329-A. ⓒ **322/113-0102.**

Mar de Sueños 𝕽𝕽   This small shop carries stunning swimsuits and exquisite lingerie. Without a doubt, the finest women's beachwear, intimate apparel, and evening wear in Vallarta for those special occasions—or just to make you feel extra special. The shop also stocks a selection of fine linen clothing—and it's one of the few places in Mexico that carries the renowned Italian line La Perla. Other name brands include Gottex, D&G, and DKNY. Open daily from 10am to 9pm. Basilio Badillo 277-B. ⓒ **322/222-7362.**

CONTEMPORARY ART

Several dozen galleries get together to offer art walks almost every week between November and April.

Corsica   Among the newest and best of Vallarta's galleries, Corsica features an exquisite collection of sculptures, installations, and paintings, from world-renown contemporary artists from Mexico. They offer professional packing and worldwide shipping with purchases. There are three locations—at Guadalupe Sanchez 735, Leona Vicario 230, and Plaza Península. Open Monday through Saturday 11am to 2pm, and by appointment 5 to 11pm. ⓒ **322/223-1821.** www.galeriacorsica.com.

Galería AL (Arte Latinoamericano)   This gallery showcases contemporary works created by young, primarily Latin American artists, as well as Vallarta favorite Marta Gilbert. Feature exhibitions take place every 2 weeks during high season. The historic building (one of Vallarta's original structures) has exposed brick walls; small rooms of exhibition spaces on the second and third floors surround an open courtyard. It's also rumored to have a friendly resident ghost, who partner Susan Burger says has been quite welcoming. Open Monday through Saturday from 10:30am to 9pm. Josefa Ortiz Domínguez 155. ⓒ **322/222-4406.** www.galeriaal.com.

Galería des Artistes   This stunning gallery features contemporary painters and sculptors from throughout Mexico, including the renowned original "magiscopes" of Feliciano Bejar. Paintings by a

Vallarta favorite Evelyn Boren, as well as a small selection of works by Mexican masters, including Orozco, can be found here, among the exposed brick walls and stylish interior spaces. It's open Monday to Saturday 11am to 10pm. Just across the street, affiliate **Galería Omar Alonso** (② 322/222-5587; www.galeriaomaralonso.com) exhibits photography by internationally renowned artists. Open Monday through Saturday 11am to 11pm. Leona Vicario 248. ② 322/223-0006.

Galería Pacífico   Since opening in 1987, Galería Pacífico has been considered one of the finest in Mexico. On display is a wide selection of sculptures and paintings in various media by midrange masters and up-and-comers alike. The gallery is 1½ blocks inland from the fantasy sculptures on the *malecón.* Among the artists whose careers Galería Pacífico has influenced are rising talent Brewster Brockman, internationally renowned sculptor Ramiz Barquet, and Patrick Denoun. Open Monday through Saturday from 10am to 8pm; Sunday by appointment. Between May and October, check for reduced hours or vacation closings. Aldama 174, 2nd floor. ② 322/222-1982. galeriapacifico@prodigy.net.mx.

Galería Uno   One of Vallarta's first galleries, the Galería Uno features an excellent selection of contemporary paintings by Latin American artists, plus a variety of posters and prints. During the high season, featured exhibitions change every 2 weeks. In a classic adobe building with open courtyard, it's also a casual, salon-style gathering place for friends of owner Jan Lavender. Open Monday through Saturday from 10am to 10pm. Morelos 561 (at Corona). ② 322/222-0908.

Gallería Dante   This gallery-in-a-villa showcases contemporary art as well as sculptures and classical reproductions of Italian, Greek, and Art Deco bronzes—against a backdrop of gardens and fountains. Works by more than 50 Mexican and international artists are represented, including the acclaimed local talent Rogelio Diaz, as well as Alejandro Colunga and Tellosa. Located on the "Calle de los Cafés," the gallery is open during the winter Monday through Saturday from 10am to 5pm, and by appointment. Basilio Badillo 269. ② 322/222-2477. www.galleriadante.com.

Studio Cathy Von Rohr   This lovely studio showcases the work of Cathy Von Rohr, one of the most respected artists in the area. For years, Cathy lived in the secluded cove of Majahuitas, on the bay's southern shore, and much of her work reflects the tranquillity and deep connection with the natural world that resulted. Paintings, prints, and sculptures are featured. It's open by appointment and does not accept credit cards. Manuel M. Diéguez 321. ℂ **866/256-2739** in the U.S., or 322/222-5875. www.cathyvonrohr.com.

CRAFTS & GIFTS

Alfarería Tlaquepaque   Opened in 1953, this is Vallarta's original source for Mexican ceramics and decorative crafts, all at excellent prices. Talavera pottery and dishware, colored glassware, birdcages, baskets, and wood furniture are just a few of the many items in this warehouse-style store. Open Monday through Saturday, 9am to 9pm, and Sundays from 9am to 3pm. Av. México 1100. ℂ **322/223-2121.**

La Casa del Feng Shui   I am enchanted by this shop's selection of crystals, candles, talismans, fountains, and wind chimes—along with many more items designed to keep the good energy flowing in your home, office, or personal space. Why not take home something to add more harmony to your life? Open Monday through Saturday from 9am to 9pm. Corona 165, around the corner from Morelos. ℂ **322/ 222-3300.**

Safari Accents   Flickering candles glowing in colored-glass holders welcome you to this highly original shop overflowing with creative gifts, one-of-a-kind furnishings, and reproductions of paintings by Frida Kahlo and Botero. Open daily from 10am to 11pm. Olas Altas 224, Loc. 4. ℂ **322/223-2660.**

DECORATIVE & FOLK ART

Banderas Bay Trading Company ✪   This shop features fine antiques and one-of-a-kind decorative objects for the home, including contemporary furniture, antique wooden doors, religious-themed items, original art, hand-loomed textiles, glassware, and pewter. This unique selection is handpicked by one of the area's most noteworthy interior designers, Peter Bowman. Open Monday to Saturday 9am to 9pm. A *bodega* (warehouse) annex of the shop is located at Constitución 319 ℂ **322/223-9817.** Lázaro Cárdenas 263 (near Ignacio L. Vallarta). ℂ **322/223-4352.**

Lucy's CuCu Cabaña *(Finds*   Owners Lucy and Gil Givens have assembled an exceptionally entertaining and eclectic collection of Mexican folk art—about 70% of which is animal-themed. Each summer they travel Mexico and personally select the handmade works created by over 100 indigenous artists and artisans. Items

> ### *Tips* Meet the Author
>
> If you're shopping at Lucy's CuCu Cabaña, you may find your-
> self attended to by Lucy's husband, and Vallarta's favorite
> author, Gil Gevins. Gil's hilarious books include *Refried Brains,
> Puerto Vallarta on 49 Brain Cells a Day,* and the follow-up
> *Puerto Vallarta on a Donkey a Day*—laugh-out-loud tales of
> life in this town, perfect for beach reading. And, natch,
> they're available for sale at the shop. You couldn't buy a bet-
> ter souvenir.

include metal sculptures, Oaxacan wooden animals, *retablos* (altars),
and fine Talavera ceramics. Open Monday through Saturday from
10am to 8pm. The store is closed from May 15 to October 15.
Basilio Badillo 295. ② 322/222-4839.

Olinala   This shop contains two floors of fine indigenous Mexican crafts and folk art, including an impressive collection of
museum-quality masks and original contemporary art by gallery
owner Brewster Brockman. Open Monday through Friday from
10am to 2pm and 5 to 8pm, Saturday from 10am to 2pm. Lázaro Cárdenas 274. ② 322/222-4995.

Puerco Azul   Set in a space that actually has a former pig-roasting
oven, Puerco Azul features a whimsical and eclectic selection of art
and home accessories, much of it created by owner and artist Lee
Chapman (aka Lencho). You'll find many animal-themed works in
bright colors, including his signature *puercos azules* (blue pigs).
Open Monday to Saturday from 10am to 8pm, closed on Sunday.
Constitución 325, just off Basilio Badillo's "restaurant row." ② 322/222-8647.

Querubines *(Finds*   This is my personal favorite for the finest-qual-
ity artisanal works from throughout Mexico. Owner Marcella Gar-
cía travels across the country to select the items, which include
exceptional artistic silver jewelry, embroidered and hand-woven
clothing, bolts of loomed fabrics, tin mirrors and lamps, glassware,
pewter frames and trays, high-quality wool rugs, straw bags, and
Panama hats. Open Monday through Saturday from 9am to 9pm.
Under the same ownership and open the same hours, **Serafina,**
Basilio Badillo 260 (② 322/223-4594), features a more extensive
selection of cotton clothing and handmade jewelry. Juárez 501A (corner of Galeana). ② 322/223-1727.

JEWELRY & ACCESSORIES

Viva ⭐⭐⭐ *(Finds)*   At Viva, both the shop and the jewelry are stunning. You enter through a long corridor lined with displays showcasing exquisite jewelry from over 450 international designers, including Mexico's finest silversmiths. Open daily from 10am to 11pm. Basilio Badillo 274. **©** **322/222-4078.** www.vivacollection.com.

3 Puerto Vallarta After Dark

Puerto Vallarta's spirited nightlife reflects the town's dual nature: part resort, part colonial town. In years past, Vallarta was known for its live music scene, but in recent years the nocturnal action has shifted to DJ clubs, spinning an array of eclectic, contemporary music. A concentration of nightspots lies along Calle Ignacio L. Vallarta (the extension of the main southbound road) after it crosses the Río Cuale. Along one 3-block stretch you'll find a live blues club, sports bar, live mariachi music, a gay dance club, a steamy live salsa dance club, and the obligatory **Señor Frog's.** Walk from place to place and take in a bit of it all!

The *malecón,* which used to be lined with restaurants, is now known more for hip dance clubs and a few more relaxed options, all of which look out over the ocean. You can first stroll the broad walkway by the water's edge and check out the action at the various clubs, which extend from **Bodeguita del Medio** on the north end to **Hooters** just off the central plaza.

Marina Vallarta's clubs offer a more upscale, indoor, air-conditioned atmosphere. South of the Río Cuale, the **Olas Altas** zone's small cafes and martini bars buzz with action. In this zone, there's also an active gay and lesbian club scene.

PERFORMING ARTS & CULTURAL EVENTS

Truth be told, cultural nightlife beyond the **Mexican Fiesta** is limited. Culture centers on the visual arts; the opening of an exhibition has great social and artistic significance. Puerto Vallarta's gallery community comes together in the central downtown area to present weekly **art walks,** where new exhibits are presented, featured artists attend, and complimentary cocktails are served. Check listings in the daily English-language newspaper, *Vallarta Today,* or the events section of www.virtualvallarta.com, to see what's on the schedule during your stay. Also of note are the free musical performances in the downtown plaza's gazebo—check with the municipal tourism office for the current schedule.

FIESTA NIGHTS

Major hotels in Puerto Vallarta feature frequent fiestas for tourists—extravaganzas with open bars, Mexican buffet dinners, and live entertainment. Some are fairly authentic and make a good introduction for first-time travelers to Mexico; others can be a bit cheesy. Shows are usually held outdoors but move indoors when necessary. Reservations are recommended.

Rhythms of the Night (Cruise to Caletas) 🎭🎭🎭 *(Moments*

This is an unforgettable evening under the stars at John Huston's former home at the pristine cove called Las Caletas. The smooth, fast Vallarta Adventures catamaran travels here, entertaining guests along the way. Tiki torches and drummers dressed in native costumes greet you at the dock. There's no electricity—you dine by the light of candles, the stars, and the moon. The buffet dinner is delicious—steak, seafood, and generous vegetarian options. Everything is first class. The entertainment showcases indigenous dances in contemporary style. The cruise departs at 6pm and returns by 11pm. Departs from Terminal Marítima. ✆ 888/303-2653 in the U.S., or 322/297-1212, ext 3. www.vallarta-adventures.com. Cost $80 (£44); includes cruise, dinner, open bar, and entertainment.

THE CLUB & MUSIC SCENE
RESTAURANT & BARS

Azul 96   Among the newest clubs to open, Azul 96 is known more for its sand-floored, rooftop Sky Bar than its sleek ground-floor restaurant, which specializes in traditional gourmet fare. The architecture is stunning, but most people pass by as they climb the stairs—or take the elevator to the bar upstairs, with its panoramic views of the city. A long glass bar borders one side and serves sushi along with cocktails. In the "sandy beach" area, partiers settle into high tables or banquettes to enjoy the energizing dance music. The Sky Bar is open daily from 8pm to 4am. Morelos 696, Col. Centro. ✆ 322/222-1022. www.azul96.com.

Bar Constantini 🎭🎭   The most sophisticated lounge in Vallarta is set in the elegant eatery, Café des Artistes. It's become a popular option for those looking for a lively yet sophisticated setting for after-dinner drinks. The plush sofas are welcoming, and the list of champagnes by the glass, signature martinis, and specialty drinks is suitably tempting. Live jazz and blues in an intimate atmosphere are drawing crowds, as are weekly wine tastings, held each Thursday at 6pm. An ample appetizer and dessert menu make it appropriate for late-night dining and drinks. Open daily from 6pm to 2am. Guadalupe Sánchez 740. ✆ 322/222-3229.

Carlos O'Brian's   Vallarta's original nightspot was once the only place for an evening of revelry. Although the competition is stiffer nowadays, COB's still packs them in—especially the 20-something set. The late-night scene resembles a college party. Open daily from noon to 2am; happy hour is from noon to 8pm. Paseo Díaz Ordaz *(malecón)* 786, at Pípila. © 322/222-1444 or -4065. Weekend cover $11 (£6.05); includes 2 drinks.

La Bodeguita del Medio   This authentic Cuban restaurant and bar is known for its casual energy, terrific live Cuban music, and mojitos. It is a branch of the original Bodeguita in Havana (reputedly Hemingway's favorite restaurant there), which opened in 1942. If you can't get to that one, the Vallarta version has successfully imported the essence—and has a small souvenir shop that sells Cuban cigars, rum, and other items. The downstairs has large wooden windows that open to the *malecón* street action, while the upstairs offers terrific views of the bay. Walls throughout are decorated with old photographs and patrons' signatures—if you can, find a spot and add yours! The food is less memorable here than the music and atmosphere, so I recommend drinks and dancing, nothing more. Open daily from 11:30am to 2am. Paseo Díaz Ordaz 858 *(malecón)*, at Allende. © 322/223-1585.

Z'Tai ⓡ   Opened in 2007, Z'Tai is a stunning array of spaces that span an entire city block. Enter from the *malecón,* and you'll discover ZBar, an upstairs lounge with chill-out music, bay views, and comfy banquettes for relaxing. Venture further into this club and you'll find an expansive open air garden area that serves cocktails as well as an array of Asian-inspired dining and snacking options, accompanied by electronic music at a level still appropriate for conversation. Seating is casual and spans several elevations, overlooking Zen gardens and flowing ponds. At the opposite end (Calle Morelos entrance), is an air-conditioned dining area. They boast a 1,000-bottle wine menu, but the favorite drink here is their signature cucumber martini. Open daily for food service from 6pm to 2am, with bar service until 4am. They also offer valet service or shuttle service to wherever you parked your car. Morelos 737, Col. Centro. © 322/222-0306.

ROCK, JAZZ & BLUES

El Faro Lighthouse Bar ⓡ   A circular cocktail lounge at the top of the Marina lighthouse, El Faro is one of Vallarta's most romantic nightspots. Live or recorded jazz plays, and conversation is manageable. Drop by at twilight for the magnificent panoramic views, but don't expect anything other than a drink and, if you get lucky, some popcorn. Open daily from 5:30pm to 2am. Royal Pacific Yacht Club, Marina Vallarta. ℂ 322/221-0541 or -0542.

Mariachi Loco   This lively mariachi club features singers belting out boleros and ranchero classics. The mariachi show begins at 9pm—the mariachis stroll and play as guests join in impromptu singing—and by 10pm it gets going. After midnight the mariachis play for pay, which is around $10 (£5.50) for each song played at your table. There's Mexican food from 8 to 10:30pm. Open daily from 8pm to 4am. Cárdenas 254 (at Ignacio Vallarta). ℂ 322/223-2205. Generally no cover, but varies depending on guest performances.

Route 66   A popular live-music club in Vallarta, Route 66 features a hot house band, playing a mix of reggae, blues, rock, and anything by Santana. Live music jams between 10pm and 2am Monday through Sunday nights. It's open daily from 6pm to 2am. Ignacio L. Vallarta 217 (between Madero and Cárdenas, south of the river). No phone.

NIGHT CLUBS & DANCING

A few of Vallarta's clubs charge admission, but generally you pay just for drinks: say, $5 (£2.75) for a margarita, $3 (£1.65) for a beer, more for whiskey and mixed drinks. Keep an eye out for discount passes frequently available in hotels, restaurants, and other tourist spots. Most clubs are open from 10pm to 4am.

Christine   This dazzling club draws a crowd with an opening laser-light show, pumped-in dry ice, flashing lights, and a dozen large-screen video panels. Once a disco—in the true sense of the word—it received a needed face-lift in 2003, and is now a more modern dance club, with techno, house, and hip-hop the primary tunes played. The sound system is truly amazing, and the mix of music can get almost anyone dancing. Dress code: No tennis shoes or flip-flops, no shorts for men. Open daily from 10pm to 4am; the light show begins at 11pm. In the Krystal Vallarta hotel, north of downtown off Av. Francisco Medina Ascencio. ℂ 322/224-0202. Cover ladies $10 (£5.50), men $20 (£11).

Collage Club   A multilevel monster of nighttime entertainment, Collage includes a pool salon, video arcade, bowling alley, and the always-packed Disco Bar, with frequent live entertainment. It's just past the entrance to Marina Vallarta, air-conditioned, and very popular with a young, mainly local crowd. Open daily from 10am to 6am. Calle Proa s/n, Marina Vallarta. ℂ 322/221-0505. Cover $5.50–$40 (£3.05–£22), which varies by theme party being offered that night.

de Santos ⟨⟨⟨   Vallarta's chic dining spot is known more for the urban, hip crowd the bar draws—it is *the* hot spot for locals. The adjacent club has become known as the place for the superchic to party, although competition opened in late 2006 to lure some regulars away. The lower level holds an air-conditioned bar and dance floor (after midnight, when dining tables have been cleared away), where a DJ spins the hottest of house and techno. Upstairs, there's an open-air rooftop bar with chill-out music and acid jazz. Enjoy the tunes and the fresh air while lounging around on one of the several oversize beds. One partner, a member of the superhot Latin rock group Maná, uses Vallarta as a home base for writing songs. The crowd, which varies in age from 20s on up, shares a common denominator of cool style. The restaurant bar is open daily from 5pm to 1am; the club is open Wednesday through Saturday from 10pm to 6am. Morelos 771. ✆ 322/223-3052 or -3053.

Hilo   You'll recognize Hilo by the giant sculptures that practically reach out the front entrance and pull you into this high-energy club, which has become a favorite with the 20-something set. Music ranges from house and electronic to rock. It seems the later the hour, the more crowded the place becomes. Open daily from 4pm to 6am. Malecón, between Aldama and Abasolo sts. ✆ 322/223-5361. Cover $7 (£3.85) weekends and holidays.

J & B Salsa Club   This is the locally popular place to go for dancing to Latin music—from salsa to samba, the dancing is hot! On Fridays, Saturdays, and holidays the air-conditioned club features live bands. Open daily from 10pm to 6am. Av. Francisco Medina Ascencio Km 2.5 (Hotel Zone). ✆ 322/224-4616. Cover $10 (£5.50).

Nikki Beach   This haven of the hip hails from South Beach, Miami, and St. Tropez, and has brought its ultracool vibe to Vallarta. It's a great choice for catching rays during the day, but its real appeal is the nocturnal action. White-draped bed-size lounges are scattered about in the outdoor lounge area, under a canopy of tall palms and umbrellas. Indoor dining and lounging is also available. The music is the latest in electronic, house, and chill, with visiting DJs often playing weekend nights. Sundays feature their signature beach brunch, and Thursday evenings feature "Beautiful People" night. Open Sunday to Wednesday from 11am to 1am (food service stops at 11pm); Thursday to Saturday from 11am to 3am (food service stops at 1am.). On the beach at the Westin Regina Resort, Marina Vallarta. ✆ 322/221-0252 or 226-1150. www.nikkibeach.com. No cover, unless for a special event, which will vary.

Señor Frog's   The sheer size of this outpost of the famed Carlos 'n' Charlie's chain is daunting, but it fills up and rocks until the early morning hours. Cute waiters are a signature of the chain, and one never knows when they'll assemble on stage and call on a bevy of beauties to join them in a tequila-drinking contest. Occasionally live bands appear. Although mainly popular with the 20s set, all ages will find the air-conditioned club fun. There's food service, but it's better known for its dance-club atmosphere. Open daily from 11am to 4am. Ignacio L. Vallarta and Venustiano Carranza. *C* **322/222-5171** or -5177. Cover–$11 (£6.05).

Zoo   Your chance to be an animal and get wild in the night. The Zoo even has cages to dance in if you're feeling unleashed. This popular club has a terrific sound system and a great variety of dance music, including techno, reggae, and rap. Every hour's happy hour, with two-for-one drinks. It opens daily at noon and closes in the wee hours. Paseo Díaz Ordaz *(malecón)* 630. *C* **322/222-4945**. www.zoobar dance.com. Cover $11 (£6.05); includes 2 drinks.

A SPORTS BAR

No Name Bar&Grill   With a multitude of TVs and enough sports memorabilia to start a minimuseum, the No Name is a great venue for catching your favorite game. It shows all NBA, NHL, NFL, and MLB broadcast events, plus pay-per-view. No Name also serves great barbecued ribs and USDA imported steaks. It's open daily from 9am to midnight. Morelos 460 *(malecón)*, at Mina. *C* **322/223-2508**.

GAY & LESBIAN CLUBS

Vallarta has a vibrant gay community with a wide variety of clubs and nightlife options, including special bay cruises and evening excursions to nearby ranches. The free *Gay Guide Vallarta* (www.gayguidevallarta.com) specializes in gay-friendly listings, including weekly specials and happy hours.

Disco Club Paco Paco   This combination dance club, cantina, and rooftop bar stages a spectacular "Trasvesty" transvestite show every Thursday, Friday, Saturday, and Sunday night at 1:30am. It's open daily from 1pm to 6am and is air-conditioned. Ignacio L. Vallarta 278. *C* **322/222-7667**. www.club-pacopaco.com. Cover $6 (£3.30) includes 1 drink 9pm to 6am.

Garbo   This small, cozy club is gay friendly, but not exclusively gay, and features great recorded music and occasional live music on weekends. It's open daily from 6pm to 2am and is air-conditioned. Pulpito 142. *C* **322/223-5753**. www.bargarbo.com.

La Noche   A casual, intimate "neighborhood bar" catering to a gay clientele, with great prices on drinks, and a menu of tequila cocktails. Beers are always two-for-one. Daily from 6pm to 2am. Lazaro Cardenas 257 (2 doors from Ignacio Vallarta). (℃ **322/222-3364.**

Ranch Disco Bar   This place is known for the "Ranch Hand's Show," Wednesday through Sunday at 11:15pm and 1am. The club also has a dance floor. Daily from 9pm to 6am. Venustiano Carranza 239 (around the corner from Paco Paco, and can also be accessed directly from Paco Paco). (℃ **322/223-0537.** Cover $6 (£3.30) includes 1 drink.

4 Side Trips from Puerto Vallarta

YELAPA: ROBINSON CRUSOE MEETS JACK KEROUAC ✸

It's a cove straight out of a tropical fantasy, and only a 45-minute trip by boat from Puerto Vallarta. Yelapa has no cars, has one sole paved (pedestrian-only) road, and got electricity just 5 years ago. It's accessible only by boat. Its tranquillity, natural beauty, and seclusion have made it a popular home for hippies, hipsters, artists, writers, and a few expats (looking to escape the stress of the world, or perhaps the law). A seemingly strange mix, but you're unlikely to ever meet a stranger—Yelapa remains casual and friendly.

To get there, travel by excursion boat or inexpensive water taxi (see "Getting Around," in chapter 2). You can spend an enjoyable day, but I recommend a longer stay—it provides a completely different perspective.

Once you're in Yelapa, you can lie in the sun, swim, snorkel, eat fresh grilled seafood at a beachside restaurant, or sample the local moonshine, *raicilla*. The local beach vendors specialize in the most amazing pies you've ever tasted (coconut, lemon, or chocolate). Equally amazing is how the pie ladies walk the beach while balancing the pie plates on their heads; they sell crocheted swimsuits, too. You can tour this tiny town or hike up a river to see one of two waterfalls; the closest to town is about a 30-minute walk from the beach. *Note:* If you use a local guide, agree on a price before you start out. Horseback riding, guided birding, fishing trips, and paragliding are also available.

For overnight accommodations, local residents frequently rent rooms, and there's also the rustic **Hotel Lagunita** ✸ (℃ **322/ 209-5056** or -5055; www.hotel-lagunita.com). Its 32 cabañas have private bathrooms, and the hotel has electricity, a saltwater pool, primitive spa with massage, an amiable restaurant and bar, as well as the Barracuda Beach lounge and brick-oven pizza cafe, plus a gourmet coffee shop. Though the prices are high for what you get, it is the most accommodating place for most visitors. Double rates run $110 (£61) during the season and $75 (£41) in the off season (MasterCard and Visa are accepted). Lagunita has become a popular spot for yoga retreats, and regularly features yoga classes.

A stylish alternative is the fashionable **Verana** ❀❀❀ (© **800/ 530-7176** or 322/222-2360; www.verana.com). See "Where to Stay," chapter 2, for details.

If you stay over Wednesday or Saturday during the winter, don't miss the regular dance at the **Yelapa Yacht Club** ❀ (no phone). Typically tongue-in-cheek for Yelapa, the "yacht club" consists of a cement dance floor and a disco ball, but the DJ spins a great range of tunes, from Glenn Miller to 50 Cent, attracting all ages and types. Dinner ($5–$12/£2.75–£6.60) is a bonus—the food may be the best anywhere in the bay. The menu changes depending on what's fresh. Ask for directions; it's in the main village, on the beach.

NUEVO VALLARTA & NORTH OF VALLARTA: ALL-INCLUSIVES

Many people assume Nuevo Vallarta is a suburb of Puerto Vallarta, but it's a stand-alone destination over the state border in Nayarit. It was designed as a megaresort development, complete with marina, golf course, and luxury hotels. Although it got off to a slow start, it is finally coming together, with a collection of mostly all-inclusive hotels on one of the widest, most attractive beaches in the bay. The biggest resort, Paradise Village, has a growing marina and an 18-hole golf course inland from the beachside strip of hotels, plus a growing selection of condos and homes for sale. The Mayan Palace also recently opened an 18-hole course. The Paradise Plaza shopping center, next to Paradise Village, adds much to the area's shopping, dining, and services. It's open daily from 10am to 10pm. To get to the beach, you travel down a lengthy entrance road from the highway, passing by a few remaining fields (great for birding) but mostly real estate under construction.

Also worthwhile is a day spent at the **Etc. Beach Club,** Paseo de los Cocoteros 38, Nuevo Vallarta (© **322/297-0174**). This beach club has a volleyball net, showers, restroom facilities, and food and drink service on the beach, both day and night. To get there, take the second entrance to Nuevo Vallarta coming from Puerto Vallarta and turn right on Paseo de los Cocoteros; it is past the Vista Bahía hotel. It's open daily from 11am to 7pm. Drinks cost $2.50 to $7 (£1.40–£3.85), entrees $4.50 to $17 (£2.50–£9.35); cash only.

A trip into downtown Puerto Vallarta takes about 30 minutes by taxi, costs about $18 to $20 (£9.90–£11), and is available 24 hours a day. The ride is slightly longer by public bus, which costs $1.20 (65p) and operates from 7am to 11pm.

Marival Grand & Club Suites   This all-inclusive hotel sits almost by itself at the northernmost end of Nuevo Vallarta. Done in Mediterranean style, it offers a complete vacation experience, from its beautiful beach to the adjacent dance club. There are a large variety of room types, ranging from standard units with no balconies to large master suites with whirlpools. The master suites have minibars and hair dryers. The broad white-sand beach is one of the real assets here—it stretches over 450m (1,476 ft.). There is also an extensive activities program, including fun for children.

Paseo de los Cocoteros and Bulevar Nuevo Vallarta s/n, 63735 Nuevo Vallarta, Nay. ⓒ 450/686-0226 in Canada, and 322/297-0100 or 226-8200. Fax 322/297-0262. www.gomarival.com. 495 units. High season $409 (£225) double, low season $208 (£114) double; upgrade to junior suite $50 (£28) per day, to master suite w/whirlpool $300 (£165) per day. Rates are all-inclusive. Ask for seasonal specials. AE, MC, V. From the Puerto Vallarta airport, enter Nuevo Vallarta from the 2nd entrance; Club Marival is the 1st resort to your right on Paseo de los Cocoteros. Free parking. **Amenities:** 6 restaurants; 8 bars; 4 outdoor pools, including an adults-only whirlpool and a children's pool with slides; 4 lighted tennis courts; spa; business center; salon. *In room:* A/C, TV, safe.

Paradise Village 𝕬𝕬   Truly a village, this self-contained resort on an exquisite stretch of beach offers a full array of services, from an on-site dance club to a full-service European spa and health club. The collection of pyramid-shaped buildings, designed in Maya-influenced style, houses well-designed all-suite accommodations in studio, one-, two-, and three-bedroom configurations. All have sitting areas and kitchenettes, making the resort ideal for families or groups of friends. The Maya theme extends to both oceanfront pools, with mythical creatures forming water slides and waterfalls. The exceptional spa is reason enough to book a vacation here, with treatments, hydrotherapy, massage (including massage on the beach), and fitness and yoga classes. Special spa packages are always available. A new and compelling attraction is their El Tigre golf course (details earlier in this chapter, under "Golf"), and their on-site marina continues to draw a growing number of boats and yachts.

Paseo de los Cocoteros 001, 63731 Nuevo Vallarta, Nay. ⓒ 800/995-5714 in the U.S., or 322/226-6770. Fax 322/226-6713. www.paradisevillage.com. 490 units. High season $185–$290 (£102–£160) junior or 1-bedroom suite, $390 (£215) 2-bedroom suite, $572 (£315) 3-bedroom suite; low season $159–$235 (£87–£129) junior or 1-bedroom suite, $290 (£160) 2-bedroom suite, $520 (£286) 3-bedroom suite. AE, DC, MC, V. Free covered parking. **Amenities:** 2 restaurants; 2 beachside snack bars; nightclub; 2 beachside pools; lap pool; championship golf club w/18-hole course; 4 tennis courts; complete fitness center; European spa; water-sports center; marina; kids' club; travel desk; guests-only rental-car fleet; basketball court; beach volleyball; petting zoo. *In room:* A/C, TV, minibar, coffeemaker, hair dryer, iron, safe.

BUCERIAS: A COASTAL VILLAGE ⍟

Only 18km (11 miles) north of the Puerto Vallarta airport, Bucerías ("boo-seh-*ree*-ahs," meaning "place of the divers") is a small coastal fishing village of 10,000 people in Nayarit state on Banderas Bay. It's caught on as an alternative to Puerto Vallarta for those who find the pace of life there too invasive. Bucerías offers a seemingly contradictory mix of accommodations—trailer-park spaces and exclusive villa rentals tend to dominate, although there's a small selection of hotels as well.

To reach the town center by car, take the exit road from the highway out of Vallarta and drive down the shaded, divided street that leads to the beach. Turn left when you see a line of minivans and taxis (which serve Bucerías and Vallarta). Go straight ahead 1 block to the main plaza. The beach, with a lineup of restaurants, is a half-block farther. You'll see cobblestone streets leading from the highway to the beach, and hints of villas and town homes behind high walls. Second-home owners and about 1,500 transplanted Americans have already sought out this peaceful getaway; tourists have discovered its relaxed pace as well.

If you take the bus to Bucerías, exit when you see the minivans and taxis to and from Bucerías lined up on the street that leads to the beach. To use public transportation from Puerto Vallarta, take a minivan or bus marked BUCERIAS (they run 6am–9pm). The last minivan stop is Bucerías's town square. There's also 24-hour taxi service.

Exploring Bucerías   Come here for a day trip from Puerto Vallarta just to enjoy the long, wide, uncrowded beach, along with the fresh seafood served at the beachside restaurants or at one of the cafes listed below. On Saturdays and Sundays, many of the streets surrounding the plaza are closed to traffic for a *mercado* (street market)—a shopping nirvana where you can buy anything from tortillas to neon-colored cowboy hats. If you are inclined to stay a few days, you can relax inexpensively and explore more of Bucerías.

The **Coral Reef Surf Shop,** Heroe de Nacozari 114-F (© **329/ 298-0261**), sells a great selection of surfboards and gear, and offers surfboard and boogie board rentals, surf lessons, and ATV and other adventure tours to surrounding areas.

Where to Stay   Unfortunately, I cannot recommend any of the hotels in Bucerías; they're run-down, and most people who choose to stay here opt for a private home rental. Check out the villa rental bulletin board at **www.sunworx.com**. **Las Palmas** in Bucerías (© **329/ 298-0060;** fax 329/298-0061) will book accommodations, including villas, houses, and condos. Call ahead, or ask for directions to the office when you get to Bucerías. It's open Monday through Friday from 9am to 2pm and 4 to 6pm, Saturday from 9am to 2pm.

Where to Dine   Besides those mentioned below, there are many seafood restaurants fronting the beach. The local specialty is *pescado zarandeado,* a whole fish smothered in tasty sauce and slow-grilled.

Karen's Place ⚜ INTERNATIONAL/MEXICAN   This casual oceanside restaurant offers classic cuisine, plus Mexican favorites in a style that appeals to North American appetites. Known for Sunday champagne brunch (9am–3pm), it is a perfect place to enjoy a light beach lunch, or a romantic dinner. The best-selling entrees are barbeque ribs and coconut shrimp. The casual, comfortable restaurant features live music on Tuesday and Friday at 7pm. It also has a decked terrace dining area with spectacular views, as well as a sushi menu.

On the beach at the Costa Dorada, Calle Lázaro Cárdenas. © 322/133-2186 or 329/298-0832. www.all.at/karens. Breakfast $4.50–$5.50 (£2.50–£3.05); Sun brunch (9am–3pm) $14 (£7.70); main courses $5.50–$13 (£3.05–£7.15). MC, V. Mon–Sat 9am–9pm, Sun 9am–3pm.

Le Fort ⚜⚜⚜ FRENCH   What an unforgettable dining experience! It's more than dinner—the evening consists of watching as Chef Gilles Le Fort prepares your gourmet meal and teaches you how to re-create it. The U-shaped bar in the intimate kitchen accommodates diners, who sip fine wines and nibble on pâté while the master works. Chef Le Fort is the winner of numerous culinary awards, and his warm conviviality is the real secret ingredient of this unusual experience. Once dinner is served, the chef and his wife, Margarita, will join the table, entertaining with stories of their experiences in Mexico. The first group of six to book for the evening chooses the menu; the maximum class size is 16, so groups often blend together. Le Fort has probably the most extensive wine cellar in the bay—some 4,000 bottles. Hand-rolled Cuban cigars, homemade sausages, pâtés, and more delicacies are available in the adjoining shop.

Calle Lázaro Cárdenas 71, 1 block from the Hotel Royal Decameron. ⓒ **329/298-1532.** www.lefort.com.mx. Reservations required. 3-course dinner, wines, and recipes $45 (£25) per person. No credit cards. Daily 8–10:30pm; cooking classes available 10am–1:30pm.

Mark's ⓡⓡ ⓕⓘⓝⓓⓢ ITALIAN/STEAK/SEAFOOD   It's worth a special trip to Bucerías just to eat at this covered-patio restaurant. The most popular American hangout in town, Mark's offers a great assortment of thin-crust pizzas and flatbread, baked in its brick oven and seasoned with fresh herbs grown in the garden. Everything has exquisite flavorings—some favorites include lobster-stuffed chile relleno, macadamia-crusted red snapper filet, ahi tuna served rare, and filet mignon with blue-cheese ravioli. Multitalented chef Jan Marie (Mark's charming wife and partner) runs an adjacent boutique, featuring elegant home accessories and unique gift items. The bar televises all major sporting events.

Calle Lázaro Cárdenas 56 (a half block from the beach). ⓒ **329/298-0303.** Pasta $8.70–$19 (£4.80–£10); main courses $13–$22 (£7.15–£12). MC, V. High season daily lunch noon–4pm and dinner 5–11pm; low season daily 5–10pm. From the highway, turn left just after bridge, where there's a small sign for Mark's; double back left at next street (immediately after you turn left) and turn right at next corner; Mark's is on the right.

Mezzogiorno ⓡⓡ ITALIAN   The owners of this elegantly casual oceanfront *trattoria* built a reputation with their Mezzaluna restaurant in Vallarta, then moved the business to their former home in Bucerías when the traffic became too much to deal with a commute. And diners on the north shore are so very grateful! It's the most attractive dining option north of Vallarta, in a sleekly restored home overlooking the bay. Choose to dine indoors or under the stars, beneath a canopy of trees on an oceanview deck or on the sand itself. But as stunning as the minimalist decor of the restaurant is, it takes second place to the savory dishes served. Salads are ample in size, and varied in combination of ingredients. My favorite combines grilled chicken with mixed greens, sun-dried tomatoes, goat cheese, and a currant-balsamic vinaigrette. For main dishes, pastas are the specialty, with best-sellers that include their calamari and saffron ravioli in a creamy sauce. Also delightful are the shrimp, clams, and fish served over black fettuccine, with black olives, capers, and a spicy tomato sauce. There is an ample wine list, full bar service, and attentive service.

Av. del Pacífico 33. ⓒ **329/298-0350.** www.mezzogiorno.com.mx. Main courses $7–$18 (£3.85–£9.90). MC, V. Daily 6–11pm.

PUNTA MITA: EXCLUSIVE SECLUSION *(*(*(*

At the northern tip of the bay is an arrowhead-shaped, 600-hectare (1,482-acre) peninsula bordered on three sides by the ocean, called Punta Mita. Considered a sacred place by the Indians, this is the point where Banderas Bay, the Pacific Ocean, and the Sea of Cortez come together. It's magnificent, with white-sand beaches and coral reefs just offshore. Stately rocks jut out along the shoreline, and the water is a dreamy translucent blue. Punta Mita is evolving into one of Mexico's most exclusive developments. The master plan calls for a total of four luxury hotels, several high-end residential communities, and up to three championship golf courses. It is the first luxury residential development in Mexico intended for the foreign market. Today, what you'll find is the elegant Four Seasons Resort, its Jack Nicklaus Signature golf course, and a selection of rental luxury villas and condos. But by early 2008, a new 100-room St. Regis Resort will open, along with Punta Mita's second Jack Nicklaus golf course.

Casa Las Brisas *(*(* *Finds*   Although not technically in Punta Mita, Casa Las Brisas is near enough to get the sense of relaxed seclusion of this area. It's located on the back road that runs from Punta Mita to Sayulita, on the small, pristine Careyeros Bay. The six rooms are set in a villa, overlooking the exquisite beach. The villa itself is a work of white stucco walls, tile floors and patios, thatch and tile roofs, and guayaba-wood balcony detailing. Patios and intimate indoor-outdoor seating areas on varying levels are ideal for an afternoon read or an evening cocktail. Interiors of the guest rooms are simple and elegant, with touches such as carved armoires, headboards, and doors from Michoacán. The colorful bathrooms feature large showers lined with hand-painted tiles. Private balconies with ocean views surround the pool, which features submerged sunning chairs and a small fountain. There are no TVs or telephones, but a cellphone in the lobby is available for guests. A big plus here is the delicious dining, included in the price of your stay.

Playa Careyeros, 63734 Punta de Mita, Nay. (© **866/740-7999** in the U.S., 329/298-4114, or 322/225-4364. www.casalasbrisas.com. 7 suites. High season $445–$575 (£245–£316) suite; low season $385–$515 (£212–£283) suite. Rates include all meals and drinks. Minimum 3-night stay. Credit cards for deposit only; cash payment upon booking. Limited street parking. **Amenities:** Restaurant; small outdoor pool; universal gym station; spa; tour services; entertainment room w/TV, DVD, and VCR. *In room:* A/C, minibar, safe, no phone.

Four Seasons Resort Punta Mita ★★★ The Four Seasons Resort has brought a new standard of luxury to Mexico's Pacific Coast. The boutique hotel artfully combines seclusion and pampering service with a welcoming sense of comfort. Accommodations are in three-story *casitas* surrounding the main building, which holds the lobby, cultural center, restaurants, shopping arcade, and oceanfront pool. Every guest room offers breathtaking views of the ocean from a large terrace or balcony. Most suites also offer a private plunge pool, a separate sitting room, a bar, and a powder room. Room interiors are typical Four Seasons—plush and spacious, with a king or two double beds, a seating area, and an oversize bathroom with a deep soaking tub, separate glass-enclosed shower, and dual vanity sink. More than the stylish luxury, this hotel boasts unerring service that is both warm and unobtrusive. At least 45 minutes from Puerto Vallarta's activities, it's the perfect getaway—but then, most guests feel so relaxed and at ease, it's hard to think of venturing beyond the resort at all. The full-service spa, tennis center, and private championship golf course seem to be reason enough. In 2006, Four Seasons unveiled an adults-only tranquillity pool, complete with champagne and caviar bar, and surrounded by cabañas available for daily rent, that come equipped with Wi-Fi, plasma TVs, and a comfy daybed. In 2007, they expanded their popular Kids for All Seasons club, plus added a building of rooms geared for family travelers, surrounded by a Lazy River, as well as yacht charters. In addition to the sumptuous rooms and suites, the resort now offers private 4- and 5-bedroom villas for guest stays, complete with private butler services.

63734 Bahía de Banderas, Nay. ⓒ **800/332-3442** in the U.S., or 329/291-6000. Fax 329/291-6060. www.fourseasons.com. 165 units. High season $545–$1,175 (£300–£646) double, $1,685–$4,485 (£927–£2,466) suite; low season $375–$925 (£206–£509) double, $1,025–$2,295 (£564–£1,262) suite. AE, DC, MC, V. Free valet parking. **Amenities:** 3 restaurants; lobby bar; beachfront bar; oceanfront pool; adults-only pool; tennis center w/4 courts of various surfaces; full-service fitness center; European-style spa; *temazcal* (pre-Hispanic sweat lodge); watersports equipment including sea kayaks, sailboards, surfboards, and sunfish sailboats; children's programs; game room, 24-hr. concierge; tour desk; room service; cultural center w/lectures and activities; complimentary video library. *In room:* A/C, TV/VCR, high-speed Internet, minibar, coffeemaker, hair dryer, iron, safe.

SAYULITA: MUCH MORE THAN A GREAT SURF SPOT
Sayulita is only 40km (25 miles) northwest of Puerto Vallarta, on Highway 200 to Tepic, yet it feels like worlds away. It captures the simplicity and tranquillity of beach life that has long since left

Vallarta—but hurry, because it seems this place is on the verge of exploding in popularity. For years, Sayulita has been principally a surfers' destination—the main beach in town is known for its consistent break and long, rideable waves. Recently, visitors and locals who find Vallarta becoming too cosmopolitan have started to flock here.

An easygoing attitude seems to permeate the air in this beach town. Yet despite its simplicity, niceties are popping up all over among the basic accommodations, inexpensive Mexican food stands, and handmade, hippie-style-bauble vendors. It's quickly becoming gentrified with new restaurants, cafes, shops, and villas for rent.

Sayulita is a popular stage for surfing tournaments; on any given weekend you might encounter perfect-swell-seeking surfers—or a Huichol Indian family that has come down to sell their wares. This eclectic mix of the cool, the unusual, and the authentic Mexican makes Sayulita a special place.

To get to Sayulita, you can rent a car, or take a taxi from the airport or downtown Vallarta. The rate is about $50 (£28) to get to the town plaza. You can also take a taxi back to Vallarta. The stand is on the main square, or you can call for pickup at your hotel. The trip from the airport to Sayulita costs $55 (£30). Guides also lead tours to Puerto Vallarta, Punta Mita, and other surrounding areas, including a Huichol Indian community.

Where to Stay   Sayulita offers several private homes for rent. One local expert on Sayulita rentals is **Upi Viteri** (upiviteri@prodigy. net.mx), who has access to some of the nicest rental properties.

Where to Dine   If you are in Sayulita, chances are you heard about it because of **Don Pedro's,** the most popular restaurant in town, in the heart of the main beach.

Don Pedro's INTERNATIONAL   Many say it's Don Pedro's that has brought so much attention to Sayulita in recent years—Vallarta area visitors came for the food, then booked their next vacation in this funky town. Choose between a two-level indoor dining area or shaded tables on the beach for breakfast, lunch, or dinner. Starters include crispy calamari, spring rolls, and fresh salads. Main courses include thin-crust pizzas, artfully prepared fresh fish, and a changing selection of savory pasta and chicken dishes, such as chicken Provençal, a whole chicken marinated in garlic and herbs, served with sautéed spinach, roasted tomatoes, and white beans. Grilled ahi tuna with mashed potatoes is also a favorite. In the bar area, TVs broadcast sporting events of any relevance, from the Super Bowl to Mexican soccer. I enjoy a relaxing lunch here, then stay for the beach. Full bar service also available.

Marlin 2, on the beachfront. ⓒ 329/291-3090. Main courses $5–$25 (£2.75–£14). MC, V. Daily 8am–11pm.

Rollie's ★★ *(finds)* BREAKFAST Breakfast heaven! This family restaurant emanates a happy aura that puts its patrons in a good mood. The menu reflects the tone of the place, with options such as Rollie's Delight (blended fresh orange and banana), Adriana's Rainbow (an omelet with cheese, tomatoes, green peppers, and onions), and my personal favorite, Indian Pipe Pancakes. All dishes come with Rollie's famous lightly seasoned, pan-fried new potatoes. Rollie's recently expanded their offerings to dinner as well, served from 5:30 to 9pm. Specialties include paella. There's also an upstairs espresso bar.

Av. Revolución, 2 blocks west of the main square. ⓒ 329/291-3567 or -3075. Breakfast $3–$8 (£1.65–£4.40); dinner $4–$15 (£2.20–£8.25). No credit cards. Daily Nov–Apr 8am–noon and 5:30–9pm. Closed May–Oct.

SAN SEBASTIAN: AN AUTHENTIC MOUNTAIN HIDEAWAY ★★★

If you haven't heard about San Sebastián yet, it probably won't be long—its remote location and historic appeal have made it the Mexican media's new darling destination. Originally discovered in the late 1500s and settled in 1603, the town peaked as a center of mining operations, swelling to a population of over 30,000 by the mid-1800s. Today, with roughly 600 year-round residents, San Sebastián retains all the charm of a village locked in time, with an old church, a coffee plantation, an underground tunnel system—and wholly without a T-shirt shop.

Getting There By car, it's a 2½-hour drive up the Sierra Madre from Puerto Vallarta on an improved road, but it can be difficult during the summer rainy season, when the road washes out frequently. **Vallarta Adventures** (ⓒ 888/303-2653 in the U.S., or 322/297-1212, ext. 3; www.vallarta-adventures.com) runs a daily plane service for half-day tours and can occasionally accommodate overnight visitors. The small private airport can arrange flights. **Aerotron** (ⓒ 322/221-1921; www.aerotron.com.mx) charges about $130 (£72) round-trip, **Aéro Taxis de la Bahía** (ⓒ 322/221-1990 and 222-2049) about $92 (£51) round-trip, depending on the type of plane and number of passengers. For more information on air tours and horseback-riding excursions, see the "Organized Tours" section, earlier in this chapter.

Where to Stay   There are two places to stay in San Sebastián. The first is the very basic **El Pabellón de San Sebastián,** which faces the town square. Its nine simply furnished rooms surround a central patio. Don't expect extras here; rates run $50 (£28) per double. The town's central phone lines handle reservations—you call © **322/ 297-0200** and leave a message or send a fax, and hopefully the hotel will receive it. Except on holidays, there is generally room at this inn. No credit cards.

A more enjoyable option is the stately **Hacienda Jalisco** ✦✦ (© **322/222-9638;** www.haciendajalisco.com), built in 1850 and once the center of mining operations in town. The beautifully land-scaped, rambling old hacienda is near the airstrip, a 15-minute walk from town. Proprietor Bud Acord has welcomed John Huston, Liz Taylor, Richard Burton, Peter O'Toole, and a cast of local characters over the years.

The five extra-clean rooms have wood floors, rustic furnishings and antiques, and working fireplaces; some are decorated with pre-Columbian reproductions. The ample bathrooms are beautifully tiled and have skylights. Hammocks grace the upstairs terrace, while a sort-of museum on the lower level attests to the celebrity guests and importance the hacienda has enjoyed over the years. Because of its remote location, all meals are included. Rates are $80 (£44) per person per night, and include full breakfast and dinner; alcoholic bever-ages are extra. Reserve through e-mail (pmt15@hotmail.com or info@haciendajalisco.com), through the town telephone (© **322/ 297-0200**), or on their website. Group rates and discounts for longer stays are available. No credit cards are accepted. Horseback, walking, or mine tours can be arranged through the Hacienda.

4

Costa Alegre: Puerto Vallarta to Barra de Navidad

By Lynne Bairstow

Costa Alegre is one of Mexico's most spectacular coastal areas, a 232km (144-mile) stretch that connects tropical forests with a series of dramatic cliff-lined coves. Tiny outpost towns line the coast, while dirt roads trail down to a succession of magical coves with pristine beaches, most of them steeped in privileged exclusivity. Considered one of Mexico's greatest undiscovered treasures, this area is becoming a favored hideaway for publicity-fatigued celebrities and those in search of natural seclusion.

The area is referred to as **Costa Alegre (Happy Coast)**—the marketer's term—and **Costa Careyes (Turtle Coast),** after the many sea turtles that nest here. It is home to an eclectic array of the most captivating and exclusive places to stay in Mexico, with a selective roster of activities that includes championship golf and polo. Along the line, however, you will encounter the funky beach towns that were the original lure for travelers who discovered the area.

Stops along Highway 200, as it meanders between Puerto Vallarta to the north and Manzanillo to the south, can be an enjoyable day trip, but travelers usually make the drive en route to a destination along the coast.

1 Along Costa Alegre (from North to South)

CRUZ DE LORETO'S LUXURY ECO-RETREAT

Hotelito Desconocido ★★★ *Moments*   The fact that the Hotelito Desconocido ("little unknown hotel") is ecologically minded is a bonus, but it's not the principal appeal. A cross between *Out of Africa* and *Blue Lagoon,* it is among my favorite places in Mexico. Think camping out with luxury linens, romantic candles everywhere, and a symphony performed by cicadas, birds, and frogs.

The rustic, open-air rooms, called *palafitos,* are in cottages perched on stilts over a lagoon. A grouping of suites is on the ample

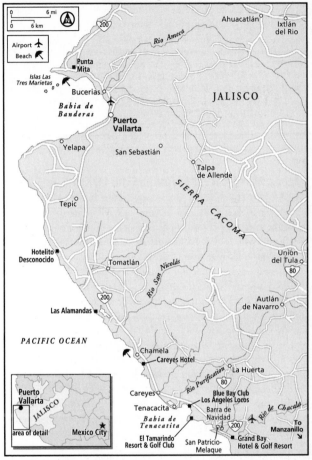

Costa Alegre & Central Pacific Coast

sand bar that separates the tranquil estuary from the Pacific Ocean. However, these are the least desirable units, and are often damp from the ocean air. Also here is a saltwater pool—the ocean is too aggressive for even seasoned swimmers.

Ceiling fans cool the air, and water is solar-heated. It's easy to disconnect here. In fact, it's mandatory: There's no electricity, no phones, no neighboring restaurants, nightclubs, or shopping—only delicious tranquillity. What the service lacks in polish it makes up for in enthusiasm. Rates do not include meals or drinks; a meal plan is mandatory, because there are no other options nearby (making the whole package somewhat pricey)—but it's a unique experience.

Playón de Mismaloya s/n, Cruz de Loreto, 48360 Tomatlán, Jal. ℭ **800/851-1143** in the U.S. and Canada (reservations: ℭ **01-800/013-1313** in Mexico, or 322/281-4010 or 222-2546). Fax 322/281-4130. www.hotelito.com. 24 units. High season $395–$478 (£217–£263) double, $520–$707 (£286–£389) suite; low season $312 (£172) double, $516–$561 (£284–£309) suite. Mandatory daily meal plan $90 (£50) per person. Children are discouraged. AE, MC, V. Take Hwy. 200 south for 1 hr., turn off at exit for Cruz de Loreto, and continue on clearly marked route on unpaved road for about 25 min. All activities are subject to an extra charge. Free parking. **Amenities:** 2 restaurant/bars; primitive-luxury spa; whirlpool; sauna; sailboards; kayaks; mountain bikes; massage; birding tours; hiking trails; horseback riding; billiards; beach volleyball. *In room:* No phone.

LAS ALAMANDAS: AN EXCLUSIVE LUXURY RESORT

Las Alamandas 𝕽𝕽𝕽   Almost equidistant between Manzanillo (1½ hr.) and Puerto Vallarta (1¾ hr.) lies Mexico's original ultra-exclusive resort. A dirt road winds for a mile through a tiny village to the guardhouse of Las Alamandas, on 28 hectares (69 acres) set against low hills. The resort consists of villas and *palapas* spread among four beaches, gardens, lakes, lagoons, and a bird sanctuary. It's designed for privacy—to the point that guests rarely catch a glimpse of one another. The resort has air-conditioning, telephones, and a new beachside massage *palapa*, yet manages to keep the experience as natural as possible. The resort accommodates only 22 guests.

The six spacious villas have brightly colored decor and tiled verandas with ocean views. They have several bedrooms (each with its own bathroom) and can be rented separately; guests who rent entire villas have preference for reservations. Some villas are on the beach, others across a cobblestone plaza. TVs with VCRs are available on request, but there's no outside reception. Van transportation to and from Manzanillo ($293/£161 one-way) and Puerto Vallarta ($289/£159 one-way) can be arranged when you reserve your room. Air transport from Puerto Vallarta is also available; call for details.

Hwy. 200, Km 83 48850 Manzanillo–Puerto Vallarta, Jal. Mailing address: Domicilio Conocido Costa Alegre QUEMARO Jalisco, Apdo. Postal 201, 48980 San Patricio Melaque, Jal. ℭ **888/882-9616** in the U.S. and Canada, or 322/285-5500. Fax 322/285-5027. www.alamandas.com. 14 units. High season $460–$910 (£253–£501) double, $1,200–$1,990 (£660–£1,095) villa; low season $360–$680 (£198–£374) double, $960–$1,400 (£374–£528) villa. Meal plans available. AE, MC, V. Free parking. **Amenities:** Restaurant; 18m (59-ft.) outdoor pool; lighted tennis court; weight room; boogie boards; mountain bikes; concierge; tour desk; birding boat tours; hiking trails; horseback riding; room service; book and video library; landing strip (make advance arrangements). *In room:* A/C, minibar.

CAREYES

The Careyes Hotel 🐢🐢   The Careyes is a gem of a resort nestled on a small, pristine cove between dramatic cliffs that are home to the exclusive villas of Careyes. This area has practically defined the architectural style of Mexico beach chic—bold washes of vibrant colors, open spaces, and gardens that showcase the tropical flowers and palms indigenous to the area.

The pampering accommodations all face the ocean and have always been stylishly simple. Although guests come here for isolation, you can enjoy many services, including a full European spa and polo. It's both rustic and sophisticated, with the room facades awash in scrubbed pastels forming a U around the center lawn and freeform pool. Rooms have a dramatic feel, from the plantation shutters and white-tile floors to the handsome loomed bedspreads and colorful pillows. Some rooms have balconies; all have ocean views. Twenty rooms have private pools, and villas are available for rent.

The hotel offers a number of special-interest activities for guests. Named after the hawksbill turtle (*carey* in Spanish), the hotel sponsors a Save the Turtle program in which guests can participate between July and December.

The Careyes is roughly 150km (93 miles) south of Puerto Vallarta. It's about a 2-hour drive north of Manzanillo on Highway 200, and about a 1-hour drive from the Manzanillo airport. Taxis from the Manzanillo airport charge around $100 (£55) one-way. Car-rental counters are at the Manzanillo and Puerto Vallarta airports. A car would be useful only for exploring the coast—Barra de Navidad and other resorts, for example—and the hotel can make touring arrangements.

Hwy. 200 Km 53.5, 48970 Careyes, Jal. CP. Mailing address: Apdo. Postal 24, 48970 Cihuatlán, Jal. (✆ **800/525-4800** in the U.S. and Canada, 315/351-0000 or -0606. Fax 315/351-0100. www.elcareyesresort.com. 51 units. High season $345–$425 (£190–£234) double, $535–$625 (£294–£343) suite; low season $305–$379 (£168–£208) double, $479–$565 (£263–£311) suite. AE, MC, V. Free parking. **Amenities:** Restaurant; bar; deli; large beachside pool; privileges at exclusive El Tamarindo resort (40km/25 miles south), w/mountaintop golf course; 2 tennis courts; paddle court; weight equipment; state-of-the-art spa; steam room; hot and cold plunge pools; sauna; sailboards; kayaks; Aquafins; children's programs (during Christmas and Easter vacations only); Internet access; room service; massage; laundry service; book and video library. *In room:* A/C, TV/VCR, minibar, minifridge, hair dryer.

TENACATITA BAY

Located an hour (53km/33 miles) north of the Manzanillo airport, this jewel of a bay is accessible by an 8km (5-mile) dirt road that passes through a small village set among banana plants and coconut palms. Sandy, serene beaches dot coves around the bay (frolicking dolphins are a common sight), and exotic birds fill a coastal lagoon. Swimming and snorkeling are good, and the bay is a popular stop for luxury yachts. Just south of the entrance to Tenacatita is a sign for the all-inclusive **Blue Bay Club Los Angeles Locos,** as well as the exclusive **El Tamarindo** resort and golf club. There is no commercial or shopping area, and dining options outside hotels are limited to a restaurant or two that may emerge during the winter months (high season). Relax—that's what you're here for.

Blue Bay Club Los Angeles Locos ✿
On a 5km (3-mile) stretch of sandy beach, Los Angeles Locos offers an abundance of activities, entertainment, and dining options, at an excellent value. It's a good choice for families and groups of friends. All rooms have ocean views, with either balconies or terraces. The three-story hotel is basic in decor and amenities, but comfortable. The attraction here is the wide array of on-site activities, plus a "Jungle River" cruise excursion (included in the room rate). **La Lagarta Disco** is a little on the dark and smoky side but can really rock, depending on the crowd—it's basically the only option on the bay.

Carretera Federal 200 Km 20, Tenacatita 48989, Municipio de la Huerta, Jal. ✆ **800/483-7986** in the U.S., **315/351-5020** or -5100. Fax 315/351-5412. www.losangeleslocos.com. 204 units. High season $130 (£72) double; low season $110 (£61) double. Children 5–12 $35 (£19) year-round. Rates are all-inclusive. Ask about family specials. AE, MC, V. Free parking. **Amenities:** 2 restaurants and snack bar (w/buffets and a la carte dining); 3 bars; dance club; adult outdoor pool; kids' outdoor pool adjacent to the beach; 3 tennis courts; exercise room; sailboards; kayaks; Hobie cats; horseback riding; basketball court; pool tables; kids' club; massage; babysitting; laundry service. *In room:* A/C, TV.

El Tamarindo (Yellowstone Club World) ✿✿✿ *Finds*
A personal favorite, El Tamarindo is a gem that combines stunning jungle surroundings with exquisite facilities, gracious service, and absolute tranquillity. In 2006, management of the resort was taken over by the prestigious Yellowstone Club World.

The bungalows exude an air of exclusivity—each thatched-roof villa has a splash pool and whirlpool, hammock, plus lounging and dining areas that overlook a private lawn and complement the stunning bedrooms. What they don't have are televisions. Service throughout the resort is exceptional. The bedrooms—with dark hardwood floors and furnishings—can be closed off for air-conditioned comfort, but the remaining areas are open to the sea breezes and heady tropical air.

The categories of bungalows denote their location—Beachfront (on a calm cove, but not as private as the others), Palm Tree, Garden, and Forest. The nonbeachside bungalows all have similar decor and amenities but feature more closed-in areas. Anyone squeamish about creepy-crawlies may be uncomfortable in the beginning, but listening to the life around you is a spectacular sensation. On 800 hectares (1,976 acres) of tropical rainforest bordering the Pacific Ocean, you'll feel as if you've found your own personal bit of heaven.

El Tamarindo has a championship 18-hole golf course designed by David Fleming; the approach to the first hole is through a forest of palms so tall they block the sun. The course has 7 oceanside holes and dramatic views. Equally exceptional are their spa services, with most massages and treatments provided in beachfront *cabañas,* or the resort's Spa Hut. The resort restaurant is the only dining option, but you won't be disappointed. The menu, which changes daily, has ample selections of fresh seafood selections, as well as pastas and beef, and all are artfully prepared. You can't leave without trying the resort's Tamarind Margarita.

Carretera Barra de Navidad–Puerto Vallarta Km 7.5, 48970 Cihuatlán, Jal. © 315/ 351-5032. Fax 315/351-5070. www.ycwtamarindo.com. 29 bungalows. High season $495–$975 (£272–£536) villas; low season $415–$839 (£228–£461) villas. AE, MC, V. From Puerto Vallarta (3 hr.) or the Manzanillo airport (40 min.), take Hwy. 200, then turn west at the clearly marked exit for El Tamarindo; follow signs for about 25 min. Free valet parking. **Amenities:** Restaurant; bar; large beachside pool w/whirlpool; 2 clay tennis courts; yoga classes; spa services; *temazcal* (pre-Hispanic sweat lodge); sailboards; kayaks; Aquafin sailboats; mountain bikes; estuary bird-watching tours; hiking trails; horseback riding; room service; TV and Internet-access room. *In room:* A/C, hair dryer, safe.

2 Barra de Navidad & Melaque

This pair of rustic beach villages (only 5km/3 miles apart) has been attracting travelers for decades. Only 30 minutes north of Manzanillo's airport and about 100km (62 miles) north of downtown Manzanillo, Barra has a few brick or cobblestone streets, good budget hotels and restaurants, and funky beach charm. All of this lies incongruously next to the superluxurious Grand Bay Hotel, which sits on a bluff across the inlet from Barra.

In the 17th century, Barra de Navidad was a harbor for the Spanish fleet; from here, galleons first set off in 1564 to find China. Located on a crescent-shaped bay with curious rock outcroppings, Barra de Navidad and neighboring Melaque are connected by a continuous beach on the same wide bay. It's safe to say that the only time Barra and Melaque hotels are full is during Easter and Christmas weeks. **Barra de Navidad** has more charm, more tree-shaded streets, better restaurants, more stores, and more conviviality between locals and tourists. Barra is very laid-back; faithful returnees adore its lack of flash. Other than the Grand Bay Hotel, on the cliff across the waterway in what is called Isla Navidad (although it's not on an island), nothing is new or modern. But there's a bright edge to Barra, with more good restaurants and limited—but existent—nightlife.

Melaque, on the other hand, is larger, rather sun-baked, treeless, and lacking in attractions. It does, however, have plenty of cheap hotels available for longer stays, and a few restaurants. Although the beach between the two is continuous, Melaque's beach, with deep sand, is more beautiful than Barra's. Both villages appeal to those looking for a quaint, quiet, inexpensive retreat rather than a modern, sophisticated destination.

Isla Navidad Resort has a manicured 27-hole golf course and the superluxurious Grand Bay Hotel, but the area's pace hasn't quickened as fast as expected. The golf is challenging and delightfully uncrowded, with another exceptional course at nearby El Tamarindo. It's a serious golfer's dream.

ESSENTIALS

GETTING THERE & DEPARTING   Buses from Manzanillo frequently run up the coast along Highway 200 on their way to Puerto Vallarta and Guadalajara. The fare is about $3.50 (£1.90). Most stop in the central villages of Barra de Navidad and Melaque. From the Manzanillo airport, it's only around 30 minutes to Barra, and **taxis** are available. The fare from Manzanillo to Barra is around $40 (£22); from Barra to Manzanillo, $30 (£17). From Manzanillo, the highway twists through some of the Pacific Coast's most beautiful mountains. Puerto Vallarta is 3 hours by **car** and 5 hours by bus, north on Highway 200 from Barra.

VISITOR INFORMATION   The **tourism office** for both villages is at Jalisco 67 (between Veracruz and Mazatlán), Barra (©/fax **315/355-5100;** www.barradenavidad.com). The office is open daily Monday through Friday from 9am to 5pm.

ORIENTATION   In Barra, hotels and restaurants line the main beachside street, **Legazpi.** From the bus station, beachside hotels are 2 blocks straight ahead, across the central plaza. Two blocks behind the bus station and to the right is the lagoon side. More hotels and

Barra de Navidad Bay Area

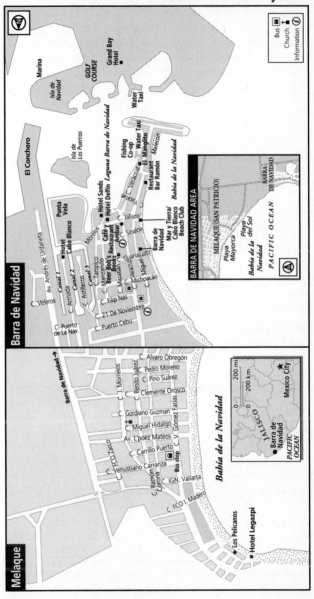

restaurants are on its main street, **Morelos/Veracruz.** Few streets are marked, but 10 minutes of wandering will acquaint you with the village's entire layout. There's a taxi stand at the intersection of Legazpi and Sinaloa streets. Legazpi, Jalisco, Sinaloa, and Veracruz streets border Barra's **central plaza.**

ACTIVITIES ON & OFF THE BEACH

Swimming and enjoying the beach and views of the bay take up most tourists' time. You can hire a small boat for a coastal ride or fishing in two ways. Go toward the *malecón* on Calle Veracruz until you reach the tiny boatmen's cooperative, with fixed prices posted on the wall, or walk two buildings farther to the water taxi ramp. The water taxi is the best option for going to Colimilla (5 min.; $2/£1.10) or across the inlet (3 min.; $1/55p) to the Grand Bay Hotel. Water taxis make the rounds regularly, so if you're at Colimilla, wait, and one will be along shortly. At the cooperative, a 30-minute **lagoon tour** costs $20 (£11), and a **sea tour** costs $25 (£14). **Sportfishing** is $80 (£44) for up to four people for a half-day in a small *panga* (open fiberglass boat, like the ones used for water taxis).

Surfing along Costa Alegre is gaining ground, thanks in large part to Germaine Badke, and the **South Swell Mex Surf Shop** (℃ **315/ 354-5497** or 100-4332; www.southswellmex.com), which he owns and operates. The shop offers boogie board and surfboard rentals, surfboard and surf supply sales, and will also create a custom-designed board. Surf lessons are also available. They're located in Suite 2 of the Hotel Alondra.

Isla Navidad Country Club (℃ **314/337-9024;** http://navidad. wyndham-hotels.com) has a beautiful and challenging 27-hole, 7,053-yard, par-72 **golf course** that is open to the public. Grand Bay Hotel guests pay greens fees of $175 (£96) for 18 holes, $192 (£106) for 27 holes; nonguests pay $207 and $230 (£114 and £127), respectively. Prices include a motorized cart. Caddies are available, as are rental clubs.

Beer Bob's Books, Avenida Tampico, between Sinaloa and Guanajuato, is a book-lover's institution in Barra and a sort of community service that the rather grouchy Bob does for fun. His policy of "leave a book if you take one" allows vacationers to select from hundreds of neatly shelved paperbacks, as long as they leave a book in exchange. It's open Monday through Friday from noon to 3pm and occasionally in the evenings. "Beer Bob" got his name because in earlier days, when beer was cheap, he kept a cooler stocked, and book browsers could sip and read. (When beer prices went up, Bob put the cooler away.)

WHERE TO STAY

Low season in Barra is any time except Christmas and Easter weeks. Except for those 2 weeks, it doesn't hurt to ask for a discount at the inexpensive hotels. To arrange **real estate rentals,** contact **The Crazy Cactus,** Veracruz 165, a half-block inland from the town church on Legazpi (℧/fax **315/355-6099;** crazycactusmx@yahoo. com). The store may be closed May through October.

VERY EXPENSIVE

Grand Bay Hotel Isla Navidad Resort (Overrated)   Across the yacht channel from Barra de Navidad, this luxurious hotel opened in 1997 on 480 hectares (1,186 acres) next to its 27-hole golf course. Now operated by Wyndham Resorts, it overlooks the village, bay, Pacific Ocean, and Navidad lagoon. The hotel's beach is narrow and on the lagoon. A better beach is opposite the hotel on the bay in Barra de Navidad. The spacious rooms are sumptuously outfitted with marble floors, large bathrooms, and hand-carved wood furnishings. Prices vary according to view and size of room, but even the modest rooms are large, and all have cable TV. Each comes with a king-size or two double beds, ceiling fans plus air-conditioning, and a balcony. All suites have a steam sauna and telephones in the bathroom as well as a sound system. The hotel is a short water-taxi ride across the inlet from Barra de Navidad; it is also on a paved road from Highway 200. Although the hotel bills itself as being on the Island of Navidad at Port Navidad, the port is the marina, and the hotel is on a peninsula.

Circuito de los Marinos s/n, 28830 Isla Navidad, Col. ℧ **01-800/849-2373** in Mexico, or 310/937-5124 or 314/331-0500. Fax 314/331-0570. www.wyndham.com/hotels/ZLOGB/main.wnt. 199 units. High season $499 (£274) double, $580–$892 (£319–£491) suite; low season $429 (£236) double, $507–$805 (£279–£443) suite. Rates include round-trip transportation to and from Manzanillo airport. AE, DC, DISC, MC, V. Free parking. **Amenities:** 2 restaurants; 2 bars; golf club w/food and bar service; outdoor pool w/water slides and swim-up bar; 27-hole, par-72 golf course; golf club w/pro shop and driving range; 3 lighted grass tennis courts; workout room; marina w/private yacht club; fishing, boat tours, and other excursions can be arranged; kids' club w/activity program; concierge; business center; salon; room service; babysitting; laundry service; dry cleaning. In room: A/C, TV, minibar, hair dryer, iron, safe.

MODERATE

Hotel Cabo Blanco ★★   Located on the point where you cross over to Isla Navidad, the Cabo Blanco is an outstanding option for family vacations or longer-term stays. Rooms are pleasantly rustic, with tile floors, large tile tubs, separate dressing areas, and stucco walls. The hotel overlooks the bay, but it's a 5-minute walk to the beach. The beamed-ceiling lobby is in its own building; rooms are in hacienda-style buildings surrounded by gardens. The atmosphere is generally tranquil, except during weekends and Mexican holidays, when this hotel tends to fill up. Because the Cabo Blanco doesn't front the beach, it has an affiliated beach club and restaurant, Mar y Tierra (p. 137).

Armada y Bahía de la Navidad s/n, 48987 Barra de Navidad, Jal. ℭ 315/355-6495 or -6496. Fax 315/355-6494. www.hotelcaboblanco.com. 101 units. $130 (£72) double; $256 (£141) suite w/kitchenette. All-inclusive plans also available. AE, MC, V. Limited street parking. **Amenities:** 2 restaurants; 4 outdoor pools (2 adults only); 2 tennis courts; concierge; tour desk; car-rental desk; laundry service. *In room:* A/C, TV.

INEXPENSIVE

Hotel Barra de Navidad ⓡ   At the northern end of Legazpi, this popular, comfortable beachside hotel is among the nicest in the town. It has friendly management, and some rooms with balconies overlooking the beach and bay. Other, less-expensive rooms afford only a street view. Only the oceanview rooms have air-conditioning. A nice swimming pool is on the street level to the right of the lobby.

Legazpi 250, 48987 Barra de Navidad, Jal. ℭ **315/355-5122.** Fax 315/355-5303. www.hotelbarradenavidad.com. 60 units. $72–$82 (£40–£45) double. MC, V. Free parking. **Amenities:** Outdoor pool. *In room:* A/C (in some rooms).

Hotel Delfín   One of Barra's better-maintained hotels, the four-story (no elevator) Delfín is on the landward side of the lagoon. It offers pleasant, basic, well-maintained, and well-lit rooms. Each has red-tile floors and a double, two double, or two single beds. The tiny courtyard, with a small pool and lounge chairs, sits in the shade of an enormous rubber tree. The fourth floor has a view of the lagoon. A breakfast buffet is served from 8:30 to 10:30am (p. 137).

Morelos 23, 48987 Barra de Navidad, Jal. ℭ **315/355-5068.** Fax 315/355-6020. www.hoteldelfinmx.com. 24 units. $49 (£27) double; ask about low-season discounts. MC, V. Free parking. **Amenities:** Restaurant; heated outdoor pool, gym.

Hotel Sands   The colonial-style Sands, across from the Hotel Delfín (see above) on the lagoon side at Jalisco, offers small but homey rooms with red-tile floors and windows with both screens and glass. The remodeled bathrooms have new tiles and fixtures. Lower rooms look onto a public walkway and wide courtyard filled with greenery and singing birds; upstairs rooms are brighter. Twelve rooms (suites or bungalows) have air-conditioning and kitchenette facilities. The hotel is known for its warm hospitality and high-season happy hour (2–6pm) at the pool terrace bar beside the lagoon. On weekends from 9pm to 4am, an adjacent patio "disco" plays recorded music for dancing. Breakfast is served from 7:30am to noon. Fishing trips can be arranged, and tours to nearby beaches are available.

Morelos 24, 48987 Barra de Navidad, Jal. ℂ/fax 315/355-5018. 42 units. High season $80 (£44) double; low season $54 (£30) double. Rates include breakfast. Room-only rates $10 (£5.50) less. Discounts for stays of 1 week or more. MC, V (6% surcharge). **Amenities:** Restaurant; bar; outdoor pool w/whirlpool overlooking lagoon beach; children's play area; tour desk. *In room:* A/C (in some rooms), kitchenette (in some rooms).

WHERE TO DINE

El Manglito 𝒦 SEAFOOD/MEXICAN   On the lagoon, with a view of the palatial Grand Bay Hotel, El Manglito serves home-style Mexican food to a growing number of repeat diners. The whole fried fish accompanied by drawn garlic butter, boiled vegetables, rice, and french fries, is a crowd-pleaser. Other enticements include boiled shrimp, chicken in orange sauce, and shrimp salad.

Veracruz 17, near the boatmen's cooperative. No phone. Main courses $5–$10 (£2.75–£5.50). No credit cards. Daily 9am–11pm.

Hotel Delfín BREAKFAST   The second-story terrace of this small hotel is a pleasant place to begin the day. The self-serve buffet offers an assortment of fresh fruit, juice, granola, yogurt, milk, pastries, and unlimited coffee. The price includes made-to-order eggs and delicious banana pancakes—for which the restaurant is known.

In the Hotel Delfín (p. 136), Morelos 23. ℂ 315/355-5068. www.hoteldelfin mx.com. Breakfast buffet $4 (£2.20). No credit cards. Daily 8:30am–noon.

Mar y Tierra INTERNATIONAL   Hotel Cabo Blanco's beach club is also a popular restaurant and bar and a great place to spend a day at the beach. On the beach are shade *palapas* and beach chairs, and a game of volleyball seems constantly in progress. The colorful restaurant is decorated with murals of mermaids. Perfectly seasoned shrimp fajitas come in plentiful portions.

Legazpi s/n (at Jalisco). ℂ 315/355-5028. Main courses $10–$17 (£5.50–£9.35). MC, V. Wed–Mon 10am–6pm.

Restaurant Bar Ambar CREPES/ITALIAN/FRENCH   This cozy, thatched-roof, upstairs restaurant is open to the breezes. The crepes are named after towns in France; the delicious *crêpe Paris,* for example, is filled with chicken, potatoes, spinach, and green sauce. International main dishes include imported (from the U.S.) rib-eye steak in Dijon mustard sauce, mixed brochettes, quiche, and Caesar salad. Ambar serves Spanish-style tapas from noon to 6pm, and adds French specialties during dinner. Pastas and pizzas are also served.

López de Legazpi 160, across from the church. (✆ **315/355-8169.** Crepes $9–$13 (£4.95–£7.15); main courses $15–$25 (£8.25–£14). No credit cards. Daily 5:30pm–midnight.

Restaurant Bar Ramón ✯ *Value* SEAFOOD/MEXICAN It seems that everybody eats at Ramón's, where the chips and fresh salsa arrive unbidden, and service is prompt and friendly. The food is especially good—however, most options are fried. Try fresh fried shrimp with french fries or any daily special that features vegetable soup or chicken-fried steak. Great value!

Legazpi 260. (✆ **315/355-6435.** Main courses $6–$12 (£3.30–£6.60). No credit cards. Daily 7am–11pm.

BARRA DE NAVIDAD AFTER DARK

When dusk arrives, visitors and locals alike find a cool spot to sit outside, sip cocktails, and chat.

During high season, the **Hotel Sands** poolside and lagoon-side bar has happy hour from 2 to 6pm. The colorful **Sunset Bar and Restaurant,** facing the bay at the corner of Legazpi and Jalisco, is a favorite for sunset watching and a game of oceanside pool or dancing to live or taped music. It's most popular with travelers ages 20 to 30. In the same vein, **Chips Restaurant,** on the second floor facing the ocean at the corner of Yucatán and Legazpi near the southern end of the *malecón,* has an excellent sunset vista. Live music follows the last rays of light, and patrons stay for hours. **Piper Lover Bar & Grill,** Legazpi 154 A (✆ **315/355-6747;** www.piperlover. com) is done in the style of the Carlos Anderson's chain—but it's not one of them. Still, it is lively, with pool tables and occasional live music.

At the **Disco El Galeón,** in the Hotel Sands on Calle Morelos, cushioned benches and cement tables encircle the round dance floor. It's all open air, and about as stylish as you'll find in Barra. It serves drinks only. Admission is $6 (£3), and it's open Friday and Saturday from 9pm to 4am.

A VISIT TO MELAQUE (SAN PATRICIO)

You may want to wander over to Melaque (aka San Patricio), 5km (3 miles) from Barra on the same bay. You can walk on the beach from Barra or take one of the frequent local buses from the bus station near the main square in Barra. The bus is marked MELAQUE. To return to Barra, take the bus marked CIHUATLAN.

Melaque's pace is even more laid-back than Barra's, and though it's a larger village, it seems smaller. It has fewer restaurants and less to do. Although there are more hotels, or "bungalows," as they are usually called, few manage the charm of those in Barra; if Barra hotels are full on a holiday weekend, Melaque would be a second choice. The paved road ends where the town begins. A few yachts bob in the harbor, and the palm-lined beach is gorgeous.

If you come by bus from Barra, you can exit anywhere in town or stay on until the last stop, which is the bus station in the middle of town a block from the beach. Restaurants and hotels line the beach. Coming into town from the main road, you'll be on the town's main street, **Avenida López Matéos.** You'll pass the main square on the way to the waterfront, where there's a trailer park. The street going left (southeast) along the bay is **Avenida Gómez Farías;** the one going right (northwest) is **Avenida Miguel Ochoa López.**

WHERE TO DINE   At the north end of Melaque beach is **Los Pelícanos** (no phone). It serves the usual seafood specialties; the tender fried squid is delectable. In addition, you can find burritos, and hamburgers. Many guests come here to stake a place on the beach and use the restaurant as headquarters for sipping and nipping. Open daily from 8am to 10pm, it's a peaceful place to watch the pelicans. The restaurant is at the far end of the bay before the **Hotel Legazpi** (© 315/355-5397), a pleasant place to stay. It has 20 rooms, charges $40 (£22) for a double, and doesn't accept credit cards.

In addition to the Los Pelícanos, many rustic *palapa* **restaurants** line the beach and farther along the bay.

5

Manzanillo

By Lynne Bairstow

Manzanillo has long been known as a resort town with wide, curving beaches, legendary sportfishing, and a highly praised diversity of scuba diving sites. Golf is also an attraction here, with two popular courses in the area.

One reason for its popularity could be Manzanillo's enticing tropical geography—vast groves of tall palms, abundant mango trees, and successive coves graced with smooth sand beaches. To the north, mountains blanketed with palms rise alongside the shoreline. And over it all lies the veneer of perfect weather, with balmy temperatures and year-round sea breezes. Even the approach by plane showcases the promise—you fly in over the beach and golf course. Once on the ground, you exit the airport through a palm grove.

Manzanillo is a dichotomous place—it is both Mexico's busiest commercial seaport and a tranquil, traditional town of multicolor houses cascading down the hillsides to meet the central commercial area of simple seafood restaurants, shell shops, and a few salsa clubs. The activity in Manzanillo divides neatly into two zones: the downtown commercial port and the luxury Santiago Peninsula resort zone to the north. The busy harbor and rail connections to Mexico's interior dominate the downtown zone. A visit to the town's waterfront *zócalo* provides a glimpse into local life. The exclusive Santiago Peninsula, home to the resorts and golf course, separates Manzanillo's two golden sand bays.

1 Essentials

256km (159 miles) SE of Puerto Vallarta; 267km (166 miles) SW of Guadalajara; 64km (40 miles) SE of Barra de Navidad

GETTING THERE & DEPARTING

BY PLANE   **Alaska Airlines** (© **800/252-7522** in the U.S., or 314/334-2211; www.alaskaair.com) offers service from Los Angeles; **US Airways** (**America West;** © **800/428-4322** in the U.S.; www.us airways.com/awa) flies from Phoenix. Ask a travel agent about the numerous **charters** from the States in the winter.

Manzanillo Area

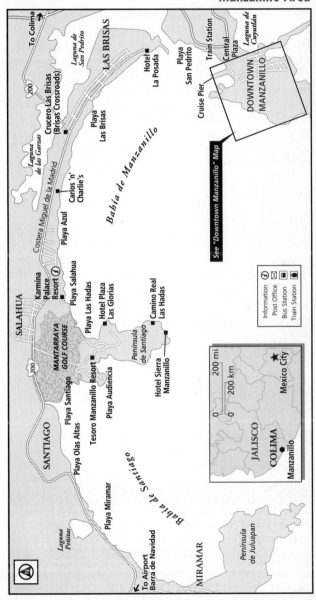

141

The **Playa de Oro International Airport** is 40km (25 miles) northwest of town. *Colectivo* (minivan) airport service is available from the airport; hotels arrange returns. Make reservations for return trips 1 day in advance. The *colectivo* fare is based on zones and runs $8 to $10 (£4.40–£5.50) for most hotels. Private taxi service between the airport and downtown area is around $25 (£14). **Budget** (© 800/472-3325 in the U.S., or 314/333-1445), **Hertz** (© 314/333-3191), and **Alamo** (© 314/334-0124) have counters in the airport open during flight arrivals; they will also deliver a car to your hotel. Daily rates run $58 to $78 (£32–£43). You need a car only if you plan to explore surrounding cities and the Costa Alegre beaches.

BY CAR   **Coastal Highway 200** leads from Acapulco (south) and Puerto Vallarta (north). From Guadalajara, take **Highway 54** through Colima into Manzanillo. Outside Colima you can switch to a toll road, which is faster but less scenic.

BY BUS   Buses run to Barra de Navidad (1½ hr. north), Puerto Vallarta (5 hr. north), Colima (1½ hr. east), and Guadalajara (4½ hr. north), with deluxe service and numerous daily departures. Manzanillo's **Central Camionera** (bus station) is about 12 long blocks east of town. If you follow Hidalgo east, the station will be on your right.

VISITOR INFORMATION

The **tourism office** (© 314/333-2277; fax 314/333-2264; www.manzanillo.com.mx) is on the Costera Miguel de la Madrid 875-A, Km 8.5. It's open Monday through Friday from 9am to 7pm, and Saturday from 9am to 2pm.

CITY LAYOUT

The town lies at one end of an 11km-long (7-mile) beach facing Manzanillo Bay and its commercial harbor. The beach has four sections—**Playa Las Brisas, Playa Azul, Playa Salahua,** and **Playa Las Hadas.** At the other end of the beaches is the high, rocky **Santiago Peninsula.** Santiago is 11km (7 miles) from downtown; it's the site of many beautiful homes and the best hotel in the area, Las Hadas, as well as the hotel's Mantarraya Golf Course. The peninsula juts out into the bay, separating Manzanillo Bay from Santiago Bay. Playa Las Hadas is on the south side of the peninsula, facing Manzanillo Bay, and **Playa Audiencia** is on the north side, facing Santiago Bay. The inland town of **Santiago** is opposite the turnoff to Las Hadas.

Activity in downtown Manzanillo centers on the *zócalo,* officially known as the Jardín Alvaro Obregón. A railroad, shipyards, and a basketball court with constant pickup games separate it from the waterfront. The plaza has flowering trees, a fountain, twin kiosks, and a view of the bay. It is a staple of local life, where people congregate on park benches to swap gossip and throw handfuls of rice to the ever-present *palomas* (doves—really just pigeons). Large ships dock at the pier nearby. **Avenida México,** the street leading out from the plaza's central gazebo, is the town's principal commercial thoroughfare. This area is currently undergoing a government-funded renaissance, so look for new improvements.

Once you leave downtown, the **Costera Miguel de la Madrid** highway (or just Costera Madrid) runs through the neighborhoods of Las Brisas, Salahua, and Santiago to the **hotel zones** on the Santiago Peninsula and at Miramar. Shell shops, mini-malls, and several restaurants are along the way.

There are two main lagoons. **Laguna de Cuyutlán,** almost behind the city, stretches south for miles, paralleling the coast. **Laguna de San Pedrito,** north of the city, parallels the Costera Miguel de la Madrid; it's behind Playa Las Brisas beach. Both are good birding sites. There are also two bays. **Manzanillo Bay** encompasses the harbor, town, and beaches. The Santiago Peninsula separates it from the second bay, **Santiago.** Between downtown and the Santiago Peninsula is **Las Brisas,** a flat peninsula with a long stretch of sandy golden beach, a lineup of inexpensive but run-down hotels, and a few good restaurants.

GETTING AROUND

BY TAXI Taxis in Manzanillo are plentiful. Fares are fixed by zones; rates for trips within town and to more distant points should be posted at your hotel. Daily rates can be negotiated for longer drives outside the Manzanillo area.

BY BUS The *camionetas* (local buses) make a circuit from downtown in front of the train station, along the Bay of Manzanillo, to the Santiago Peninsula and the Bay of Santiago to the north; the fare is 10¢ (5p). The ones marked LAS BRISAS go to the Las Brisas crossroads, to the Las Brisas Peninsula, and back to town; MIRAMAR, SANTIAGO, and SALAHUA buses go to outlying settlements along the bays and to most restaurants mentioned below. Buses marked LAS HADAS go to the Santiago Peninsula and pass the Las Hadas resort and the Tesoro Manzanillo and Plaza Las Glorias hotels. This is an inexpensive way to see the coast as far as Santiago and to tour the Santiago Peninsula.

FAST FACTS: Manzanillo

American Express There is no local office for American Express in Manzanillo. However, a highly recommendable agency (and American Express's former representative) is **Bahías Gemelas Travel Agency,** Blvd. Costero Miguel de la Madrid 1556, Las Gaviotas (© **314/333-1000;** fax 314/333-0649). It's open Monday through Friday from 9am to 2pm and 4 to 7pm, Saturday from 9am to 2pm.

Area Code The telephone area code is **314.**

Bank **Banamex,** just off the plaza on Avenida Juárez, downtown (© **314/332-0115**), is open Monday through Friday from 9am to 4pm, Saturday 10am to 2pm.

Hospital Contact the **Cruz Roja (Red Cross)** at © **314/336-5770** or the **General Hospital** at © **314/332-1903.**

Internet Access **Digital Center,** Bulevar Miguel de la Madrid 96-B (© **314/333-9191;** www.digitalcenter.manzanillo.com), is located in the hotel zone, near the Hotel Marbella and Fiesta Americana hotels. It charges $2 (£1.10) per hour, and also has printers. It's open Monday through Friday from 9am to 8pm, Saturday from 9am to 2pm. They also have computer repair services available.

Police Both the general police and Tourism Police are available by calling © **314/332-1004** or -1002.

Post Office The *correo,* Dr. Miguel Galindo 30, opposite Farmacia de Guadalajara, downtown (© **314/332-0022**), is open Monday through Friday from 8:30am to 4pm, Saturday from 9am to 1pm.

2 Activities On & Off the Beach

Activities in Manzanillo revolve around its golden sand beaches, which frequently accumulate a film of black mineral residue from nearby rivers. Most of the resort hotels are completely self-contained. Manzanillo's public beaches provide an opportunity to see more local color and scenery. They are the daytime playground for those staying at places off the beach or without pools.

BEACHES   Playa Audiencia, on the Santiago Peninsula, offers the best swimming as well as snorkeling, but **Playa San Pedrito,**

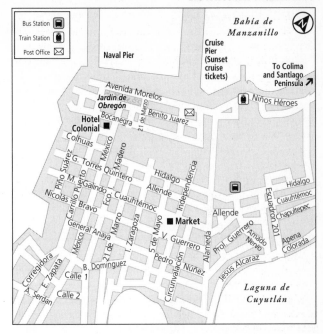

Downtown Manzanillo

Bus Station
Train Station
Post Office

Bahía de
Manzanillo

Naval Pier

Cruise
Pier
(Sunset
cruise
tickets)

To Colima
and Santiago
Peninsula ↗

Avenida Morelos

Niños Héroes

Jardin de
Obregón

Hotel
Colonial

Bocanegra
Benito Juarez

21 de Marzo

Colhuas

México
Madero

G. Torres Quintero

Hidalgo

Piño Suárez
M. Galindo
Fco. Cuauhtémoc

Allende

Independencia

Carrillo Puerto

Nicolás Bravo

Allende

Hidalgo

Escuadron 201

Cuauhtémoc

Chapultepec

General Anaya

México

21 de Marzo

I. Zaragoza

5 de Mayo

Market

V. Guerrero

Alameda

Prol. Guerrero

Amado
Nervo

Apena
Colorada

Corregidora

E. Zapata

B. Domínguez

Calle 1

Pedro
Núñez

Circunvalación

Jesús Alcaraz

A. Serdán

Calle 2

Laguna de
Cuyutlán

shallow for a long way out, is the most popular beach for its prox-
imity to downtown. **Playa Las Brisas,** located south of Santiago
Peninsula as you're heading to downtown Manzanillo, offers an
optimal combination of location and good swimming. **Playa Miramar,** on the Bahía de Santiago past the Santiago Peninsula, is popular with bodysurfers, windsurfers, and boogie boarders. It's
accessible by local bus from town. The major part of **Playa Azul,**
also south of the Santiago Peninsula, drops off sharply but is noted
for its wide stretch of golden sand.

BIRDING Several lagoons along the coast offer good birding. As
you go from Manzanillo past Las Brisas to Santiago, you'll pass
Laguna de Las Garzas (Lagoon of the Herons), also known as
Laguna de San Pedrito, where you can see many white pelicans and
huge herons fishing in the water. They nest here in December and
January. Directly behind downtown is the **Laguna de Cuyutlán**
(follow the signs to Cuyutlán), where you'll usually find birds in
abundance; species vary between summer and winter.

DIVING **Underworld Scuba** 🐟🐟 (©/fax **314/333-3678;** cell 314/358-0327; www.gomanzanillo.com), owned by longtime resident and local diving expert Susan Dearing, conducts highly professional diving expeditions and classes. Susan's warm enthusiasm and intimate knowledge of the area make this one of my top recommendations for dive outfitters in Mexico. Many locations are so close to shore that there's no need for a boat. Close-in dives include the jetty with coral growing on the rocks at 14m (46 ft.) and a nearby sunken frigate downed in 1959 at 8m (26 ft.). Divers can see abundant sea life, including coral reefs, seahorses, giant puffer fish, and moray eels. A dive requiring a boat costs $60 (£33) per person for one tank (with a three-person minimum) or $80 (£44) for two tanks ($10/£5.50 discount if you have your own equipment). You can also rent weights and a tank for beach dives for $10 (£5.50). A three-stop snorkel trip costs $45 (£25). All guides are certified divemasters, and the shop offers certification classes (PADI, YMCA, and CMAS) in very intensive courses of various durations. The owner offers a 10% discount on your certification when you mention Frommer's. MasterCard and Visa are accepted.

ESCORTED TOURS Because Manzanillo is so spread out, you might consider a city tour. Reputable local tour companies include **HECtours** (© **314/333-1707;** www.hectours.com) and **Bahías Gemelas Travel Agency** (© **314/333-1000;** fax 314/333-0649). Schedules are flexible; a half-day city tour costs around $25 (£14). Other tours include the daylong Colima Colonial Tour ($67/£37), which stops at Colima's Archaeological Museum and principal colonial buildings, and passes the active volcano. Offerings change regularly, so ask about new tours.

FISHING Manzanillo is famous for its fishing, particularly sailfish. Marlin and sailfish are abundant year-round. Winter is best for dolphin fish and dorado (mahimahi); in summer, wahoo and rooster fish are in greater supply. The international sailfish competition is held around the November 20 Revolution Day holiday, and the national sailfish competition is in February. You can arrange fishing through travel agencies or directly at the fishermen's cooperative (© **314/332-1031**), located downtown where the fishing boats moor. Call from 6am to 2pm or 5 to 8pm. A fishing boat is approximately $40 (£22) for 8 people to $50 (£28) for 12 people per hour, with most trips lasting about 5 hours.

GOLF The 18-hole **La Mantarraya Golf Course** (© 314/ 331-0101) is open to nonguests as well as guests of Las Hadas. At one time, La Mantarraya was among the top 100 courses in the world, but newer entries have passed it. Still, the compact, challenging 18-hole course designed by Roy and Pete Dye is a beauty, with banana trees, blooming bougainvillea, and coconut palms at every turn. A lush and verdant place (12 of the 18 holes are played over water), it remains a favorite.

When the course was under construction, workers dug up pre-Hispanic ceramic figurines, idols, and beads where the 14th hole now lies. It is believed to have been an important ancient burial site. The course culminates with its signature 18th hole, with a drive to the island green off El Tesoro (the treasure) beach, directly in front of the Karminda Palace Resort. Local lore says this beach still may hold buried treasure from Spanish galleons, whose crews were the first to recognize the perfection of this natural harbor, and who used it during the 16th century as their starting point for voyages to the Pacific Rim. Greens fees are $150 (£83) for 18 holes, $90 (£50) for 9 holes; cart rental costs $50 (£28) for 18 holes and $30 (£17) for 9 holes.

The fabulous Isla Navidad Country Club 27-hole golf course associated with the **Grand Bay Hotel** (© 314/337-9024) in Barra de Navidad, an easy distance from Manzanillo, is also open to the public. The Robert von Hagge design is long and lovely, with each hole amid rolling, tropical landscapes. It is wide open, with big fairways and big greens, and features plenty of water (2 lagoon holes, 13 lakeside holes, and 8 holes along the Pacific). The greens fees, including a motorized cart, are $166 (£91) for 18 holes, $192 (£106) for 27 holes for hotel guests; it's $207 and $230 (£114 and £127), respectively, for nonguests. Barra is about a 1- to 1½-hour drive north of Manzanillo on Highway 200.

A MUSEUM The **Museum of Archaeology and History** (© 314/332-2256) is a small but impressive structure that houses exhibits depicting the region's history, plus rotating displays of contemporary Mexican art. It's on Avenida Niños Héroes at Avenida Teniente Azueta, on the road leading between the downtown and Las Brisas areas. Every Friday evening, the museum hosts free cultural events, which might be a trio playing romantic ballads or a chamber music ensemble. Performances begin at 8pm. Hours are Tuesday through Saturday from 10am to 2pm and 5 to 8pm,

Sunday from 10am to 1pm. The museum completed an extensive renovation in November 2006.

SHOPPING   Manzanillo has a selection of shops carrying Mexican crafts and clothing, mainly from nearby Guadalajara. Almost all are downtown on the streets near the central plaza. Shopping downtown is an experience—for example, you won't want to miss the shop bordering the plaza that sells a combination of shells, religious items (including shell-framed Virgin of Guadalupe nightlights), and orthopedic supplies. The Plaza Manzanillo is an American-style mall on the road to Santiago, and there's a traditional *tianguis* (outdoor) market in front of the entrance to Club Maeva, with touristy items from around Mexico. Most resort hotels also have boutiques or shopping arcades.

SUNSET CRUISES   To participate in this popular activity, buy tickets from a travel agent or your hotel tour desk. Most cost around $25 (£14). The trips vary in their combinations of drinks, music, and entertainment and last 1½ to 2 hours. Departing from Las Hadas are the **El Explorer** and **Antares.**

3 Where to Stay & Dine

Manzanillo's strip of coastline consists of three areas: **downtown,** with its shops, markets, and commercial activity; **Las Brisas,** the hotel-lined beach area immediately north of the city; and **Santiago,** the town and peninsula, now virtually a suburb, to the north at the end of Playa Azul. Transportation by bus or taxi makes all three areas fairly convenient to each other. Reservations are recommended during the Easter, Christmas, and New Year's holidays.

WHERE TO STAY
DOWNTOWN

Hotel Colonial ✦   An old favorite, this three-story colonial-style hotel is in the central downtown district. Popular for its consistent quality, ambience, and service, it has beautiful blue-and-yellow tile and colonial-style carved doors and windows in the lobby and restaurant. Rooms are decorated with minimal furniture, red-tile floors, and basic comforts. The hotel is 1 block inland from the main plaza at the corner of Juárez and Galindo.

Av. México 100 and González Bocanegra, 28200 Manzanillo, Col. ✆ **314/332-1080,** 0668, or -1230. 42 units. $45 (£25) double. MC, V. Limited street parking. **Amenities:** Restaurant; bar. *In room:* A/C, cable TV.

LAS BRISAS

Some parts of the Las Brisas area look run-down; however, it still lays claim to one of the best beaches in the area and is known for its constant gentle sea breezes—a pleasure in the summer.

Hotel La Posada ⭐   This small inn has a bright-pink stucco facade with a large arch that leads to a broad tiled patio right on the beach. The rooms have exposed brick walls and simple furnishings with Mexican decorative accents. It remains popular with longtime travelers to Manzanillo. The atmosphere is casual and informal—help yourself to beer and soft drinks, and at the end of your stay, owners Juan and Lisa Martinez will count the bottle caps you deposited in a bowl labeled with your room number. The restaurant, which is open to nonguests, is open daily during high season from 8 to 11am and 1:30 to 8pm. A meal costs around $7 (£3.85). During low season, the restaurant is open from 8am to 3pm. Stop by for a drink at sunset; the bar's open until 9pm all year. The hotel is at the end of Las Brisas Peninsula, closest to downtown, and is on the local Las Brisas bus route.

Av. Lázaro Cárdenas 201, Las Brisas (Apdo. Postal 135), 28200 Manzanillo, Col. ℂ/fax **314/333-1899**. www.hotel-la-posada.info. 23 units. High season $78 (£43) double; low season $58 (£32) double. Rates include full breakfast. MC, V. Free parking. **Amenities:** Restaurant; bar; Internet cafe; laundry service; currency exchange; safe.

SANTIAGO

Five kilometers (3 miles) north of Las Brisas is Santiago Peninsula. The settlement of Salahua is on the highway where you enter the peninsula to reach the hotels Las Hadas, Plaza Las Glorias, and Tesoro Manzanillo, as well as the Mantarraya Golf Course. Buses from town marked LAS HADAS pass by these hotels every 20 minutes. Past the Salahua turnoff, at the end of the settlement of Santiago, an obscure road on the left is marked ZONA DE PLAYAS and leads to the hotels on the other side of the peninsula and Playa de Santiago.

Barceló Karmina Palace ⭐⭐⭐ *Kids*   The quality of rooms and services at this all-inclusive resort makes the newest of Manzanillo's hotels one of the area's best values. It's the best choice for families

---

Film Fact

The movie *10* featured Manzanillo's signature property, Las Hadas—along with Bo Derek.

visiting Manzanillo. The buildings resemble Maya pyramids, and even though the architecture at first might seem a little overdone, somehow it works. Rooms are all very large suites, with rich wood accents, comfortable recessed seating areas with pull-out couches, and two 27-inch TVs in each room. The extra-large bathrooms have marble floors, twin black marble sinks, separate tubs, and glassed-in showers. Most rooms have terraces or balconies with views of the ocean, overlooking the tropical gardens and swimming pools. Master suites have spacious sun terraces with private splash pools, plus a full wet bar, full refrigerator, and a large living room area with a 42-inch TV. Two full-size bedrooms close off from the living/dining area.

The kids' club offers a host of activities, while adults have numerous choices for fun—all included in the price. There's also an exceptionally well-equipped gym and European-style spa.

Av. Vista Hermosa 13, Fracc. Península de Santiago, 28200 Manzanillo, Col. **888/234-6222** in the U.S. and Canada, or 314/334-1300, 331-1313, or 01-800/507-4930 in Mexico. Fax 314/334-1108. www.barcelokarminapalace.com. 324 units. $278–$338 (£153–£186) double; $908 (£499) 2-bedroom suites for quad occupancy. Rates are all-inclusive. Special packages and Web specials available; ask about seasonal specials. 2 children younger than 8 stay free in parent's room. AE, MC, V. Free parking. **Amenities:** 2 restaurants; snack bar; 5 bars; 8 connected pools; tennis courts; health club w/treadmills and Cybex equipment; full spa facilities; men's and women's sauna and steam rooms; sailboards; beach volleyball; kids' activity program; concierge; car rental; room service; currency exchange; safe. *In room:* A/C, TV, minibar, hair dryer, iron, safe ($2/£1.10).

Brisas Las Hadas Golf Resort & Marina 𝕯𝕯   For me, Las Hadas is synonymous with a visit to Manzanillo. This elegant beachside resort is built in Moorish style into the side of the rocky peninsula. The service is gracious, warm, and unobtrusive. Rooms were just updated in 2006, and are spread over landscaped grounds and overlook the bay; cobbled lanes lined with colorful flowers and palms connect them. The resort is large but maintains an air of seclusion. (Motorized carts are on call for transportation within the property.)

Views, room size, and amenities differentiate the six types of accommodations, which can vary greatly. If you're not satisfied with your room, ask to be moved—a few of the rooms are significantly less attractive than others. Understated and spacious, the better units have white-marble floors, sitting areas, and large, comfortably furnished balconies. Nine suites have private pools. The lobby is a popular place for curling up in one of the overstuffed seating areas or, at night, for enjoying a drink and live music. Pete and Roy Dye designed La Mantarraya, the hotel's 18-hole, par-71 golf course.

One of the three restaurants, **Legazpi** (p. 153), is the most elegant dining choice in Manzanillo.

If you are visiting on a cruise ship or staying at another hotel, you can enjoy Las Hadas beach for a day by purchasing a day pass from the hotel's gate guard. In exchange, you'll receive coupons for beach chairs and towels.

Av. de los Riscos s/n, Santiago Peninsula, 28200 Manzanillo, Col. ℂ **888/559-4329** in the U.S. and Canada, or 314/331-0101. www.brisas.com.mx. 234 units. High season $206–$327 (£113–£180) double, $386–$626 (£212–£344) Fantasy Suite; low season $175–$379 (£96–£208) double, $386–$626 (£212–£344) Fantasy Suite. AE, DC, MC, V. Free guarded parking. **Amenities:** 3 restaurants; 3 lounges and bars; 2 outdoor pools; small workout room; marina for 70 vessels; scuba diving; snorkeling; water-skiing; sailing and trimaran cruises; concierge; tour desk; travel agency; car rental; shopping arcade; room service; in-room massage; babysitting; laundry service; dry cleaning. *In room:* A/C, TV, minibar, hair dryer, safe.

Plaza Tucanes ℱ The sunset-colored walls of this pueblolike hotel ramble over a hillside on the Santiago Peninsula. The restaurant on top and most rooms afford a broad vista of other red-tiled rooftops and either the palm-filled golf course or the bay. It's one of Manzanillo's undiscovered resorts, known more to wealthy Mexicans than to Americans. Originally conceived as private condominiums, the accommodations were designed for living; each spacious unit is stylishly furnished, and very comfortable. Each has a huge living room; a small kitchen/bar; one, two, or three large bedrooms with tile or brick floors; large bathrooms with Mexican tiles; huge closets; and large furnished private patios with views. Some units contain whirlpool tubs, and a few rooms can be partitioned off and rented by the bedroom only. Rooms can be a long walk from the main entrance, through a succession of stairways and paths. If stair climbing bothers you, try to get a room by the restaurant and pool—you'll have a great view, and a hillside rail elevator goes straight from top to bottom.

Av. de Tesoro s/n, Santiago Peninsula, 28200 Manzanillo, Col. ℂ **314/334-1098.** Fax 314/334-0090. www.plazatucanes.com.mx. 112 units. $146 (£80) double; $250 (£138) double all-inclusive. Packages available. AE, MC, V. Free parking. **Amenities:** 2 restaurants, including Argentine steakhouse; outdoor pool; mini golf; recreational park; kids' club; game area; room service; babysitting (w/advance notice); beach club on Las Brisas beach, w/pool and small restaurant; transportation to and from beach club (once daily in each direction). *In room:* A/C, TV, safe.

Tesoro Manzanillo Resort ℱ *Kids* This hotel (formerly the Gran Costa Real and Sierra) with all-inclusive package options, has 21 floors overlooking La Audiencia beach, and a full program of activities, dining, and entertainment. Its excellent kids' program makes it a top choice for families. Architecturally, it mimics the white Moorish style of Las Hadas that has become so popular in Manzanillo. Inside, it's palatial in scale and awash in pale-gray marble. Room decor picks up the pale-gray theme with armoires that conceal the TV and minibar. Most standard rooms have two double beds or a king-size bed, plus a small table, chairs, and desk. Several rooms at the end of most floors are small, with one double bed, small porthole-size windows, no balcony, and no view. Most rooms, however, have balconies and ocean or hillside views. The 10 honeymoon suites have king-size beds and chaises. Junior suites have sitting areas with couches and large bathrooms. Scuba-diving lessons take place in the pool, and excellent scuba-diving sites are within swimming distance of the shore.

Av. La Audiencia 1, Los Riscos, 28200 Manzanillo, Col. © **800/543-7556** in the U.S., or 314/333-2000. Fax 314/333-2611. www.tesororesorts.com. 332 units. High season $230–$340 (£127–£187) double, $240–$370 (£132–£204) suite; low season $200 (£110) double, $220 (£121) suite. Rates are all-inclusive. AE, MC, V. Free parking. **Amenities:** 3 restaurants; 4 bars; grand pool on the beach; children's pool; 4 lighted tennis courts; health club w/exercise equipment, aerobics, and hot tub; men's and women's sauna and steam rooms; travel agency; salon w/massage; room service; laundry service; currency exchange. *In room:* A/C, TV, minibar, hair dryer.

WHERE TO DINE
DOWNTOWN

Roca del Mar MEXICAN/INTERNATIONAL   Join the locals at this informal cafe facing the plaza. The large menu includes club sandwiches, hamburgers, *carne asada a la tampiqueña* (thin grilled steak served with rice, poblano pepper, an enchilada, and refried beans), fajitas, fish, shrimp, and vegetable salads. A specialty is its paella (served on Sun and Tues), and the economical *pibil* tacos are outstanding. This cafe is very clean and offers sidewalk dining.

Blvd. Costero. © **314/336-9097.** Main courses $3–$12 (£1.65–£6.60). No credit cards. Daily 7:30am–11pm.

LAS BRISAS

The **Hotel La Posada** (see "Where to Stay," above) offers breakfast to nonguests at its beachside restaurant; it's also a great place to mingle with other tourists and enjoy the sunset and cocktails.

La Toscana (Finds SEAFOOD   You're in for a treat at La Toscana (by the same owner of the now-closed Willy's), one of Manzanillo's most popular restaurants, located on the beach in Las Brisas. It's homey, casual, and small, so reservations are highly recommended.

The exquisite cuisine belies the atmosphere, with starters that include escargot and salmon carpaccio. Among the grilled specialties are shrimp imperial wrapped in bacon, red snapper tarragon, sea bass with mango and ginger, and tender fresh lobsters (four to a serving). Live music frequently sets the scene.

Bulevar Miguel de la Madrid 3177. © 314/333-2515. Reservations highly recommended. Main courses $8–$20 (£4.40–£11). MC, V. Daily 6pm–2am. 100m (328 ft.) from Hotel Fiesta Mexicana.

SANTIAGO ROAD

The restaurants below are on the Costera Madrid between downtown and the Santiago Peninsula, including the Salahua area.

Benedetti's Pizza PIZZA   There are several branches in town, so you'll probably find a Benedetti's not far from where you are staying. The variety is extensive; add some *chimichurri* sauce to your sesame-crust pizza to enhance the flavor. Benedetti's specializes in seafood pizzas, such as smoked oyster and anchovy. You can also select from pastas, sandwiches, burgers, fajitas, salads, Mexican soups, cheesecake, and pie.

Bulevar Miguel de la Madrid, near the Las Brisas Glorietta on the ocean side (west). © 314/333-1592 or 334-0141. Pizza $9–$12 (£4.95–£6.60); main courses $2–$5.55 (£1.10–£3.05). AE, MC, V. Daily 10am–11:30pm.

Bigotes II *(Finds* SEAFOOD   Locals flock to this large, breezy restaurant (the name translates as "Mustaches") by the water for the good food and festive atmosphere. Strolling singers serenade diners as they dig into large portions of grilled seafood.

Puesta del Sol 3. © 314/333-1236. Main courses $9.50–$23 (£5.25–£13). MC, V. Daily noon–10pm. From downtown, follow the Costera Madrid past the Las Brisas turnoff; the restaurant is behind the Penas Coloradas Social Club, across from the beach.

SANTIAGO PENINSULA

Legazpi ✺✺ INTERNATIONAL   This is a top choice in Manzanillo for sheer elegance, gracious service, and outstanding food. The candlelit tables are set with silver and flowers. Enormous bell-shaped windows on two sides show off the sparkling bay below. The sophisticated menu includes prosciutto with melon marinated in port wine, crayfish bisque, broiled salmon, roast duck, lobster, veal, and flaming desserts.

In the Brisas Las Hadas hotel (p. 150), Santiago Peninsula. © 314/331-0101. Main courses $8.50–$16 (£4.70–£8.80). AE, MC, V. High season daily 7–11:30pm; closed low season.

4 Manzanillo after Dark

Nightlife in Manzanillo is much more exuberant than you might expect, but then Manzanillo is not only a resort town—it's also a thriving commercial center. Clubs and bars tend to change from year to year, so check with your concierge for current hot spots. Some area clubs have a dress code prohibiting shorts or sandals, principally applying to men.

El Bar de Félix, between Salahua and Las Brisas by the Avis rental-car office (© 314/333-1875), is open Tuesday through Sunday from 2pm to midnight, and has an $8 (£4.40) minimum consumption charge. Music ranges from salsa and ranchero to rock and house—it's the most consistently lively place in town, with pool tables. The adjacent (and related) **Vog Disco** (© 314/333-1875), Bulevar Costera Miguel de la Madrid Km 9.2, features alternative music in a cavernous setting, with a midnight light show; it's Manzanillo's current late-night hot spot, open until 5am, but only on Friday and Saturday. The cover charge for women is $10 (£5.50), for men $15 (£8.25). Also very popular—with a built-in crowd—is the nightclub at the **Club Maeva Hotel & Resort** (© 01-800/849-1987 in Mexico), on the inland side of the main highway, north of the Santiago Peninsula. It's open Tuesday, Thursday, and Saturday from 11pm to 2am. Couples are given preferential entrance. Nonguests are welcome but must pay an entrance fee, typically $20 to $30 (£11–£17), after which all drinks are included. Note that when Club Maeva is fully booked, entrance to nonguests may be difficult to impossible—ask your hotel front desk if they can secure a pass for you. The fee varies depending on the night of the week and the time of year.

6

Settling into Guadalajara

By David Baird

Guadalajara is the second-largest city in Mexico (with 3.5 million inhabitants, it's a very distant second to Mexico City), but because it's the homeland of mariachi music, the *jarabe tapatío* (the Mexican hat dance), and tequila, many consider it the most Mexican of cities. Despite its size, Guadalajara isn't hard to navigate, and the people are friendly and helpful. And unlike in Mexico City, visitors can enjoy big-city pleasures without big-city hassles.

While in Guadalajara, you will undoubtedly come across the word *tapatío* (or *tapatía*). In the early days, people from the area were known to trade in threes, called *tapatíos*. Gradually, the locals came to be called Tapatíos, too, and the word now signifies Guadalajaran when referring to a thing, a person, or a manner of doing something.

1 Orientation

452km (281 miles) NW of Mexico City; 339km (210 miles) E of Puerto Vallarta

GETTING THERE & DEPARTING

BY PLANE   Guadalajara's international airport is a 25- to 45-minute ride from the city. Taxi tickets to Guadalajara, priced by zone, are for sale in front of the airport ($15/£8.25 to downtown area). Taxis are the only transport.

See chapter 2 for a list of toll-free numbers for international airlines serving Mexico. Local numbers for airlines serving Guadalajara are: **AeroMar** (© 33/3615-8509), **AeroMéxico** (© 01-800/021-4010), **American** (© 01-800/904-6000), **Click** (© 01-800/122-5425), **Continental** (© 01-800/900-5000), **Delta** (© 33/3630-3530), **Mexicana** (© 01-800/502-2000), and **United** (© 33/3616-9489).

Aviacsa (© 33/3123-1751) connects to Los Angeles, Las Vegas, Houston, and Chicago. **Azteca** (© 33/3630-4615) offers service to and from Mexico City, and from there to several cities in Mexico. **Allegro** (© 33/3647-7799) operates flights to and from Oakland

and Las Vegas via Tijuana. **Alaska Airlines** (© 01-800/426-0333) flies to Los Angeles and Reno.

BY CAR Guadalajara is at the hub of several four-lane toll roads (called *cuotas* or *autopistas*), which cut travel time considerably but are expensive. From Nogales on the **U.S. border,** follow Highway 15 south (21 hr.). From **Tepic,** a quicker route is toll road 15D (5 hr.; $31/£17). From **Puerto Vallarta,** go north on Highway 200 to Compostela; toll road 68D heads east to join the Tepic toll road. Total time is 5½ hours, and the tolls add up to $29 (£16). From **Barra de Navidad,** on the coast southeast of Puerto Vallarta, take Highway 80 northeast (4½ hr.). From **Manzanillo,** you might also take this road, but toll road 54D through Colima to Guadalajara (3½ hr.; $26/£14) is faster. From **Mexico City,** take toll road 15D (7 hr.; $55/£30).

BY BUS Two bus stations serve Guadalajara. The old one, south of downtown, is for buses to Lake Chapala and other nearby areas; the new one, 10km (6¼ miles) southeast of downtown, is for longer trips.

The Old Bus Station For destinations within 100km (62 miles) of town, including the Lake Chapala area, go to the old bus terminal, on Niños Héroes off Calzada Independencia Sur. For Lake Chapala, take **Transportes Guadalajara-Chapala,** which runs frequent buses and *combis* (minivans).

The New Bus Station The **Central Camionera** is 15 to 30 minutes from downtown. The station has seven terminals connected by a covered walkway. Each terminal houses different bus lines, offering first- and second-class service for different destinations. You can buy bus tickets from several travel agents in Guadalajara. Ask at your hotel for the closest to you. There are several major bus lines. The best service (big seats and lots of room) is provided by **ETN.**

VISITOR INFORMATION

The **State of Jalisco Tourist Information Office** is at Calle Morelos 102 (© **33/3668-1600** or -1601; http://visita.jalisco.gob.mx) in the Plaza Tapatía, at Paseo Degollado and Paraje del Rincón del Diablo. It's open Monday through Friday from 9am to 8pm, and Saturday, Sunday, and festival days 10am to 2pm. You can get maps, a monthly calendar of cultural events, and good information. The city operates several tourist information booths—one in Plaza Liberación (directly behind the cathedral), another in Plaza Guadalajara (directly in front of the cathedral). These are open daily from 9am to 1pm and 3 to 7pm.

Greater Guadalajara

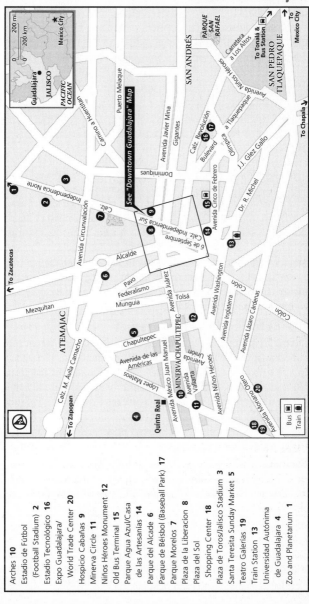

Arches 10
Estadio de Fútbol
(Football Stadium) 2
Estadio Tecnológico 16
Expo Guadalajara/
World Trade Center 20
Hospicio Cabañas 9
Minerva Circle 11
Niños Héroes Monument 12
Old Bus Terminal 15
Parque Agua Azul/Casa
de las Artesanías 14
Parque del Alcalde 6
Parque de Béisbol (Baseball Park) 17
Parque Morelos 7
Plaza de la Liberacion 8
Plaza del Sol
Shopping Center 18
Plaza de Toros/Jalisco Stadium 3
Santa Teresita Sunday Market 5
Teatro Galerías 19
Train Station 13
Universidad Autónima
de Guadalajara 4
Zoo and Planetarium 1

CITY LAYOUT

The **Centro Histórico** (city center), with all its plazas, churches, and museums, will obviously be of interest to the visitor. The **west side** is Guadalajara's modern, cosmopolitan district. In the northwest corner is **Zapopan,** home of Guadalajara's patron saint. On the opposite side of the city from Zapopan, in the southeast corner, are the craft centers of **Tlaquepaque** and **Tonalá.**

The main artery for traffic from downtown to the west side is **Avenida Vallarta.** It starts downtown as **Juárez.** The main arteries for returning to downtown are **México** and **Hidalgo,** both north of Vallarta. Vallarta heads due west, where it intersects another major artery, **Avenida Adolfo López Mateos,** at **Fuente Minerva** (or simply La Minerva, or Minerva Circle). Minerva Circle, a 15-minute drive from downtown, is the central point of reference for the west side. To go to Zapopan from downtown, take **Avenida Avila Camacho,** which you can pick up on Alcalde; it takes 20 minutes by car. To Tlaquepaque and Tonalá, take **Calzada Revolución.** Tlaquepaque is 8km (5 miles) from downtown and takes 15 to 20 minutes by car; Tonalá is 5 minutes farther. Another major viaduct, **Calzada Lázaro Cárdenas,** connects the west side to Tlaquepaque and Tonalá, bypassing downtown.

THE NEIGHBORHOODS IN BRIEF

Centro Histórico The heart of the city contains many plazas, the cathedral, and several historic buildings and museums. Here, too, are the striking murals of José Clemente Orozco, one of the great Mexican muralists. Theaters, restaurants, shops, and clubs dot the area, and an enormous market rounds out the attractions. All of this is in a space roughly 12 blocks by 12 blocks, an easy area for a good walker to explore and enjoy the several plazas and pedestrian-only areas. To the south is a large green space called Parque Agua Azul.

West Side This is the swanky part of town, with the fine restaurants, luxury hotels, boutiques, and galleries, as well as the American, British, and Canadian consulates. It's a large area best navigated by taxi.

Zapopan Founded in 1542, Zapopan is a suburb of Guadalajara. In its center is the 18th-century basilica, the home of Guadalajara's patron saint, the Virgin of Zapopan. The most interesting part of Zapopan is clustered around the temple and can be explored by foot. It has a growing arts and nightlife scene.

Tlaquepaque This was a village of artisans (especially potters) that grew into a market center. In the last 30 years, it has attracted designers from all over Mexico. Every major form of art and craft is for sale here: furniture, pottery, glass, jewelry, woodcarvings, leather goods, sculptures, and paintings. The shops are sophisticated, yet Tlaquepaque's center retains a small-town feel that makes door-to-door browsing enjoyable and relaxing.

Tonalá This has remained a town of artisans. Plenty of stores sell mostly local products from the town's more than 400 workshops. You'll see wrought iron, ceramics, blown glass, and papier-mâché. A busy street market operates each Thursday and Sunday.

2 Getting Around

BY TAXI Taxis are the easiest way to get around town. Most have meters, and, though some drivers are reluctant to use them, you can insist that they do. There are three rates: for day, night, and suburbia. On my last visit, typical fares were: downtown to the west side, $6 to $8 (£3.30–£4.40); downtown or west side to Tlaquepaque, $7 to $9 (£3.85–£4.95); to the new bus station, $7 (£3.85); to the airport, $15 to $20 (£8.25–£11).

BY CAR Keep in mind the several main arteries (see "City Layout," above). Several important freeway-style thoroughfares crisscross the city. **González Gallo** leads south from the town center and connects with the road to Lake Chapala. **Avenida Vallarta** continues past La Minerva and eventually feeds onto **Highway 15,** bound for Tequila and Puerto Vallarta.

BY BUS For the visitor, the handiest route is the TUR **706,** which runs from the Centro Histórico southeast to Tlaquepaque, the Central Camionera (the new bus station), and Tonalá. You can catch this bus on Avenida 16 de Septiembre. The same bus runs in the reverse direction back to the downtown area. The fare is $1.50 (83p).

The **electric bus** is handy for travel between downtown and the Minerva area and only costs 40¢. It bears the sign PAR VIAL and runs east along Hidalgo and west along Calle Independencia (not Calzada Independencia). Hidalgo passes the north side of the cathedral. The Par Vial goes as far east as Mercado Libertad and as far west as Minerva Circle. The city also has a light rail system, **Tren Ligero,** but it doesn't serve areas of interest to visitors.

FAST FACTS: Guadalajara

American Express The local office is at Av. Vallarta 2440, Plaza los Arcos, Local A-1 (© 33/3818-2323); it's open Monday through Friday from 9am to 6pm, Saturday from 9am to noon.

Area Code The telephone area code is **33**.

Books, Newspapers & Magazines **Gonvil,** a popular bookstore chain, has a branch across from Plaza de los Hombres Ilustres on Avenida Hidalgo, and another a few blocks south at Av. 16 de Septiembre 118 (Alcalde becomes 16 de Septiembre south of the cathedral). It carries few English selections. **Sanborn's,** at the corner of Juárez and 16 de Septiembre, does a good job of keeping English-language periodicals in stock, but most are specialty magazines. Many newsstands sell the two English local papers, the *Guadalajara Reporter* and the *Guadalajara Weekly.* For the widest selection of English-language books, try **Sandi Bookstore,** Av. Tepeyac 718 (© 33/3121-0863), in the Chapalita neighborhood on the west side.

Business Hours Store hours are Monday through Saturday from 10am to 2pm and 4 to 8pm.

Climate & Dress Guadalajara's weather is mostly mild. From November through March, you'll need a sweater in the evening. The warmest months, April and May, are hot and dry. From June to September, the city gets afternoon and evening showers that keep the temperature a bit cooler, but it seems to me that the local climate is getting warmer. Dress is conservative; attention-getting sportswear (short shorts, halters, and the like) is out of place.

Consulates The **American consular offices** are at Progreso 175 (© 33/3268-2200 or -2100). Other consulates include the **Canadian consulate,** Hotel Fiesta Americana, Local 31 (© 33/3615-6215); the **British consulate,** Calle Jesús Rojas 20, Col. Los Pinos (© 33/3343-2296); and the **Australian consulate,** López Cotilla 2018, Col. Arcos Vallarta (© 33/3615-7418). These offices all keep roughly the same hours: Monday through Friday from 8am to 1pm.

Currency Exchange Three blocks south of the cathedral, on López Cotilla, between Corona and Degollado, are more than 20 *casas de cambio.* Almost all post their rates, which are usually better than bank rates and without the long lines.

Elevation Guadalajara sits at 1,700m (5,576 ft.).

Emergencies The emergency phone number is ⓒ 060.

Hospitals For medical emergencies, visit the **Hospital México-Americano,** Cólomos 2110 (ⓒ **33/3642-7152** or 33/3641-3141).

Internet Access Most of the big hotels have business centers that you can use. There are many Internet cafes in the Centro Histórico; the easiest way to find one is to ask a young person.

Language Classes Foreigners can study Spanish at the **Foreign Student Study Center,** University of Guadalajara, Calle Tomás V. Gómez 125, 44100 Guadalajara, Jal. (ⓒ **33/3616-4399**). **IMAC** is a private Spanish school at Donato Guerra 180 in the Centro Histórico (ⓒ **33/3613-1080**).

Police Tourists should first try to contact the Jalisco tourist information office in Plaza Tapatía (ⓒ **33/3668-1600**). If you can't reach the office, call the municipal police at ⓒ **33/ 3668-7983.**

Post Office The *correo* is at the corner of Carranza and Calle Independencia, about 4 blocks northeast of the cathedral. Standing in the plaza behind the cathedral, facing the Degollado Theater, walk to the left and turn left on Carranza; walk past the Hotel Mendoza, cross Calle Independencia, and look for the post office on the left. It's open Monday through Thursday from 9am to 5pm, Saturday from 10am to 2pm.

Safety Guadalajara doesn't have as much crime as Mexico City. Rarely do you hear of muggings. Crimes against tourists and foreign students are infrequent and most often take the form of purse snatching. Criminals usually work in teams and target travelers in busy places, such as outdoor restaurants. Keep jewelry out of sight. Should anyone spill something on you, be alert to your surroundings and step away from them—this is a common method for distracting the victim.

3 Where to Stay

Rates shown are the standard rack rates and include the 17% tax. In slow periods, look for discounts; the big hotels often give business discounts. I've noticed that in some of the cheaper hotels, air-conditioning is a relative concept.

Almost all of the luxury hotels in Guadalajara are on the west side, which has the majority of the shopping malls, boutiques, fashionable restaurants, and clubs. There is also a lot to do in the Centro Histórico, making it a good place to stay. Finally, Tlaquepaque is a comfortable suburb and is perfect for shoppers; the only drawback is that almost everything shuts down by 7 or 8pm. Chain hotels not included below are Hilton, Marriott, Camino Real, Howard Johnson, Crowne Plaza, and Best Western.

VERY EXPENSIVE

Hotel Presidente InterContinental ★★★ Housed in a 14-story glass building with an atrium lobby, this hotel offers the most comprehensive list of services and amenities in Guadalajara. There is little turnover in staff, and the concierge has proven more capable and knowledgeable than any other in the city. The health club here is a standout among other hotels. The rooms are comfortable and quiet, with modern furnishings that include a desk and a small table with two chairs. Club rooms have discreet check-in and are on limited-access hallways; rates include continental breakfast, newspaper, and evening cocktails. The extra privacy and services are good for Mexican soap opera stars or repeat guests who like having their preferences known in advance. If you're neither of these, opt for one of the other rooms. The lobby bar is popular; during the season, bullfighters relax here after *la corrida*. Standard rooms come as "superior" or "deluxe," although differences in prices aren't that pronounced. The rooms are about the same size and come with attractive midsize bathrooms. Deluxe rooms have a few more amenities. The suites are very large and come with large, very attractive bathrooms.

Av. López Mateos Sur and Moctezuma (west side), 45050 Guadalajara, Jal. ⓒ **800/ 327-0200** in the U.S. and Canada, or 33/3678-1234. Fax 33/3678-1222. www. interconti.com. 409 units. $276–$290 (£152–£160) double; $317 (£174) club; $414 (£228) and up for suite. Internet promotional rates available. AE, DC, MC, V. Valet parking $5 (£2.75). **Amenities:** 2 restaurants; bar; outdoor heated pool; golf at nearby clubs; health club w/saunas, steam rooms, and whirlpools; concierge; tour desk; car rental; large business center; executive business services; salon; room service; in-room massage; babysitting; laundry service; dry cleaning; nonsmoking rooms; executive-level rooms. *In room:* A/C, TV w/pay movies, Wi-Fi, minibar, coffeemaker, hair dryer, iron, safe.

Quinta Real ★★★ This chain specializes in building properties that are suggestive of Mexico's heritage, in contrast to the comfortable but generic luxury hotels. No glass skyscraper here—two five-story buildings made of stone, wood, plaster, and tile occupy lush grounds. Suites vary quite a bit: Eight have brick cupolas, and some have balconies. All are large, with a split-level layout and antique decorative touches. And all come with large, great bathrooms with tub/shower combinations. The "grand-class" suites have even bigger bathrooms with Jacuzzi tubs. They are also a bit larger and come with a few extras, such as a stereo. You can choose between two doubles or one king-size bed. The hotel is 2 blocks from Minerva Circle in western Guadalajara. Ask for a room that doesn't face López Mateos.

Av. México 2727 (at López Mateos, west side), 44690 Guadalajara, Jal. ℂ 866/621-9288 in the U.S. and Canada, or 33/3669-0600. Fax 33/3669-0601. www.quintareal.com. 76 suites. $418 (£230) master suite; $439 (£241) grand-class suite. AE, DC, MC, V. Free secure parking. **Amenities:** Restaurant; bar; small outdoor heated pool; golf at local club; fitness room; discounts at local day spa; concierge; tour desk; car rental; business center; executive business services; room service; in-room massage; babysitting; laundry service; dry cleaning; nonsmoking rooms. In room: A/C, TV, high-speed Internet, minibar, hair dryer, iron, safe.

Villa Ganz 𝘼𝘼𝘼   This small, all-suite hotel is one of Guadalajara's most comfortable places to stay. Located in the near west side of the city, near Avenida Chapultepec, it's rooms are big, well furnished, and decorated with flair. Each holds a basket of fruit and a small bottle of wine on check-in. Bathrooms are large and well lit—some have tubs, others just showers. Bed choices include a king, queen, or two twins. Beds come with down comforters (hypoallergenic option available). Rooms facing the garden are the quietest, but those facing the street are set back from the traffic and have double-glazed windows. The common rooms and rear garden are agreeable places to relax. Service is personal and helpful. In-room dining can be arranged with one of three nearby restaurants or arrangements can be made to bring in a chef. Villa Ganz is a member of the Boutique Hotels of Mexico.

López Cotilla 1739 (between Bolivar and San Martín, west side), 44140 Guadalajara, Jal. ℂ 800/728-9098 in the U.S. and Canada, 866/818-8342 in Canada, or 33/3120-1416. www.villaganz.com. 10 suites. $234 (£129) junior suite; $269 (£148) master suite; $304 (£167) grand master suite. Rates include continental breakfast. Internet specials often available. AE, MC, V. Free secure parking. Children 11 and under not accepted. **Amenities:** Golf and tennis at local club; concierge; tour desk; room service; in-room massage; laundry service; dry cleaning. In room: A/C, TV, Wi-Fi, hair dryer, safe.

EXPENSIVE

Holiday Inn Hotel and Suites Centro Histórico 𝘼𝘼   This six-story downtown property has comfortable guest rooms and a good location—just a few blocks from the main square. Standard rooms are carpeted and decorated in Mexican architectural colors. The furniture is modern Mexican with a few wrought-iron pieces—the overall effect is cheerful. The size and lighting are good; bathrooms are midsize, recently upgraded, and well equipped, with ample

counter space. For quiet, ask for a room off the street. The suites are larger, but otherwise not much different. Room rates include transportation to (but not from) the airport.

Av. Juárez 211, Centro Histórico, 44100 Guadalajara. Jal. © 800/465-4329 in the U.S. and Canada, 01-800/009-9900 in Mexico, or 33/3560-1200. www.holiday-inn.com. 90 units. $140–$150 (£77–£83) double; $175 (£96) suite. Ask about promotional rates. AE, MC, V. Free secure parking. **Amenities:** Restaurant; bar; fitness room; business center; room service; laundry service; dry cleaning; nonsmoking rooms. *In room:* A/C, TV, Wi-Fi, minibar, coffeemaker, hair dryer, iron, safe.

Hotel de Mendoza ⓖ   On a quiet street next to the Degollado Theater and Plaza Tapatía, 2 blocks from the cathedral, the Mendoza has the best location of any downtown hotel. The decor would best be described as a stab at old Spanish, with wood paneling and old-world accents. Standard rooms are midsize. Bed choices are one queen, two full, or two queens. Bathrooms are midsize, with better than average lighting. Suites have an additional sitting area and larger bathrooms with the recent addition of Jacuzzi tubs. Rooms face the street, an interior courtyard, or the pool. *Note:* The bath towels are the narrowest I've ever seen—obviously the brainchild of a demented cost-cutting expert. If the hotel hasn't changed these, ask for a couple extra after you check in.

Carranza 16, Centro Histórico, 44100 Guadalajara, Jal. © 33/3492-5151. Fax 33/3613-7310. www.demendoza.com.mx. 104 units. $125 (£69) double; $145 (£80) suite. Discounts sometimes available. AE, MC, V. Secure parking $4 (£2.20). **Amenities:** Restaurant; bar; small outdoor pool; fitness room; Jacuzzi; tour desk; business center; room service; laundry service; dry cleaning; nonsmoking rooms. *In room:* A/C, TV, Wi-Fi, hair dryer, safe.

MODERATE

Hotel Cervantes ⓖ ⓥ𝘢𝘭𝘶𝘦   This six-story downtown hotel offers modern amenities at a great price. The rooms are attractive and midsize. They have wall-to-wall carpeting and tile bathrooms with ample sink areas and shower/tub combinations. The air-conditioning is more in theory than in practice. The lower price is for one double bed; the higher price, for a king or two doubles. This is not a noisy hotel, but if you require absolute quiet, request an interior room. The Cervantes is 6 blocks south and 3 blocks west of the cathedral.

Prisciliano Sánchez 442, Centro Histórico, 44100 Guadalajara, Jal. ©/fax 33/3613-6686. www.hotelcervantes.com.mx. 100 units. $72–$80 (£40–£44) double; $105 (£58) suite. AE, MC, V. Free secure parking. **Amenities:** Restaurant; lobby bar; small outdoor heated pool; tour desk; room service; babysitting; laundry service; dry cleaning. *In room:* A/C, TV.

Hotel Morales ★★ *Value* A historical hotel that's attractive and comfortable, the Morales is a good choice for anyone wishing to stay downtown. Guest rooms are comparable to the Holiday Inn Hotel & Suites but a good bit cheaper. The standard rooms are called either "suite sencilla" (one queen bed) or "suite doble" (2 double beds). The beds are firm. The rooms are medium or large and have Pergo floors. The bathrooms are quite attractive, with ceramic tile floors and good looking countertops. The showers are strong. The rooms that face the street have balconies with really good double-glazed windows that do a marvelous job at screening the noise. The imperial suites offer a lot for the money, with super large bathrooms equipped with a two-person Jacuzzi tub and a separate shower. All rooms are set around an arcaded lobby holding an attractive bar area. There's live music on Thursday and Friday evenings.

Av. Corona 243 (corner with Prisciliano Sánchez) Centro Histórico, 44100 Guadalajara, Jal. ⓒ **33/3658-5232.** Fax 33/3658-5239. www.hotelmorales.com.mx. 64 units. $105 (£58) suite double; $135 (£74) junior suite; $165 (£91) imperial suite. AE, MC, V. Free sheltered parking. **Amenities:** Restaurant; bar; fitness room; tour info; business center; room service; babysitting; laundry service; dry cleaning; nonsmoking rooms. *In room:* A/C, TV, high-speed Internet, coffeemaker, hair dryer, iron, safe.

La Villa del Ensueño ★★ This B&B in central Tlaquepaque is a lovely alternative to big-city hotels. A modern interpretation of traditional Mexican architecture, it is a delight to the eye—small courtyards and beautiful gardens bordered by old stucco walls, which have been painted in muted shades of orange oxide or covered in carefully trimmed ivy, with an occasional wrought-iron balcony or stone staircase. The rooms are individually decorated and have more character than most hotel lodgings. All contain ceiling fans and Wi-Fi connections. Doubles have either two twin or two double beds. Guests receive a complimentary cocktail on arrival. The hotel is about 8 blocks from the main plaza.

Florida 305, 45500 Tlaquepaque, Jal. ⓒ **800/220-8689** in the U.S., or 33/3635-8792. Fax 818/597-0637. www.villadelensueno.com. 18 units. $88 (£48) double; $100 (£55) deluxe double; $117 (£64) 2-bedroom unit; $140 (£77) suite. Rates include full breakfast and light laundry service. AE, MC, V. Free valet parking. **Amenities:** Bar; indoor and outdoor pool; laundry service. *In room:* A/C, TV, Wi-Fi, hair dryer.

Old Guadalajara ★★ This downtown bed-and-breakfast recommends itself in many ways. It's in a colonial house, and it's well located, quiet, and beautiful. The rooms reflect the local scene and speak of Mexico without shouting it. They are large and airy with high ceilings, tile floors, and comfortable bathrooms. The colonial architecture makes it possible to live without A/C in the warm months, and every room is equipped with a ceiling fan. The central courtyard is cool and shaded by tall bamboo. The common rooms are open to the courtyard and are stocked with material for readers curious about the city. Paul Callahan prepares filling breakfasts for his guests using only natural ingredients.

Belén 236, Centro Histórico, 44100 Guadalajara, Jal. ℂ/fax **33/3613-9958.** www.oldguadalajara.com. 5 units. $125 double (£69). Rates include full breakfast. AE, MC, V for deposit; no credit cards at B&B. No children 17 or under. **Amenities:** Tour info; nonsmoking rooms. *In room:* Hair dryer, no phone.

Quinta Don José 𝒢𝒢 (*Value*)   Good value, great location, friendly English-speaking owners—there are a lot of reasons to like this small establishment just 2 blocks from Tlaquepaque's main square. Rooms run the gauntlet from midsize to extra large. They are comfortable, attractive, and quiet, with some nice local touches. Most of the standard and deluxe doubles have a king or two double beds and an attractive, midsize bathroom. A couple have small private outdoor spaces. Some of the suites in back come with a full kitchen and lots of space—more than twice the size of the usual suite, with one king and one double bed. The breakfasts are good, and plans are in the works to install a full restaurant. Some lodgings just have a good feel to them, and this is one.

Reforma 139, 45500 Tlaquepaque, Jal. ℂ **866/629-3753** in the U.S. and Canada, or 33/3635-7522. www.quintadonjose.com. 15 units. $93 (£51) standard; $105 (£58) deluxe; $128–$163 (£70–£90) suite. Rates include full breakfast. AE, MC, V. Free secure parking. **Amenities:** Restaurant; bar; heated outdoor pool; tour info; in-room massage; babysitting; laundry service; nonsmoking rooms. *In room:* A/C, TV, Wi-Fi, hair dryer, iron.

INEXPENSIVE

Hotel San Francisco Plaza (*Value*)   This colonial-style downtown hotel is both pleasant and a bargain. Its rooms are big and comfortable, with attractive furnishings. All have rugs or carpeting, and most have tall ceilings (except in the remodeled area behind the reception desk). The hotel is built in colonial style around four courtyards, which contain fountains and potted plants. Rooms along the Sánchez Street side are much quieter now that the management has installed double windows. Some units along the back wall of the rear patio have small bathrooms. The San Francisco Plaza is 6 blocks south and 2 blocks east of the cathedral. The air-conditioning is being upgraded.

Degollado 267, Centro Histórico, 44100 Guadalajara, Jal. ℂ **33/3613-8954** or -8971. Fax 33/3613-3257. www.sanfranciscohotel.com.mx. 76 units. $65 (£36) double. AE, MC, V. Free sheltered parking. **Amenities:** Restaurant; room service; laundry service; dry cleaning; ironing service. *In room:* A/C, TV.

Plaza Los Reyes (Value) Okay, so the rooms in this 10-story down-town hotel aren't anything special to look at, but they do have good, individually controlled A/C and strong showers, all for not a lot of money. It's central, downtown near the market, but it's not the prettiest part of town; it's not dangerous. For entertainment, there's a fancy new multiplex cinema across the street that shows first-run Hollywood movies. Guest rooms are midsize and come with either two doubles or a king-size bed. Those on the mezzanine level are larger and often cost the same. Ask for a room facing away from the busy Calzada Independencia. Midsize bathrooms are clean, with good water pressure and plenty of hot water.

Calzada Independencia Sur 168, 44100 Guadalajara, Jal. ℂ 33/3613-9770 or -9775. 189 units. $55 (£30) double. AE, MC, V. Free valet parking. **Amenities:** Restaurant; outdoor heated pool; tour info; room service; laundry service; nonsmoking rooms. *In room:* A/C, TV, Wi-Fi.

4 Where to Dine

Guadalajara has many excellent restaurants either for fine dining or for typical local fare. Most of the fine-dining spots are on the west side. Those in the Centro Histórico are uniformly bad, excepting **La Fonda de San Miguel.** Tlaquepaque has some good choices, but most close by 8pm. Popular eateries serving good local fare are abundant, especially in the Centro Histórico. For a quick bite, there are several **Sanborn's** in the city. This is a popular national chain of restaurants known for their *enchiladas suizas* (enchiladas in cream sauce). If you're downtown and looking for baked goods and coffee, go to **El Globo** (ℂ 33/3613-9926), an upscale bakery at the corner of Pedro Moreno and Degollado. This is also a chain with a couple more locations around Guadalajara. *Tip:* When taking a taxi, keep the address of the restaurant handy because taxi drivers cannot be relied upon to know where even the most popular restaurants are.

Local dishes include *birria* (goat or lamb covered in maguey leaves and roasted). It comes in a tomato broth or with the broth on the side. Another favorite is the *torta ahogada,* a sandwich with pork bathed in a tomato sauce. I'm not particularly fond of them. The most popular drink here is the *paloma,* which combines tequila, lots of lime juice, and grapefruit soda on ice. I am fond of these.

EXPENSIVE
Adobe Fonda (★★) NOUVELLE MEXICAN This restaurant shares space with a large store on pedestrian-only Independencia. The dining area is open and airy. Homemade bread and tostadas

come to the table with an olive oil-based chile sauce, pico de gallo, and *requezón de epazote* (ricotta-like cheese with a Mexican herb). Among the soups are *crema de cilantro* and an interesting mushroom soup with a dark-beer broth. The main courses present some difficult decisions, with intriguing combinations of Mexican, Italian, and Argentine ingredients. Shrimp quesadillas accompanied by *chimichurri* with *nopal* cactus, filet in creamy ancho sauce, and the crab salad tower were all excellent. Sample the margaritas, too.

Francisco de Miranda 27 (corner of Independencia, Tlaquepaque). ℂ **33/3657-2792**. Reservations recommended on weekends. Main courses $13–$19 (£7.15–£10). AE, MC, V. Daily 12:30–6:30pm.

Chez Nené 𝕶𝕶𝕶 FRENCH   In a small and pleasant open-air dining room, you can enjoy a quiet and leisurely meal of delicious French food. After doing just this, I had to meet the owner to see who was behind such work. He turned out to be a French expatriate (whose Mexican wife, Nené, is the restaurant's namesake) with clear ideas about food and dining. Shorn of fads and pretense, his cooking aims at the essential in a dish. Freshness and quality of ingredients are what matter most, and everything (except stews and such) is cooked to order. The daily menu is on a chalkboard and depends on what the owner finds that morning at the market. There are always at least a dozen main courses. The waiter answered every question I put to him and provided excellent service.

Juan Palomar y Arias 426 (continuación Rafael Sanzio, west side). ℂ **33/3673-4564**. Reservations recommended on weekends. Main courses $10–$20 (£5.50–£11). AE, MC, V. Tues 4–11pm; Wed–Sat 1–5:30pm and 7:30–11:30pm; Sun 1–6pm.

El Sacromonte 𝕶𝕶𝕶 MEXICAN HAUTE CUISINE   The food here is so exquisite that I try to dine here every time I'm in Guadalajara. El Sacromonte emphasizes artful presentation and design: Order "Queen Isabel's crown," and you'll be served a dish of shrimp woven together in the shape of a crown and covered in divine lobster-and-orange sauce. Or try quesadillas with rose petals in a deep-colored strawberry sauce. For soup, consider *el viejo progreso* for its unlikely combination of flavors (blue cheese and chipotle chile). The menu features amusing descriptions in verse. The main dining area is a shaded, open-air patio. The restaurant isn't far from the downtown area, on the near west side.

In the building next door, the owners have opened an updated version of the classic Mexican bar where one drinks while snacking on complimentary *botanas* (the Mexican equivalent of tapas). There is also a menu, which is simpler than the restaurant's. The place is called **El Duende.**

Pedro Moreno 1398 (corner of Calle Colonias, west side). ✆ **33/3825-5447** or 3827-0663. Reservations recommended. Main courses $11–$18 (£6.05–£9.90). MC, V. Mon–Sat 1:30pm–midnight; Sun 1:30–6pm.

La Tequila 🏵🏵 MEXICAN   In its new location, about a block from where it used to be, this restaurant churns out Mexican standards such as *chalupas poblanas* (hand-made tortillas lightly fried and topped with a chile sauce), as well as versions of trendy contemporary Mexican cooking, including pasta stuffed with shrimp and *huitlacoche* (a salty and mild-tasting corn fungus), grilled-vegetable salad, and *molcajetes de arrachera* (fajitas with slices of chiles and onions that are cooked and served in a three-legged stone vessel). The cooking is great, the place is lively (the locals love it), and the decorative touches, such as trimmed agaves, give the dining areas a regional point of reference. Indoor/outdoor dining areas and a popular upstairs bar make up the majority of the restaurant. *Tip:* If this place is too crowded, or you're simply looking for quieter dining, go to the original site (Av. Mexico 2916) where you'll find a new restaurant called **La Divina Tentación** (✆ **33/3642-7242**). The menu is similar, and the cooking, from what I sampled, was even a little better, but I suspect it might not survive for long (though I hope I'm wrong). It's a little more sedate, but well run.

Av. México 2830 (at Napoleón, west side). ✆ **33/3640-3440** or 33/3640-3110. Reservations recommended. Main courses $10–$18 (£5.50–£9.90). AE, MC, V. Mon–Sat 1pm–midnight; Sun 1–6pm.

MODERATE

Hostería del Angel 🏵🏵 TAPAS/SPANISH DELI/WINE BAR
Sip wine and munch on a few tapas in this comfortable and casual restaurant and wine bar just a few blocks from the basilica in Zapopan. The chef-owner cooked for years in Spain and Italy, where he became fascinated with the making of cheeses and deli meats such as prosciutto and Spanish *jamón serrano.* He serves a variety of tapas, and his baguette sandwiches are very popular with the locals. The menu doesn't do a good job of explaining the dishes, so don't hesitate to ask the waitperson for explanations. The house specialty is the *rotolata*—vegetables and cold cuts surrounded by a thin layer of crispy cheese. Live music plays from 9 to 11pm Monday through Saturday. The restaurant is a half-block off the pedestrian-only *calzada,* which leads to the plaza in front of the basilica.

5 de Mayo 260, Zapopan (west side). ℂ/fax **33/3656-9516.** Reservations recommended. Menu items $5–$10 (£2.75–£5.50). MC, V. Mon–Sat 9am–midnight; Sun 9am–8pm.

I Latina FUSION   Warehouse chic with a porcine motif (the owner tells me that the pig is a symbol of abundance in Thailand) is the look here. The menu is absurdly small but is supplemented with lots of daily specials. On my last visit, I sampled a steak with a coffee crust sitting on a bed of mashed sweet potatoes with shoe-string sweet potato fries and tossed greens scattered about the plate (quite good), a chicken in peanut sauce that was okay, and a stuffed filet of snapper that was quite tasty. This is a good place for people-watching—you get to see a portion of Guadalajara's hip, intellectual crowd, who enjoy the antiestablishment surroundings, including the metal and plastic tables and chairs. My main problem is the noise, which at times gets to be too much. If you're looking for quiet dining, go elsewhere. Cabs have a hard time finding this place despite being almost right off of Minerva Circle. It's not that difficult. Inglaterra faces the railroad tracks.

Av. Inglaterra (west side). ℂ **33/3647-7774.** Reservations recommended. Main courses $9–$15 (£4.95–£8.25). MC, V. Wed–Sat 7:30pm–1am; Sun 2–6pm.

La Fonda de San Miguel *Moments* MEXICAN   My favorite way to enjoy a good meal in Mexico is to have it in an elegant colonial courtyard. I love the contrast between the bright, noisy street and the cool, shaded patio. This restaurant is in the former convent of Santa Teresa de Jesús. While you enjoy the stone arches and gurgling fountain, little crisp tacos and homemade bread appear at the table. For main courses, try *chiles en nogada* (stuffed chile in a white wal-nut cream sauce) if it's in season, or perhaps a traditional *mole poblano.* The restaurant is 4 blocks west and 1 block south of the cathedral, between Pedro Moreno and Morelos. Thursday to Satur-day musicians perform from 3 to 5pm and 9 to 11pm.

Donato Guerra 25 (between Morelos and Pedro Moreno, downtown). ℂ **33/3613-0809.** Reservations recommended on weekends. Breakfast $4–$8 (£2.20–£4.40); main courses $9–$16 (£4.95–£8.80). AE, MC, V. Sun–Mon 8:30–11:30am, 1:30–6pm; Tues–Sat 8:30–11:30am, 1:30pm–midnight.

La Trattoria Pomodoro Ristorante ℱ ITALIAN   Good food, good service, and moderate prices make this restaurant perennially popular. The price of pastas and main courses includes a visit to the well-stocked salad bar. Recommendable menu items include the combination pasta plate (lasagna, fettuccini Alfredo, and spaghetti), shrimp linguine, and chicken parmigiana. The Italian owner likes to stock lots of wines from the motherland. The dining room is attractive and casual, with comfortable furniture and separate seating for smokers and nonsmokers.

Niños Héroes 3051 (west side). ℂ **33/3122-1817**. Reservations recommended, but not accepted during holidays. Pasta $7–$9 (£3.85–£4.95); main courses $8–$10 (£4.40–£5.50). AE, MC, V. Daily 1pm–midnight.

Mariscos Progreso SEAFOOD   Out on a large shaded patio, waiters carrying large platters of delicious seafood navigate among the tables. Mexicans do a wonderful job with seafood, and this popular restaurant does the tradition proud. Grilling over wood is the specialty here, but the kitchen's repertoire includes all the Mexican standards. For a sampling of grilled favorites, try the *parrillada* (a platter of grilled dishes) for two. Sometimes there's quite a bit of ambience, with mariachis adding to the commotion. At other times, the crowd thins and one can rest peacefully from the exertions of shopping with a cold drink. It's a half-block from the Parián.

Progreso 80, Tlaquepaque. ℂ **33/3657-4995**. Main courses $7–$15 (£3.85–£8.25). AE, MC, V. Daily 11am–7pm.

INEXPENSIVE

Café Madrid MEXICAN   This little coffee shop is like many coffee shops used to be—a social institution where people come in, greet each other and the staff by name, and chat over breakfast or coffee and cigarettes. Change comes slowly here. For example, despite the fact that it's an informal place, the waiters wear white jackets with black bow ties, as they did 20 years ago. The coffee and Mexican breakfasts are good, as is the standard Mexican fare served in the afternoon. The front room opens to the street, with a small lunch counter and another room in the back.

Juárez 264 (between Corona and 16 de Septiembre, downtown). ℂ **33/3614-9504**. Breakfast $2–$4 (£1.10–£2.20); main courses $5–$7 (£2.75–£3.85). No credit cards. Daily 7:30am–10:30pm.

La Chata Restaurant REGIONAL/MEXICAN   If you're staying downtown, don't let this place slip off your radar. It does a good job with all the Mexican classics and some regional specialties as well. Unlike most restaurants, this one has the kitchen in front and the dining area in back. For a reasonable sum you can get a filling bowl of *pozole* (chicken, pork, and hominy in a broth to which you add onions, radishes, chile, and oregano). They also offer *flautas* (flour tortillas that are rolled up around a filling and deep fried), *sopes* (little fried masa cakes topped with savory meats and veggies), quesadillas, and guacamole. There's also traditional *mole* and a couple of combination plates. The chairs are comfortable, and you hang out with lots of locals.

Corona 126 (between Juárez and López Cotilla, downtown). ⓒ **33/3613-0588.** Breakfast $4–$6 (£2.20–£3.30); main courses $6–$9 (£3.30–£4.95). AE, DC, MC, V. Daily 8am–midnight.

La Fonda de la Noche ⭐⭐ *Finds* MEXICAN   For a host of reasons this is my favorite place in the city for a simple supper. The limited menu is excellent, the surroundings are comfortable and inviting, the lighting is perfect, and there's a touch of nostalgia for the Mexico of the '40s, '50s, and '60s. It's not far from downtown or the west side; take a cab to the intersection of Jesús and Reforma, and, when you get there, look for a door behind a small hedge. There's no sign. It's a house with five fun dining rooms. Only Spanish is spoken, but the menu is simple. To try a little of everything, order the *plato combinado,* a combination plate that comes with an *enchilada de "medio mole,"* an empanada called a *media luna,* a tostada, and a *sope.* The owner is Carlos Ibarra, an artist from the state of Durango. He has decorated the place with traditional Mexican pine furniture and cotton tablecloths and his personal collection of paintings, mostly the works of close friends. On weekends, La Fonda offers *chiles en nogada.*

Jesús 251 (corner with Reforma, Col. El Refugio). ⓒ **33/3827-0917.** Main courses $6–$8 (£3.30–£4.40). MC, V. Tues–Sun 7:30pm–midnight.

Los Itacates Restaurant ⭐ *Value* MEXICAN   The Mexican equivalent of down-home cooking at reasonable prices. Office workers pack the place between 2 and 4pm weekdays, and there's a good crowd weekend nights, but at other times there's no problem finding a table. You can dine outdoors in a shaded sidewalk area or in one of the three dining rooms. Specialties include *lomo adobado* (baked pork in dark chile sauce), and chiles rellenos. *Pollo Itacates* is a quarter of a chicken, two cheese enchiladas, potatoes, and rice. Los Itacates is 5 blocks north of Avenida Vallarta. In the evenings they serve tacos and other *antojitos.*

Chapultepec Norte 110 (west side). ⓒ **33/3825-1106** or -9551. Reservations accepted on weekends and holidays. Breakfast buffet $6 (£3.30); tacos $1 (55p); main courses $5–$7 (£2.75–£3.85). MC, V. Mon–Sat 8am–11pm; Sun 8am–7pm.

7

Exploring Guadalajara & Beyond

By David Baird

Guadalajara is one of the most Mexican of Mexico's cities. Spend a few days exploring its historic downtown area, with all its cultural and architectural highlights, parks, attractions, and even the most hardcore resort tourist will realize there is much more to Mexico than sandy beaches and souvenir shops.

1 What to See & Do

SPECIAL EVENTS

There's always something going on from September to December. In September, when Mexicans celebrate independence from Spain, Guadalajara goes all out, with a full month of festivities. The celebrations kick off with the **Encuentro Internacional del Mariachi** (www.mariachi-jalisco.com.mx), in which mariachi bands from around the world play before knowledgeable audiences and hold sessions with other mariachis. Bands come from as far as Japan and Russia, and the event takes on a curious postmodern hue. Concerts are held in several venues. In the Degollado Theater, you can hear orchestral arrangements of classic mariachi songs with solos by famous mariachis. You might be acquainted with many of the classics without even knowing it. The culmination is a parade of thousands of mariachis and *charros* (Mexican cowboys) through downtown. It starts the first week of September.

On **September 15,** a massive crowd assembles in front of the Governor's Palace to await the traditional *grito* (shout for independence) at 11pm. The *grito* commemorates Father Miguel Hidalgo de Costilla's cry for independence in 1810. The celebration features live music on a street stage, spontaneous dancing, fireworks, and shouts of *"¡Viva México!"* and *"¡Viva Hidalgo!"* The next day is the official Independence Day, with a traditional parade; the plazas downtown resemble a country fair and market, with booths, games of chance, stuffed-animal prizes, cotton candy, and candied apples. Live entertainment stretches well into the night.

On **October 12,** a **procession** 𝕲𝕲 honoring Our Lady of Zapopan celebrates the feast day of the Virgin of Zapopan. Around dawn, her small, dark figure begins the 5-hour ride from the Cathedral of Guadalajara to the suburban Basilica of Zapopan (see "Other Attractions," below). The original icon dates from the mid-1500s; the procession began 200 years later. Today, crowds spend the night along the route and vie for position as the Virgin approaches. She travels in a gleaming new car (virginal in that it must never have had the ignition turned on), which her caretakers pull through the streets. During the months leading up to the feast day, the figure visits churches all over the city. You will likely see neighborhoods decorated with paper streamers and banners honoring the Virgin's visit to the local church.

The celebration has grown into a month-long event, **Fiestas de Octubre,** which kicks off with an enormous parade, usually on the first Saturday or Sunday of the month. Festivities include performing arts, *charreadas* (rodeos), bullfights, art exhibits, regional dancing, a food fair, and a Day of Nations incorporating all the consulates in Guadalajara. By the time this is over, you enter the **holiday season of November and December,** with Revolution Day (Nov 20), the Virgin of Guadalupe's feast day (Dec 12), and other celebrations.

DOWNTOWN GUADALAJARA

The most easily recognized building in the city is the **cathedral** 𝕲, around which four open plazas make the shape of a Latin cross. Later, a long swath of land was cleared to extend the open area from Plaza Liberación east to the Instituto Cultural Cabañas, creating **Plaza Tapatía.**

Construction on the cathedral started in 1561 and continued into the 18th century. Over such a long time, it was inevitable that remodeling would take place before the building was ever completed. The result is an unusual facade that is an amalgam of several architectural styles, including baroque, neoclassical, and Gothic. An 1818 earthquake destroyed the original large towers; their replacements were built in the 1850s, inspired by designs on the bishop's dinner china. Blue and yellow are Guadalajara's colors. The nave is airy and majestic. Items of interest include a painting in the sacristy ascribed to the 17th-century Spanish artist Bartolomé Estaban Murillo (1617–82).

On the cathedral's south side is the **Plaza de Armas,** the oldest and loveliest of the plazas. A cast-iron Art Nouveau bandstand is its

Cathedral **3**
Instituto Cultural Cabañas **12**
Church of Santa María de Gracia **7**
Mercado Libertad **11**
Museo Regional de Guadalajara **5**
Palacio del Gobierno **2**
Plaza de Armas **1**

Plaza Guadalajara **4**
Quetzalcoatl Fountain **10**
Rotonda de los Hombres Ilustres **4**
Teatro Degollado **8**
Universidad de Guadalajara Facultad de Música
& Iglesia de San Agustín **9**

dominant feature. Made in France, it was a gift to the city from the dictator Porfirio Díaz in the 1890s. The female figures on the bandstand exhibited too little clothing for conservative Guadalajarans, who clothed them. The dictator, recognizing when it's best to let the people have their way, said nothing.

Facing the plaza is the **Palacio del Gobierno** 𝒦𝒦, a broad palace two stories high, built in 1774. The facade blends Spanish and Moorish elements and holds several eye-catching details. Inside the central courtyard, above the staircase to the right, is a spectacular mural of Hidalgo by the modern Mexican master José Clemente Orozco. The Father of Independence appears high overhead, bearing directly down on the viewer and looking as implacable as a force of nature. On one of the adjacent walls Orozco painted *The Carnival of Ideologies,* a dark satire on the prevailing fanaticisms of his day. Another of his murals is inside the second-floor chamber of representatives, depicting Hidalgo again, this time in a more conventional posture, writing the proclamation to end slavery in Mexico. The *palacio* is open daily from 10am to 8pm.

In the plaza on the opposite side of the cathedral from the Plaza de Armas is the **Rotonda de los Hombres Ilustres.** Sixteen white columns, each supporting a bronze statue, stand as monuments to Guadalajara's and Jalisco's distinguished sons. Across the street from the plaza, in front of the Museo Regional, you will see a line of horse-drawn buggies. A carriage ride around the Centro Histórico lasts about an hour and costs $20 (£11) for one to four people.

Facing the east side of the rotunda is the **Museo Regional de Guadalajara,** Liceo 60 (© 33/3613-2703). Originally a convent, it was built in 1701 in the churrigueresque (Mexican baroque) style and contains some of the region's important archaeological finds, fossils, historic objects, and art. Among the highlights are a giant reconstructed mammoth's skeleton and a meteorite weighing 1,715 pounds, discovered in Zacatecas in 1792. On the first floor holds a fascinating exhibit of pre-Hispanic pottery, and exquisite pottery and clay figures recently unearthed near Tequila during the construction of the toll road. On the second floor is a small ethnography exhibit of the contemporary dress of the state's indigenous peoples, including the Coras, Huicholes, Mexicaneros, Nahuas, and Tepehuanes. It's open Tuesday through Saturday from 9am to 5:30pm and Sunday from 9am to 4:30pm. Admission is $4 (£2.20).

Behind the Cathedral is the Plaza Liberación, with the **Teatro Degollado** (deh-goh-*yah*-doh) on the opposite side. This neoclassical 19th-century opera house was named for Santos Degollado, a local patriot who fought with Juárez against Maximilian and the French. Apollo and the nine muses decorate the theater's pediment, and the interior is famous for both the acoustics and the rich decoration. It hosts a variety of performances during the year, including the Ballet Folclórico on Sunday at 10am. It's open Monday through Friday from 10am to 2pm and during performances.

To the right of the theater, across the street, is the sweet little **church of Santa María de Gracia,** built in 1573 as part of a convent for Dominican nuns. On the opposite side of the Teatro Degollado is the **church of San Agustín.** The former convent is now the **University of Guadalajara School of Music.**

Behind the Teatro Degollado begins the Plaza Tapatía, which leads to the Instituto Cabañas. It passes between a couple of low, modern office buildings. The **Tourism Information Office** is in a building on the right-hand side.

Beyond these office buildings, the plaza opens into a large expanse, now framed by department stores and offices and dominated by the abstract modern **Quetzalcoatl Fountain.** This fluid steel structure represents the mythical plumed serpent Quetzalcoatl, who figured so prominently in pre-Hispanic religion and culture, and exerts a presence even today.

At the far end of the plaza is the Hospicio Cabañas, formerly an orphanage and known today as the **Instituto Cultural Cabañas** 🏵🏵, Cabañas 8 (© **33/3617-4322**). This vast structure is impressive for both its size (more than 23 courtyards) and its grandiose architecture, especially the cupola. Created by the famous Mexican architect Manuel Tolsá, it housed homeless children from 1829 to 1980. Today, it's a thriving cultural center offering art shows and classes. The interior walls and ceiling of the main building display murals painted by Orozco in 1937. His *Man of Fire,* in the dome, is said to represent the spirit of humanity projecting itself toward the infinite. Other rooms hold additional Orozco works, as well as excellent contemporary art and temporary exhibits.

Just south of the Hospicio Cabañas (to the left as you exit) is the **Mercado Libertad** 🏵, Guadalajara's gigantic covered central market, the largest in Latin America. This site has been a market plaza since the 1500s; the present buildings date from the early 1950s (see "Shopping," below).

Guadalajara Bus Tours

Two companies offer bus tours of the city. One is a local company, **Tranvías Turísticos** (no phone), which offers two tours on small buses that look like trolley cars. Get info and buy tickets from the kiosk in Plaza Guadalajara (in front of the cathedral) starting at 10am. One tour is a circuit through downtown and surrounding neighborhoods. It lasts 1 hour and 10 minutes. The second is a slightly longer tour, going to Tlaquepaque. It lasts 1½ hours. Both cost $9 (£4.95). The other company, **Tapatío Tours** (© **33/3613-0887**), has modern, bright red double-decker buses. Its tour goes from downtown to western Guadalajara to Tlaquepaque. The tour costs $9 (£4.95) on weekdays, $11 (£6.05) on weekends. It goes farther out, into western Guadalajara. There are 10 stops; you can get off at any and catch the next bus when it passes by, which is every 35 minutes. Catch the bus in the plaza on the north side of the cathedral. It also starts at 10 in the morning.

OTHER ATTRACTIONS

At **Parque Agua Azul (Blue Water Park),** plants, trees, shrubbery, statues, and fountains create a perfect refuge from the bustling city. Many people come here to exercise early in the morning. The park is open daily from 7am to 6pm. Admission is $1 (55p) for adults, 50¢ (30p) for children.

Across Independencia from the park, cater-cornered from a small flower market, is the **Museo de Arqueología del Occidente de México,** Calzada Independencia at Avenida del Campesino. It houses a fine collection of pre-Hispanic pottery from Jalisco, Nayarit, and Colima. The museum is open Tuesday through Sunday from 10am to 2pm and 4 to 7pm. There's a small admission charge.

The state-run **Instituto de la Artesanía Jalisciense** (**© 33/3619-4664**) is at the Instituto de la Artesanía Jalisciense, just past the park entrance at Calzada Independencia and González Gallo.

Also near the park is Guadalajara's rodeo arena, **Lienzo Charro de Jalisco** (**© 33/3619-0315**). Mexican cowboys, known as *charros,* are famous for their riding and lasso work, and the arena in Guadalajara is considered the big time. There are shows and competitions every Sunday at noon. The arena is at Av. Dr. R. Michel 577, between González Gallo and Las Palomas.

Basílica de la Virgen de Zapopan ★ A wide promenade several blocks long leads to a large, open plaza and the basilica. This is the religious center of Guadalajara. On the Virgin's feast day (p. 174) the plaza fills with thousands of *tapatíos.* The 18th-century church is a lovely (and somewhat anachronistic) combination of baroque and plateresque styles. The cult of the Virgin of Zapopan practically began with the foundation of Guadalajara itself. She is much revered and the object of many pilgrimages. In front of the church are several stands selling religious figures and paraphernalia. On one side of the church is a lovely museum and store dedicated to the betterment of the Huichol Indians. It is well worth a visit.

Main Plaza, Zapopan (10km/6¼ miles northwest of downtown). No phone. Free admission. Daily 7am–7pm; museum daily 10am–7pm.

Museo de la Ciudad This museum, in a former convent, chronicles Guadalajara's past. The rooms, beginning on the right and proceeding in chronological order, cover the period from just before the city's founding to the present. Unusual artifacts, including rare Spanish armaments and equestrian paraphernalia, give a sense of what day-to-day life was like. Descriptive text is in Spanish only.

Independencia 684 (at M. Bárcenas). ☎ **33/3658-2531.** 50¢ (30p). Tues–Sun 10am–5pm.

Museo de las Artes de la Universidad de Guadalajara

Inside the main lecture hall of this building are more murals by Orozco. On the wall behind the stage is a bitter denunciation of corruption called *The People and Their False Leaders.* But in the cupola is a more optimistic work—*The Five-fold Man,* who works to create a better society and better self. There is also a small permanent collection of modern art, which will look all too familiar because the works seem so derivative of many of the modern masters.

Juárez 975 (enter on López Cotilla). ☎ **33/3134-2222.** 50¢ (30p). Tues–Sun 10am–8pm.

Museo Pantaleón Panduro ✷✷✷

This is the greatest collection of ceramic works I've ever seen. Collectors and connoisseurs of pottery will love it, but so will casual students of Mexican popular culture and the arts. This could be one of the great museums of Mexico, but someone in authority needs to come up with the money and the curators to exhibit the collection properly. Right now pieces are organized by state, which makes no sense because the collection is much more about individual artistic achievement than it is about tracing local and regional traditions in ceramics. Every year a prestigious competition is held in Tlaquepaque among ceramists from across the nation. Prizes are awarded in seven categories and a best of show among these. (*Tip:* The competition is held every June, which is a good time for visiting Tlaquepaque.) The president of Mexico even comes to town to give out the awards. After the competition, many of the winning pieces become part the museum's collection. The virtuosity manifested in some of them will take your breath away. It would be wonderful if they were organized by category, and exhibited with enough light and explanatory text to get a better appreciation and understanding of them. But for now, the best thing you can do is cajole someone into showing you around and explain something about the pieces that you're viewing. The staff is actually quite knowledgeable, and at least one speaks English. The museum occupies a third of a large complex that in colonial times was a large religious community. It's now called **Centro Cultural El Refugio,** and it's very much worth exploring after you've seen the museum's collection.

P. Sánchez 191 (at Calle Florida, Tlaquepaque). ☎ **33/3639-5656.** Free admission. Tues–Sun 10am–6pm.

2 Shopping

Many visitors to Guadalajara come specifically for the shopping in Tlaquepaque and Tonalá (see below). If you have little free time, try the government-run **Instituto de la Artesanía Jalisciense** *✿*, González Gallo 20 at Calzada Independencia (© **33/3619-4664**), in Parque Agua Azul, just south of downtown. This place is perfect for one-stop shopping, with two floors of pottery, silver jewelry, dance masks, glassware, leather goods, and regional clothing from around the state and the country. As you enter, on the right are museum displays showing crafts and regional costumes from the state of Jalisco. The craft store is open Monday through Friday from 10am to 6pm, Saturday from 10am to 5pm, Sunday from 10am to 3pm.

Guadalajara is known for its shoe industry; if you're in the market for a pair, try the **Galería del Calzado,** a shopping center made up exclusively of shoe stores. It's on the west side, about 6 blocks from Minerva Circle, at avenidas México and Yaquis.

Mariachis and *charros* come to Guadalajara from all over Mexico to buy highly worked belts and boots, wide-brimmed sombreros, and embroidered shirts. Several tailor shops and stores specialize in these outfits. One is **El Charro,** which has a store in the Plaza del Sol shopping center, across the street from the Hotel Presidente InterContinental, and one downtown on Juárez.

For a good look at the material world for most Mexicans, try the mammoth **Mercado Libertad** *✿* downtown. Besides food and produce, you'll see crafts, household goods, clothing, magic potions, and more. Although it opens at 7am, the market isn't in full swing until around 10am. Come prepared to haggle.

SHOPPING IN TLAQUEPAQUE & TONALA

Almost everyone who comes to Guadalajara for the shopping has Tlaquepaque (tlah-keh-*pah*-keh) and Tonalá in mind. These two suburbs are traditional handicraft centers that produce and sell a wide variety of *artesanía* (crafts).

TLAQUEPAQUE

Located about 20 minutes from downtown, **Tlaquepaque** *✿✿✿* has the best shopping for handicrafts and decorative arts in all of Mexico. Over the years, it has become a fashionable place, attracting talented designers in a variety of fields. Even though it's a suburb of a large city, it has a cozy, small-town feel; it's a pleasure simply to stroll through the central streets from shop to shop. No one hassles you;

no one does the hard sell. There are some excellent places to eat (see "Where to Dine," in chapter 6), or you can grab some simple fare at **El Parián,** a building in the middle of town that houses a number of small eateries.

A taxi from downtown Guadalajara costs $5 (£2.75), or you can take one of the TUR 706 buses from downtown to Tlaquepaque and Tonalá (see "Getting Around," in chapter 6).

The **Tlaquepaque Tourism Office** (© **33/3562-7050,** ext. 2320 or turismotlaquepaque@yahoo.com.mx) has an information booth in the main square by El Parián. It's staffed from 9:30am to 8pm daily.

If you are interested in pottery and ceramics, make sure to see the Pantaleón Panduro Museum, reviewed on p. 179. Another is the **Regional Ceramics Museum,** Independencia 237 (© **33/3635-5404**), which displays several aspects of traditional Jalisco pottery as produced in Tlaquepaque and Tonalá. The examples date back several generations and are grouped according to the technique used to produce them. Note the crosshatch design known as *petatillo* on some of the pieces; it's one of the region's oldest traditional motifs

---

Tips Packing It In

If you need your purchases packed safely so that you can check them as extra baggage, or if you want them shipped, talk to **Margaret del Río**. She is an American who runs a large packing and shipping company at Juárez 347, Tlaquepaque (© **33/3657-5652**). Paying the excess baggage fee usually is cheaper than shipping, but less convenient.

---

and is, like so many other motifs, a real pain to produce. Look for the wonderful old kitchen and dining room, complete with pots, utensils, and dishes. The museum is open Tuesday through Saturday from 10am to 6pm, Sunday from 10am to 3pm; admission is free.

The following list is just a small fraction of what you'll find; the best approach might be to just follow your nose. The main shopping is along **Independencia,** a pedestrian-only street that starts at El Parián. You can go door-to-door visiting the shops until the street ends, then work your way back on **Calle Juárez,** the next street over, south of Independencia.

Agustín Parra   So you bought an old hacienda and are trying to restore its chapel—where do you go to find traditional baroque sculpture, religious art, gold-leafed objects, and even entire *retablos* (altarpieces)? Parra is famous for exactly this kind of work, and the store is lovely. It's open Monday through Saturday from 10am to 7pm. Independencia 158. © **33/3657-8530.**

Bazar Hecht   One of the village's longtime favorites. Here you'll find wood objects, handmade furniture, and a few antiques. It's open Monday through Saturday from 10am to 2:30pm and 3:30 to 7pm. Juárez 162. © **33/3657-0316.**

Sergio Bustamante   Sergio Bustamante's imaginative, original bronze, ceramic, and papier-mâché sculptures are among the most sought-after in Mexico—as well as the most copied. He also designs silver jewelry. This exquisite gallery showcases his work. It's open Monday through Saturday from 10am to 7pm, Sunday from noon to 4pm. Independencia 238 at Cruz Verde. © **33/3639-5519.**

Teté Arte y Diseño   Architectural decorative objects, especially hand-wrought iron hardware for the "Old Mexico" look, is what this store is mainly known for. It also has a large collection of wrought-iron chandeliers. It's open Monday through Saturday from 10am to 7:30pm. Juárez 173. © **33/3635-7347.**

TONALÁ: A TRADITION OF POTTERY MAKING

Tonalá ✦✦ is a pleasant town 5 minutes from Tlaquepaque. The streets were paved only recently, and there aren't fancy shops here. The village has been a center of pottery making since pre-Hispanic times; half of the more than 400 workshops here produce a wide variety of high- and low-temperature pottery. Other local artists work with forged iron, cantera stone, brass and copper, marble, miniatures, papier-mâché, textiles, blown glass, and gesso. This is a good place to look for custom work in any of these materials; you can locate a large pool of craftspeople by asking around.

Market days are Thursday and Sunday. Expect large crowds, and blocks of stalls displaying locally made pottery and glassware, as well as cheap manufactured goods, food, and all kinds of bric-a-brac. "Herb men" sell a rainbow selection of dried medicinal herbs from wheelbarrows; magicians entertain crowds with sleight-of-hand; and craftspeople spread their colorful wares on the plaza's sidewalks. I prefer to visit Tonalá on non–market days, when it's much easier to get around and see the stores and workshops. This is the place for buying sets of margarita glasses, the widely seen blue-rimmed hand-blown glassware, as well as the pottery typically associated with Mexico and finely painted *petatillo* ware.

The **Tonalá Tourism Office** (✆ **33/3284-3092**) is in the Arte-sanos building, set back from the road at Atonaltecas 140 Sur (the main street leading into Tonalá) at Matamoros. There is an information booth in front. Hours are Monday through Friday from 9am to 3pm, Saturday from 9am to 1pm. The office offers **free walking tours** on Monday, Tuesday, Wednesday, and Friday at 9am and 2pm, and Saturday at 9am and 1pm. They include visits to arti-sans' workshops (where you'll see ceramics, stoneware, blown glass, papier-mâché, and the like). Tours last 3 to 4 hours and require a minimum of five people. Visitors can request an English-speaking guide. Also in Tonalá, cater-cornered from the church, you'll see a small tourism information kiosk that's staffed on market days and provides maps and useful information.

The **Museo Nacional de Cerámica,** Constitución 104, between Hidalgo and Morelos (✆ **33/3284-3000,** ext. 1194) occupies a two-story mansion and displays work from Jalisco and all over the country. There's a large shop in the front on the right as you enter. The museum is open Tuesday through Friday from 10am to 5pm, Saturday and Sunday from 10am to 2pm. Admission is free; the fee for using a video or still camera is $8.50 (£4.70) per camera.

Tonalá

On the map:
- Police
- Museo Nacional de Cerámica
- Plaza Principal
- Casa de Artesanías
- Cruz Blanca

Streets and labels: Morelos, Hidalgo, Lopez Cotilla, Angulo, Nicolás Bravo, Ramon Corona, Cuitlahuac, Independencia, Constitución, Lende, Alvaro Obregón, Emiliano Zapata, Cuauhtémoc, Av. Río Nilo, Juárez, Pedro Moreno, Av De Los Tonaltecas, Zaragoza, Degollado, FCO. I Madero, W. Carranza, 16 De Sept, Pino Suares, 5 De Mayo, Moctezuma, Ingurgentes, Santes Degollado, Matamoros, Javier Mina, Colón, Cruz Blanca, Anesagasti, Galeana, Av Tonala

Information ☒
Post Office ⓘ

3 Guadalajara After Dark

MARIACHIS

You can't go far in Guadalajara without coming across some mariachis, but seeing really talented performers takes some effort. Try **Casa Bariachi,** Av. Vallarta 2221 (ⓒ **33/3615-0029**). In Tlaquepaque, go to **El Parián,** the building on the town square where mariachis serenade diners under the archways.

THE CLUB & MUSIC SCENE

Guadalajara, as you might expect, has a lot of variety in entertainment. For the most extensive listing of clubs and performances, get your hands on a copy of *Ocio,* the weekly insert of *Público.* You'll find listings in the back, categorized by type of music. Across the street from Casa Bariachi, mentioned above, is **La Bodeguita del Medio** (ⓒ **33/3630-1620**) at Av. Vallarta 2320. It offers live old-school Cuban son. The groups come from Cuba and rotate every few months. The last night I visited the place, a small combo was playing in a little corner partly mixing in with the crowd. The place is on the small side, but people were making room to dance. Another thing to do is track down Cuban diva **Rosalia,** who lives in Guadalajara. She's a great talent and always has a tight band playing with her as she belts out salsa and merengue tunes. The last time I was in Guadalajara she was singing weekends at the bar at the Hotel Presidente InterContinental.

Tequila: The Name Says It All

Tequila is an entertaining (and intoxicating) town, well worth a day trip from Guadalajara. Several taxi drivers charge about $55 (£30) to take you to the town, get you into a tour of a distillery, take you to a restaurant, and haul you back to Guadalajara. A few of them speak English. One recommended driver is José Gabriel Gómez (© 33/3649-0791; jgabriel-taxi@hotmail.com); he has a new car and drives carefully. Call him in the evening. Tour companies also arrange bus trips to Tequila; ask at the ticket kiosk of Tranvías Turísticos, mentioned on p. 177. That company has started a weekend tour to Tequila, taking people to the Cofradía distillery.

Tequila has many distilleries, including the famous brands **Sauza** and **José Cuervo.** All the distilleries—the big, modern ones and the small, more traditional ones—offer tours. If you're on your own, a good place to hook up with a tour is at the little booth outside the city hall on the main square; two young English-speaking women run tours to any of the local factories. Tours cost only $5 (£2.75) and last about 2 hours. All tours show how tequila is made, what traditions the process follows, and what differences exist between tequilas; they end, of course, with a tasting. Avenida Vallarta runs straight to the highway to Tequila, which is about an hour outside of Guadalajara.

Another approach is to take the **Tequila Express** to the town of Amatitán, home of the Herradura distillery. This excursion is more about having a good time and enjoying some of the things this area is known for than it is about sampling tequila. Serious tequila enthusiasts will be disappointed. There's a nice tour of the distillery, but most of the time is spent watching mariachis and Mexican cowboys perform. The tequila tastings are limited. Everyone has a good time and drinks a fair share, but a trip to the town proper is more informative and offers a greater opportunity for trying different tequilas.

The Tequila Express leaves from the train station on Friday and Saturday, and sometimes on Sunday during vacation and holiday season. You need to be there by 10am. The Guadalajara Chamber of Commerce (Cámara de Comercio), at Vallarta and Niño Obrero (© **33/3880-9099**), organizes this trip. Buy tickets ahead of time at the main office; at the small office in the Centro Histórico at Morelos 395, at Calle Colón (no phone); or through Ticketmaster (© **33/3818-3800**). Office hours are Monday through Friday from 9am to 2pm and 4 to 6pm. Tickets cost $65 (£36) for adults, $35 (£19) for children 6 to 12. The tour includes food and drink. It returns to Guadalajara at about 8pm. Travel time is 1¾ hours each way. For more information, see www.tequilaexpress.com.mx.

Appendix:
Useful Terms & Phrases

Most Mexicans are very patient with foreigners who try to speak their language; it helps a lot to know a few basic phrases. Included in this appendix are simple phrases for expressing basic needs, followed by some common menu items.

1 Basic Vocabulary

ENGLISH-SPANISH PHRASES

English	Spanish	Pronunciation
Good day	**Buen día**	bwehn *dee*-ah
Good morning	**Buenos días**	*bweh*-nohss dee-ahss
How are you?	**¿Cómo está?**	*koh*-moh ehss-*tah?*
Very well	**Muy bien**	mwee byehn
Thank you	**Gracias**	*grah*-syahss
You're welcome	**De nada**	deh *nah*-dah
Good-bye	**Adiós**	ah-*dyohss*
Please	**Por favor**	pohr fah-*vohr*
Yes	**Sí**	see
No	**No**	noh
Excuse me	**Perdóneme**	pehr-*doh*-neh-meh
Give me	**Déme**	*deh*-meh
Where is . . . ?	**¿Dónde está . . . ?**	*dohn*-deh ehss-*tah?*
the station	**la estación**	lah ehss-tah-*syohn*
a hotel	**un hotel**	oon oh-*tehl*
a gas station	**una gasolinera**	*oo*-nah gah-soh-lee-*neh*-rah

English	Spanish	Pronunciation
a restaurant	**un restaurante**	oon res-tow-*rahn*-teh
the toilet	**el baño**	el *bah*-nyoh
a good doctor	**un buen médico**	oon bwehn *meh*-dee-coh
the road to . . .	**el camino a/hacia . . .**	el cah-*mee*-noh ah/*ah*-syah
To the right	**A la derecha**	ah lah deh-*reh*-chah
To the left	**A la izquierda**	ah lah ees-*kyehr*-dah
Straight ahead	**Derecho**	deh-*reh*-choh
I would like	**Quisiera**	key-*syeh*-rah
I want	**Quiero**	*kyeh*-roh
to eat	**comer**	koh-*mehr*
a room	**una habitación**	*oo*-nah ah-bee-tah-*syohn*
Do you have . . . ?	**¿Tiene usted . . . ?**	tyeh-neh oo-*sted?*
a book	**un libro**	oon *lee*-broh
a dictionary	**un diccionario**	oon deek-syow-*nah*-ryo
How much is it?	**¿Cuánto cuesta?**	*kwahn*-toh *kwehss*-tah?
When?	**¿Cuándo?**	*kwahn*-doh?
What?	**¿Qué?**	keh?
There is (Is there . . . ?)	**(¿)Hay (. . . ?)**	eye?
What is there?	**¿Qué hay?**	keh eye?
Yesterday	**Ayer**	ah-*yer*
Today	**Hoy**	oy
Tomorrow	**Mañana**	mah-*nyah*-nah
Good	**Bueno**	*bweh*-noh
Bad	**Malo**	*mah*-loh
Better (best)	**(Lo) Mejor**	(loh) meh-*hohr*

English	Spanish	Pronunciation
More	**Más**	mahs
Less	**Menos**	*meh*-nohss
No smoking	**Se prohibe fumar**	seh proh-*ee*-beh foo-*mahr*
Postcard	**Tarjeta postal**	tar-*heh*-ta pohs-*tahl*
Insect repellent	**Repelente contra insectos**	reh-peh-*lehn*-te *cohn*-trah een-*sehk*-tos

MORE USEFUL PHRASES

English	Spanish	Pronunciation
Do you speak English?	**¿Habla usted inglés?**	*ah*-blah oo-*sted* een-*glehs?*
Is there anyone here who speaks English?	**¿Hay alguien aquí que hable inglés?**	eye *ahl*-gyehn ah-*kee* keh *ah*-bleh een-*glehs?*
I speak a little Spanish.	**Hablo un poco de español.**	*ah*-bloh oon *poh*-koh deh ehss-pah-*nyohl*
I don't understand Spanish very well.	**No (lo) entiendo muy bien el español.**	noh (loh) ehn-*tyehn*-doh mwee byehn el ehss-pah-*nyohl*
The meal is good.	**Me gusta la comida.**	meh *goo*-stah lah koh-*mee*-dah
What time is it?	**¿Qué hora es?**	keh *oh*-rah ehss?
May I see your menu?	**¿Puedo ver el menú (la carta)?**	*pueh*-do vehr el meh-*noo* (lah *car*-tah)?
The check, please.	**La cuenta, por favor.**	lah *quehn*-tah pohr fa-*vorh*

English	Spanish	Pronunciation
What do I owe you?	¿Cuánto le debo?	*kwahn*-toh leh *deh*-boh?
What did you say?	¿Mande? (formal)	*mahn*-deh?
	¿Cómo? (informal)	*koh*-moh?
I want (to see) . . .	Quiero (ver) . . .	*kyeh*-roh (vehr)
a room	un cuarto or una habitación	oon *kwar*-toh, *oo*-nah ah-bee-tah-*syohn*
for two persons	para dos personas	*pah*-rah dohss pehr-*soh*-nahs
with (without) bathroom	con (sin) baño	kohn (seen) *bah*-nyoh
We are staying here only . . .	Nos quedamos aquí solamente . . .	nohs keh-*dah*-mohss ah-*kee* soh-lah-*mehn*-teh
one night.	una noche.	*oo*-nah *noh*-cheh
one week.	una semana.	*oo*-nah seh-*mah*-nah
We are leaving . . .	Partimos (Salimos) . . .	pahr-*tee*-mohss (sah-*lee*-mohss)
tomorrow.	mañana.	mah-*nya*-nah
Do you accept . . . ?	¿Acepta usted . . . ?	ah-*sehp*-tah oo-*sted*
traveler's checks?	cheques de viajero?	*cheh*-kehss deh byah-*heh*-roh?
Is there a laundromat . . . ? near here?	¿Hay una lavandería . . . ? cerca de aquí?	eye *oo*-nah lah-*vahn*-deh-*ree*-ah *sehr*-kah deh ah-*kee*

English	Spanish	Pronunciation
Please send these clothes to the laundry.	Hágame el favor de mandar esta ropa a la lavandería.	*ah*-gah-meh el fah-*vohr* deh mahn-*dahr* ehss-tah *roh*-pah a lah lah-*vahn*-deh-*ree*-ah

NUMBERS

1	**uno** (*ooh*-noh)	17	**diecisiete** (dyess-ee-*syeh*-teh)
2	**dos** (dohss)	18	**dieciocho** (dyess-ee-*oh*-choh)
3	**tres** (trehss)	19	**diecinueve** (dyess-ee-*nweh*-beh)
4	**cuatro** (*kwah*-troh)	20	**veinte** (*bayn*-teh)
5	**cinco** (*seen*-koh)	30	**treinta** (*trayn*-tah)
6	**seis** (sayss)	40	**cuarenta** (kwah-*ren*-tah)
7	**siete** (*syeh*-teh)	50	**cincuenta** (seen-*kwen*-tah)
8	**ocho** (*oh*-choh)	60	**sesenta** (seh-*sehn*-tah)
9	**nueve** (*nweh*-beh)	70	**setenta** (seh-*tehn*-tah)
10	**diez** (dyess)	80	**ochenta** (oh-*chehn*-tah)
11	**once** (*ohn*-seh)	90	**noventa** (noh-*behn*-tah)
12	**doce** (*doh*-seh)	100	**cien** (syehn)
13	**trece** (*treh*-seh)	200	**doscientos** (do-*syehn*-tohs)
14	**catorce** (kah-*tohr*-seh)	500	**quinientos** (kee-*nyehn*-tohs)
15	**quince** (*keen*-seh)	1,000	**mil** (meel)
16	**dieciseis** (dyess-ee-*sayss*)		

TRANSPORTATION TERMS

English	Spanish	Pronunciation
Airport	**Aeropuerto**	ah-eh-roh-*pwehr*-toh
Flight	**Vuelo**	*bweh*-loh
Rental car	**Arrendadora de autos**	ah-rehn-da-doh-rah deh ow-tohs
Bus	**Autobús**	ow-toh-*boos*
Bus or truck	**Camión**	ka-*myohn*
Lane	**Carril**	kah-*reel*
Nonstop (bus)	**Directo**	dee-*rehk*-toh

English	Spanish	Pronunciation
Baggage (claim area)	**Equipajes**	eh-kee-*pah*-hehss
Intercity	**Foraneo**	foh-rah-*neh*-oh
Luggage storage area	**Guarda equipaje**	gwar-dah eh-kee-*pah*-heh
Arrival gates	**Llegadas**	yeh-*gah*-dahss
Originates at this station	**Local**	loh-*kahl*
Originates elsewhere	**De paso**	deh *pah*-soh
Stops if seats available	**Para si hay lugares**	*pah*-rah see eye loo-*gah*-rehs
First class	**Primera**	pree-*meh*-rah
Second class	**Segunda**	seh-*goon*-dah
Nonstop (flight)	**Sin escala**	seen ess-*kah*-lah
Baggage claim area	**Recibo de equipajes**	reh-see-boh deh eh-kee-*pah*-hehss
Waiting room	**Sala de espera**	*sah*-lah deh ehss-*peh*-rah
Toilets	**Sanitarios**	sah-nee-*tah*-ryohss
Ticket window	**Taquilla**	tah-*kee*-yah

2 Menu Glossary

Achiote Small red seed of the *annatto* tree.

Achiote preparado A Yucatecan prepared paste made of ground *achiote,* wheat and corn flour, cumin, cinnamon, salt, onion, garlic, and oregano.

Agua fresca Fruit-flavored water, usually watermelon, cantaloupe, chia seed with lemon, hibiscus flour, rice, or ground melon-seed mixture.

Antojito Typical Mexican supper foods, usually made with *masa* or tortillas and having a filling or topping such as sausage, cheese, beans, and onions; includes such things as *tacos, tostadas, sopes,* and *garnachas.*

Atole A thick, lightly sweet, hot drink made with finely ground corn and usually flavored with vanilla, pecan, strawberry, pineapple, or chocolate.

Botana An appetizer.

Buñuelos Round, thin, deep-fried crispy fritters dipped in sugar.

Carnitas Pork deep-cooked (not fried) in lard, and then simmered and served with corn tortillas for tacos.

Ceviche Fresh raw seafood marinated in fresh lime juice and garnished with chopped tomatoes, onions, chiles, and sometimes cilantro.

Chayote A vegetable pear or mirliton, a type of spiny squash boiled and served as an accompaniment to meat dishes.

Chiles en nogada Poblano peppers stuffed with a mixture of ground pork and beef, spices, fruits, raisins, and almonds. Can be served either warm—fried in a light batter—or cold, sans the batter. Either way it is then covered in walnut-and-cream sauce.

Chiles rellenos Usually poblano peppers stuffed with cheese or spicy ground meat with raisins, rolled in a batter, and fried.

Churro Tube-shaped, breadlike fritter, dipped in sugar and sometimes filled with *cajeta* (milk-based caramel) or chocolate.

Cochinita pibil Pork wrapped in banana leaves, pit-baked in a *pibil* sauce of *achiote,* sour orange, and spices; common in the Yucatán.

Enchilada A tortilla dipped in sauce, usually filled with chicken or white cheese, and sometimes topped with *mole* (*enchiladas rojas* or *de mole*), or with tomato sauce and sour cream (*enchiladas suizas*—Swiss enchiladas), or covered in a green sauce *(enchiladas verdes),* or topped with onions, sour cream, and guacamole *(enchiladas potosinas).*

Escabeche A lightly pickled sauce used in Yucatecan chicken stew.

Frijoles refritos Pinto beans mashed and cooked with lard.

Garnachas A thickish small circle of fried *masa* with pinched sides, topped with pork or chicken, onions, and avocado, or sometimes chopped potatoes and tomatoes, typical as a *botana* in Veracruz and Yucatán.

Gorditas Thick, fried corn tortillas, slit and stuffed with choice of cheese, beans, beef, chicken, with or without lettuce, tomato, and onion garnish.

Horchata Refreshing drink made of ground rice or melon seeds, ground almonds, cinnamon, and lightly sweetened.

Huevos mexicanos Scrambled eggs with chopped onions, hot green peppers, and tomatoes.

Huitlacoche Sometimes spelled "cuitlacoche." A mushroom-flavored black fungus that appears on corn in the rainy season; considered a delicacy.

Manchamantel Translated, means "tablecloth stainer." A stew of chicken or pork with chiles, tomatoes, pineapple, bananas, and jicama.

Masa   Ground corn soaked in lime; the basis for tamales, corn tortillas, and soups.

Mixiote   Rabbit, lamb, or chicken cooked in a mild chile sauce (usually chile *ancho* or *pasilla*), and then wrapped like a tamal and steamed. It is generally served with tortillas for tacos, with traditional garnishes of pickled onions, hot sauce, chopped cilantro, and lime wedges.

Pan de muerto   Sweet bread made around the Days of the Dead (Nov 1–2), in the form of mummies or dolls, or round with bone designs.

Pan dulce   Lightly sweetened bread in many configurations, usually served at breakfast or bought in any bakery.

Papadzules   Tortillas stuffed with hard-boiled eggs and seeds (pumpkin or sunflower) in a tomato sauce.

Pibil   Pit-baked pork or chicken in a sauce of tomato, onion, mild red pepper, cilantro, and vinegar.

Pipián   A sauce made with ground pumpkin seeds, nuts, and mild peppers.

Poc chuc   Slices of pork with onion marinated in a tangy sour orange sauce and charcoal-broiled; a Yucatecan specialty.

Pozole   A soup made with hominy in either chicken or pork broth.

Pulque   A drink made of fermented juice of the maguey plant; best in the state of Hidalgo and around Mexico City.

Quesadilla   Corn or flour tortillas stuffed with melted white cheese and lightly fried.

Queso relleno   "Stuffed cheese," a mild yellow cheese stuffed with minced meat and spices; a Yucatecan specialty.

Rompope   Delicious Mexican eggnog, invented in Puebla, made with eggs, vanilla, sugar, and rum.

Salsa verde   An uncooked sauce using the green tomatillo and puréed with spicy or mild hot peppers, onions, garlic, and cilantro; on tables countrywide.

Sopa de flor de calabaza   A soup made of chopped squash or pumpkin blossoms.

Sopa de lima   A tangy soup made with chicken broth and accented with fresh lime; popular in Yucatán.

Sopa de tortilla   A traditional chicken broth–based soup, seasoned with chiles, tomatoes, onion, and garlic, served with crispy fried strips of corn tortillas.

Sopa tlalpeña (or *caldo tlalpeño*)   A hearty soup made with chicken, carrots, zucchini, corn, onions, garlic, and cilantro.

Sopa tlaxcalteca   A hearty tomato-based soup filled with cooked nopal cactus, cheese, cream, and avocado, with crispy tortilla strips floating on top.

Sope   Pronounced "*soh*-peh." An *antojito* similar to a *garnacha,* except topped with refried beans, crumbled cheese and onions.

Tacos al pastor   Thin slices of flavored pork roasted on a revolving cylinder dripping with onion slices and juice of fresh pineapple slices. Served in small corn tortillas, topped with chopped onion and cilantro.

Tamal   Incorrectly called a tamale (*tamal* singular, *tamales* plural). A meat or sweet filling rolled with fresh *masa,* wrapped in a corn husk or banana leaf, and steamed.

Tikin xic   Also seen on menus as "tik-n-xic" and "tikik chick." Charbroiled fish brushed with *achiote* sauce.

Torta   A sandwich, usually on *bolillo* bread, typically with sliced avocado, onions, tomatoes, with a choice of meat and often cheese.

Xtabentun   Pronounced "shtah-behn-*toon*." A Yucatecan liquor made of fermented honey and flavored with anise. It comes *seco* (dry) or *crema* (sweet).

Zacahuil   Pork leg tamal, packed in thick *masa,* wrapped in banana leaves, and pit-baked, sometimes pot-made with tomato and *masa;* a specialty of mid- to upper Veracruz.

Index

See also Accommodations and Restaurant indexes below.

A

AA, 12
AARP, 28–29
Abbreviations, 47
Above and Beyond Tours, 26
Access-Able Travel Source, 27
Access America, 18
Accessible Journeys, 27
Accommodations. *See also* Accommodations Index
  Barra de Navidad, 135–137
  Bucerías, 119
  chains, 44–45
  Cruz de Loreto, 126–128
  gay-friendly, 25–26
  Guadalajara, 161–167
  house and villa rentals, 45–46
  Manzanillo, 148–152
  Melaque, 139
  Nuevo Vallarta, 117–118
  out-of-the-ordinary, 45
  Puerto Vallarta, 67–74
  Punta Mita, 121–122
  rating system, 44
  Sayulita, 123, 125
  surfing for, 46
  Tenacatita Bay, 130–131
  Yelapa, 115–116
Aeromexico Vacations, 37
Agustín Parra (Tlaquepaque), 182
AIM (newsletter), 28
AirAmbulanceCard.com, 27
Airport taxes, 40
Air tours, 92–93
Air travel, 10, 39–40
Alaska Airlines Vacations, 37
Alfarería Tlaquepaque (Puerto Vallarta), 107
Ambulance services, 65–66
American Airlines Vacations, 37
American Express
  emergency number, 54
  Guadalajara, 160
  Manzanillo, 144
  Puerto Vallarta, 64–65
  traveler's checks, 17
American Express Travelers Cheque Card, 17
American Express Travel Services, 88
American Foundation for the Blind (AFB), 27
Ameri-Med, 22, 66
Año Nuevo, 6
Apple Vacations, 37
Art galleries, 105–107, 109
Arts, crafts, and gifts
  Guadalajara and environs, 180–183
  Puerto Vallarta, 102–104, 107
Ash Wednesday, 7
Auto insurance, 12
Azul 96 (Puerto Vallarta), 110

B

Bahías Gemelas Travel Agency (Manzanillo), 144, 146
Banderas Bay Trading Company (Puerto Vallarta), 107
Banks and ATMs, 15, 144
Barceló La Jolla de Mismaloya, 88
Bar Constantini (Puerto Vallarta), 110
Barra de Navidad, 2, 131–138
Basílica de la Virgen de Zapopan (Guadalajara), 178
Bayside Properties, 25–26, 67
Bazar Hecht (Tlaquepaque), 182
Beaches. *See also entries starting with "Playa"*
  Barra de Navidad, 134
  Manzanillo, 144–145
  Puerto Vallarta, 88–90
Beaded pieces, Huichol, 103
Beer Bob's Books (Barra de Navidad), 134–135
Birding, Manzanillo, 145
Boat tours and excursions, 64, 90–91, 134, 148
Boca de Tomatlán, 88–89
Bookstores, Guadalajara, 160
Bribes and scams, 23–24
Brisas Hotels & Resorts, 44
Bucerías, 62, 118–120
Bugs and bites, 20

Bullfights, Puerto Vallarta, 99
Business hours, 47–48
Bus travel, 13, 43

Calendar of events, 6–10
Caletas, 91, 110
Cameras and film, 48
Candlemas, 6–7
Canopy tours, 94–95
Canto del Sol Tennis Club (Puerto
    Vallarta), 99
Car documents, 11–12
Carlos O'Brian's (Puerto Vallarta),
    111
Carnaval, 7
Car rentals, 41–43
    for disabled travelers, 27–28
Car travel, 10–13, 40–43
Casa Bariachi (Guadalajara), 184
Cathedral, Guadalajara, 174
Cellphones, 34
Centers for Disease Control and
    Prevention, 19
Central Camionera de Puerto
    Vallarta, 60
Centro Cultural El Refugio
    (Guadalajara), 179
Chico's Dive Shop (Puerto Vallarta),
    94
Children, families with, 24–25
Chips Restaurant (Barra de Navidad),
    138
Christine (Puerto Vallarta), 112
Christmas, 9, 10
Cigars, 104
Cinco de Mayo, 7
Classic Custom Vacations, 37
Climate, 6
Clothing, Puerto Vallarta, 104–105
Club Maeva Hotel & Resort
    (Manzanillo), 154
CMQ Farmacia (Puerto Vallarta), 65
Collage Club (Puerto Vallarta), 112
Coming About, 98
Consulates, 65, 160
Consumer assistance, 65
Continental Vacations, 37
Cooperativa de Pescadores (Puerto
    Vallarta), 95
Copper Canyon, 93
Coral Reef Surf Shop (Bucerías),
    118–119
Corsica (Puerto Vallarta), 105

Costa Alegre (Costa Careyes),
    126–139
    brief description of, 2
The Crazy Cactus (Barra de Navidad),
    135
Credit cards, 16
    lost or stolen, 54
Crime. *See* Safety
Cruz Roja (Red Cross), 66, 144
Culinary Adventures, 30
Currency and exchange, 13–15
    Guadalajara, 160
    Puerto Vallarta, 65
Customs regulations, 48–50

Dance clubs and discos
    Barra de Navidad, 138
    Manzanillo, 154
    Puerto Vallarta, 112–114
    Yelapa, 116
Daylight saving time, 56
Day of the Dead, 8
Decorative and folk art, 107–108
Dentists, 50
De Santos (Puerto Vallarta), 113
Día de la Santa Cruz, 7
Día de los Reyes, 6
Día de San Pedro, 7–8
Diarrhea, travelers' *(turista)*, 21
Disabilities, travelers with, 26–28
Disco Club Paco Paco (Puerto
    Vallarta), 114
Disco El Galeón (Barra de Navidad),
    138
Doctors, 50
Dolphin Adventure, 98
Dolphin Encounter, 98–99
Dolphin Kids program, 99
Dolphins, swimming with, 98–99
Drug laws, 50–51
Drugstores, 51, 65

Ecotourism/sustainable tourism,
    30–32, 94–95
Ecotours de México, 94
El Bar de Félix (Manzanillo), 154
El Charro (Guadalajara), 180
Elderhostel, 29
ElderTreks, 29
Electricity, 51
El Faro Lighthouse Bar (Puerto
    Vallarta), 111–112

El Globo (Guadalajara), 167
El Parián (Tlaquepaque), 181, 184
El Tigre course at Paradise Village
    (Puerto Vallarta), 97
El Tuito, 92
Embassies
    of foreign countries, 51–52
    Mexican, 4
Emergencies, 52, 65–66
Emergency medical care, 22–23
Encuentro Internacional del Mariachi
    (Guadalajara), 173
Entry requirements, 4–5
Etc. Beach Club (Nuevo Vallarta),
    116–117

Families with children, 24–25
Farmacias Guadalajara (Puerto Val-
    larta), 65
Feast of the Virgin of Guadalupe, 9
Fiesta Americana and Fiesta Inn, 44
Fiesta nights, 110
Fiestas de Octubre, 8
    Guadalajara, 174
Film Festival, Puerto Vallarta, 8–9
Fishing, 95–96, 134, 146
Fishing with Carolina (Puerto
    Vallarta), 95–96
Flying Wheels Travel, 27
Flying with Disability, 27
FMT (Mexican Tourist Permit), 4–5
Frommers.com, 32
Funjet Vacations, 38

Galería AL (Arte Latinoamericano;
    Puerto Vallarta), 105
Galería del Calzado (Guadalajara), 180
Galería des Artistes (Puerto Vallarta),
    105–106
Galería Omar Alonso (Puerto
    Vallarta), 106
Galería Pacífico (Puerto Vallarta), 106
Galería Uno (Puerto Vallarta), 106
Gallería Dante (Puerto Vallarta), 106
Garbo (Puerto Vallarta), 114
Gasoline, 40
Gay and lesbian travelers, 25–26,
    114–115
Gay.com Travel, 26
Global Lifeline, 22
GOGO Worldwide Vacations, 38
Golf, 96–97, 134, 147

Gonvil (Guadalajara), 160
Gourmet Festival, 9
Grand Bay Hotel golf course
    (Barra de Navidad), 147
Green Angels, 41
Greyhound-Trailways, 13
Guadalajara, 155–186
    accommodations, 161–167
    brief description of, 2
    bus tours, 177
    climate and dress, 160
    emergencies, 161
    getting around, 159
    getting there and departing,
        155–156
    layout of, 158
    neighborhoods, 158–159
    nightlife, 184–186
    restaurants, 167–172
    safety, 161
    shopping, 180–183
    sights and attractions, 173–179
    special events, 173–174
    visitor information, 156

Health concerns, 19–23
Health insurance, 18–19
HECtours (Manzanillo), 146
Hilo (Puerto Vallarta), 113
Holland's, 67
Holy Cross Day, 7
Holy Week, 7
Horseback riding, Puerto Vallarta, 97
Hospitals, 66, 144, 161
Hoteles Camino Real, 45
Hoteles Krystal NH, 45
Hotels. See Accommodations
House and villas rentals, 45–46
Huichol Collection (Puerto Vallarta),
    104
Huichol Indians, 86, 93, 103, 178
    art, 102–104

Independence Day, 8
Insect repellent, 20
Instituto Cultural Cabañas (Guadala-
    jara), 177
Instituto de la Artesanía Jalisciense
    (Guadalajara), 178, 180
Insurance, 17–19
    auto, 12
    car-rental, 42–43

International Friendship Club (Puerto Vallarta), 93
International Gay and Lesbian Travel Association (IGLTA), 26
International Legal Defense Counsel, 53
Internet access/e-mail, 35
  Guadalajara, 161
  Manzanillo, 144
  Puerto Vallarta, 66
InTouch USA, 34
Isla Navidad Country Club, 134
Isla Navidad Resort, 132
IVA (value-added tax), 14, 56

J & B Salsa Club (Puerto Vallarta), 113
Jazz, 111, 113
Jewelry and accessories, Puerto Vallarta, 109
John Huston's Bar & Grill (Puerto Vallarta), 88
Journeywoman, 30
Juárez, Benito, Birthday of, 7
Jungle restaurants, 85

La Bodeguita del Medio
  Guadalajara, 184
  Puerto Vallarta, 111
Labor Day, 7
La Casa del Feng Shui (Puerto Vallarta), 107
La Casa del Habano (Puerto Vallarta), 104
La Casa del Tequila (Puerto Vallarta), 104
Laguna de Cuyutlán, 145
Laguna de Las Garzas, 145
La Lagarta Disco (Tenacatita Bay), 130
La Mantarraya Golf Course (Manzanillo), 147
Language, 53
Language classes, Guadalajara, 161
La Noche (Puerto Vallarta), 115
LANS (Puerto Vallarta), 104
Las Brisas. See Playa Las Brisas
Las Caletas, 91, 110
Las Palmas (Bucerías), 119
Laura López Labra Designs (Puerto Vallarta), 104–105

Legal aid, 53
Liberty Travel, 38
Lienzo Charro de Jalisco (Guadalajara), 178
Liquor laws, 53
Los Arcos, 90
Los Flamingos Club de Golf (near Puerto Vallarta), 96
Lost and found, 53–54
Lost-luggage insurance, 19
Lucy's CuCu Cabaña (Puerto Vallarta), 107–108

Mail, 54
Manzanillo, 140–154
  accommodations, 148–152
  beaches and outdoor activities, 144–147
  brief description of, 1–2
  getting around, 143
  getting there and departing, 140–142
  layout of, 142–143
  nightlife, 154
  restaurants, 152–153
  shopping, 148
  visitor information, 142
Mar de Sueños (Puerto Vallarta), 105
Mariachi Festival, 8
Mariachi Loco (Puerto Vallarta), 112
Marietas Islands, 89–90
Marigalante, 90–91
Marina Vallarta, 61, 67, 101
  accommodations, 67–69
  beaches at, 89
  restaurants, 75
Marina Vallarta Golf Club, 96
Markets
  Guadalajara, 177, 180
  Puerto Vallarta, 100, 101
Mascota, 93
MasterCard, 17, 54
May Day, 7
Mealtimes, 46
MEDEX Assistance, 18
Medical insurance, 18–19
Medjet Assist, 22
Melaque, 132
Melaque (San Patricio), 138–139
Menu glossary, 192–195
Mercado Libertad (Guadalajara), 177, 180

Mexcaltitan, 93
Mexicana Vacations, 38
Mexican embassies, 4
Mexican Government Tourist Board,
    2, 4
Mexican Tourist Permit (FMT), 4–5
Mexico Boutique Hotels, 45
Mexico Hot Line, 2
Mita Residential, 67
Money matters, 13–17
"Montezuma's revenge" *(turista)*, 21
MossRehab, 27
Museo de Arqueología del Occidente
    de México (Guadalajara), 178
Museo de la Ciudad (Guadalajara), 178
Museo de las Artes de la Universidad
    de Guadalajara, 179
Museo Nacional de Cerámica
    (Tonalá), 183
Museo Pantaleón Panduro (Guadala-
    jara), 179
Museo Regional de Guadalajara, 176
Museo Río Cuale (Puerto Vallarta),
    100
Museum of Archaeology and History
    (Manzanillo), 147–148

National Ceramics Fair and Fiesta
    (Tlaquepaque), 7
Newspapers and magazines, Puerto
    Vallarta, 66
New Year's Day, 6
New Year's Eve, 10
Night clubs, 112–114
Nightlife
    Barra de Navidad, 138
    Guadalajara, 184–186
    Manzanillo, 154
    Puerto Vallarta, 109–115
    Yelapa, 116
Nikki Beach (Puerto Vallarta), 69, 113
No Name Bar & Grill (Puerto Vallarta),
    114
Now, Voyager, 26
Nuevo Vallarta, 62, 116–118

October Festivals, 8
Olinala (Puerto Vallarta), 108
Olivia, 26
Open Air Expeditions (Puerto
    Vallarta), 91, 94

Out & About magazine, 26
Outdoor activities, Puerto Vallarta,
    94–99

Package tours, 36–38
Palacio del Gobierno (Guadalajara),
    175
Papantla Flyers (Puerto Vallarta), 100
Parasailing, 98
Parish of Nuestra Señora de
    Guadalupe church (Puerto Vallarta),
    99–100
Parque Agua Azul (Guadalajara), 178
Passports, 4, 53–55
Pets, 55
Peyote People (Puerto Vallarta), 104
Piper Lover Bar & Grill (Barra de
    Navidad), 138
Playa Anclote, 89
Playa Audiencia, 144
Playa Azul, 145
Playa Destiladeras, 89
Playa Las Animas, 89
Playa Las Brisas, 145
    accommodations, 149
    restaurant, 152–153
Playa Los Muertos, 88
Playa Miramar, 145
Playa Mismaloya, 88
Playa Piedras Blancas, 89
Playa Quimixto, 89
Playa San Pedrito, 144–145
Playa Yelapa, 89
Plaza de Armas (Guadalajara),
    174–175
Plaza Peninsula (Puerto Vallarta), 101
Plaza Tapatía (Guadalajara), 174
Pleasant Mexico Holidays, 38
Police, 55
Post offices, 66, 144, 161
Pottery and ceramics, 181–183
Prescription medications, 22
PROFECO, 65
Public Sculptures tour (Puerto Val-
    larta), 94
Puerco Azul (Puerto Vallarta), 108
Puerto Vallarta, 57–125
    accommodations, 67–74
    American Express, 64–65
    beaches, 88–90
    brief description of, 1
    consulates, 65

consumer assistance, 65
currency exchange, 65
emergencies, 65–66
exploring, 99–100
getting around, 62–64
getting to and from, 58, 60
layout of, 61–62
nightlife, 109–115
organized tours, 90–94
outdoor activities, 94–99
restaurants, 74–85
shopping, 100–109
side trips from, 115–125
travel agencies, 86
visitor information, 60–61
Puerto Vallarta Film Festival, 8–9
Punta Mita, 2, 62, 90, 121–122
Punta Mita Golf Club, 96

Querubines (Puerto Vallarta), 108
Quetzalcoatl Fountain (Guadalajara),
176–177
Quinta Real Grand Class Hotels and
Resorts, 45

Ranch Disco Bar (Puerto Vallarta),
115
Rancho Altamira, 92
Rancho El Charro, 97
Rancho Ojo de Agua, 97
Rancho Palma Real, 97
Regional Ceramics Museum
(Tlaquepaque), 181–182
Restaurants, 46–47. See also
Restaurant Index
Barra de Navidad, 137–138
Bucerías, 119–120
Guadalajara, 167–172
Manzanillo, 152–153
Melaque, 139
menu glossary, 192–195
Puerto Vallarta, 74–85
Sayulita, 123–124
Revolution Day, 9
Rhythms of the Night (Cruise to
Caletas), 110
RoadPost, 34
Rosalia, 185
Rotonda de los Hombres Ilustres
(Guadalajara), 176
Route 66 (Puerto Vallarta), 112

Safari Accents (Puerto Vallarta), 107
Safety, 23–24
Guadalajara, 161
Puerto Vallarta, 66
Sailing, Puerto Vallarta, 98
San Blas, 91
Sanborn's (Guadalajara), 160
Sanborn's Mexico Insurance, 12
Sanborn Tours, 28
Sandi Bookstore (Guadalajara), 160
San Sebastián, 124–125
San Sebastián Air Expedition, 92
Santiago Peninsula
accommodations, 149–152
restaurant, 153
SATH (Society for Accessible Travel
& Hospitality), 27
Sayulita, 122–124
Scams, 24
Scuba diving
Manzanillo, 146
Puerto Vallarta, 94
Seasons, 5–6
Senior travel, 28–29
Señor Frog's (Puerto Vallarta), 114
Sergio Bustamante (Tlaquepaque), 182
Shipping your purchases, 182
Shoe stores, Guadalajara, 180
Shopping
Guadalajara, 180–183
Manzanillo, 148
Puerto Vallarta, 100–109
Silver scam, 101
Single travelers, 29
Small Vallarta, 101–102
Smoking, 56
Snorkeling, Puerto Vallarta, 94
South Swell Mex Surf Shop (Barra de
Navidad), 134
Spanish language classes, Guadala-
jara, 161
Special-interest trips, 30
Sports bar, 114
St. Peter and St. Paul's Day, 7–8
Studio Cathy Von Rohr (Puerto
Vallarta), 106–107
Sunset Bar and Restaurant (Barra
de Navidad), 138
Suntrips, 38
Surfing, Barra de Navidad, 134
Sustainable tourism/ecotourism,
30–32, 94–95

Talpa de Allende, 93
Tapatío Tours (Guadalajara), 177
Taxes, 56
Taxis, 43
    Guadalajara, 159
    Manzanillo, 143
    Puerto Vallarta, 62–63
Teatro Degollado (Guadalajara), 176
Telephones, 32–34
Tenacatita Bay, 129–131
Tennis, 99
Tequila (town), 185
Tequila distilleries, 185
Tequila Express, 185
Terra Noble Art & Healing Center, 92
Teté Arte y Diseño (Tlaquepaque), 182
Three Kings Day, 6
Time zone, 56
Tipping, 47, 56
Tlaquepaque, 91, 159
    shopping, 180–182
Toilets, 56
Toll roads, 41
Tonalá, 91–92, 159, 183
Tourist Help Line, 52
Tours, organized
    air tours, 92–93
    boat tours, 64, 90–91, 134, 148
    Guadalajara, 177
    land tours, 91–92
    Manzanillo, 146
    package deals, 36–38
    Puerto Vallarta, 93
    Tonalá, 183
Town and Country, 38
Transportation, 38–43
Tranvías Turísticos (Guadalajara), 177
Travel Assistance International, 18
Travel Companion Exchange (TCE), 29
Traveler's checks, 16–17
Travelex Insurance Services, 18
Travel Guard International, 18
Travel Health Online, 19
Travel insurance, 17–19
Travel Insured International, 18
TravelSafe, 18
Trek America, 30
Trip-cancellation insurance, 18
Tukari Servicios Turísticos (Puerto Vallarta), 86
Turista (travelers' diarrhea), 21

Underworld Scuba (Manzanillo), 146

Vacation Rentals by Owner (VRBO), 45
VacationSpot, 45–46
Vallarta Adventures, 88, 91–94, 124
Value-added tax (IVA), 14, 56
Visa, 17, 54
Visas, 4–5
Visitor information
    Barra de Navidad, 132
    Guadalajara, 156
    Manzanillo, 142
    for Mexico, 2, 4
    Puerto Vallarta, 60–61
Vista Vallarta Golf Club, 96–97
Viva (Puerto Vallarta), 109
Vog Disco (Manzanillo), 154
Voice over Internet protocol (VoIP), 34
Voladores de Papantla (Puerto Vallarta), 100
VRBO (Vacation Rentals by Owner), 45

Wallet, lost or stolen, 53–54
Water, drinking, 56
Water taxis, Puerto Vallarta, 64
Weather, 6
Websites
    for health-related travel advice, 20
    traveler's toolbox, 35
    for vacation packages, 36
Western Union, 54
Whale-watching cruises, 91
Wheelchair accessibility, 26–28
Wi-Fi access, 35
Women travelers, 29–30
Worldwide Assistance Services, 18

Xplora Adventours (Puerto Vallarta), 86, 88

Yarn paintings, Huichol, 103, 104
Yelapa, 115–116
    accommodations, 74
Yelapa Yacht Club, 116

Zapopan, 158
Zoo (Puerto Vallarta), 114
Z'Tai (Puerto Vallarta), 111

ACCOMMODATIONS

Barceló Karmina Palace (Manzanillo), 149–150
Blue Bay Club Los Angeles Locos (Tenacatita Bay), 130
Brisas Las Hadas Golf Resort & Marina (Manzanillo), 150–151
The Careyes Hotel, 129
Casa Las Brisas (Punta Mita), 121
Casa Tres Vidas (Puerto Vallarta), 72
Casa Velas (Puerto Vallarta), 67–68
Dreams Puerto Vallarta Resort & Spa, 72–73
El Pabellón de San Sebastián (Sayulita), 125
El Planeta Vegetariano (Puerto Vallarta), 75
El Tamarindo (Yellowstone Club World; Tenacatita Bay), 130–131
Fiesta Americana Puerto Vallarta, 69
Four Seasons Resort Punta Mita, 122
Grand Bay Hotel Isla Navidad Resort, 135
Hacienda Jalisco (Sayulita), 125
Hacienda San Angel (Puerto Vallarta), 70–71
Holiday Inn Hotel and Suites Centro Histórico (Guadalajara), 163–164
Hotel Barra de Navidad, 136
Hotel Cabo Blanco (Barra de Navidad), 135–136
Hotel Cervantes (Guadalajara), 164
Hotel Colonial (Manzanillo), 148
Hotel Delfín (Barra de Navidad), 136
Hotel de Mendoza (Guadalajara), 164
Hotelito Desconocido (Cruz de Loreto), 126–128
Hotel Lagunita (Yelapa), 115–116
Hotel La Posada (Manzanillo), 149
Hotel Legazpi (Melaque), 139
Hotel Morales (Guadalajara), 165
Hotel Playa Los Arcos (Puerto Vallarta), 71–72
Hotel Presidente InterContinental (Guadalajara), 162
Hotel Sands (Barra de Navidad), 136–137

Hotel San Francisco Plaza (Guadalajara), 166
Las Alamandas, 128
La Villa del Ensueño (Guadalajara), 165
Marival Grand & Club Suites (Nuevo Vallarta), 117
Old Guadalajara, 165–166
Paradise Village (Nuevo Vallarta), 117–118
Plaza Los Reyes (Guadalajara), 167
Plaza Tucanes (Manzanillo), 151
Premier Hotel & Spa (Puerto Vallarta), 70
Quinta Don José (Guadalajara), 166
Quinta María Cortez (Puerto Vallarta), 73–74
Quinta Real (Guadalajara), 162–163
Tesoro Manzanillo Resort, 151–152
Velas Vallarta Grand Suite Resort (Puerto Vallarta), 68
Verana (Yelapa), 74, 116
Villa Ganz (Guadalajara), 163
Westin Resort & Spa Puerto Vallarta, 68–69

RESTAURANTS

Adobe Fonda (Guadalajara), 167–168
Agave Grill (Puerto Vallarta), 80
Archie's Wok (Puerto Vallarta), 82–83
Barcelona Tapas (Puerto Vallarta), 79
Benedetti's Pizza (Manzanillo), 153
Benitto's (Puerto Vallarta), 75
Bigotes II (Manzanillo), 153
Café des Artistes/Thierry Blouet Cocina de Autor (Puerto Vallarta), 76
Café Kaiser Maximilian (Puerto Vallarta), 81–82
Café Madrid (Guadalajara), 171
Café San Angel (Puerto Vallarta), 84
Chez Nené (Guadalajara), 168
Chico's Paradise (Puerto Vallarta), 85
Daiquiri Dick's (Puerto Vallarta), 77
de Santos (Puerto Vallarta), 77
Don Pedro's (Sayulita), 123–124
El Arrayán (Puerto Vallarta), 80–81
El Manglito (Barra de Navidad), 137
El Nogalito (Puerto Vallarta), 85
El Sacromonte (Guadalajara), 168–169
Espresso (Puerto Vallarta), 83
Fajita Republic (Puerto Vallarta), 84

Hacienda San Angel (Puerto Vallarta), 77–78
Hostería del Angel (Guadalajara), 169–170
Hotel Delfín (Barra de Navidad), 137
I Latina (Guadalajara), 170
Karen's Place (Bucerías), 119
La Chata Restaurant (Guadalajara), 171–172
La Esquina de los Caprichos (Puerto Vallarta), 79
La Fonda de la Noche (Guadalajara), 172
La Fonda de San Miguel (Guadalajara), 170
La Noche de la Iguana Set Restaurant (Puerto Vallarta), 88
La Palapa (Puerto Vallarta), 83
Las Palomas (Puerto Vallarta), 78
La Tequila (Guadalajara), 169
La Toscana (Manzanillo), 152–153
La Trattoria Pomodoro Ristorante (Guadalajara), 170–171
Le Bistro (Puerto Vallarta), 82
Le Fort (Bucerías), 119–120

Legazpi (Manzanillo), 153
Los Itacates Restaurant (Guadalajara), 172
Los Pelícanos (Melaque), 139
Mañana (Puerto Vallarta), 89
Mariscos Progreso (Guadalajara), 171
Mark's (Bucerías), 120
Mar y Tierra (Barra de Navidad), 137
Mezzogiorno (Bucerías), 120
Pink Bonsai (Puerto Vallarta), 89
Porto Bello (Puerto Vallarta), 75
Red Cabbage Café (El Repollo Rojo; Puerto Vallarta), 84–85
Restaurant Bar Ambar (Barra de Navidad), 137–138
Restaurant Bar Ramón (Barra de Navidad), 138
Roca del Mar (Manzanillo), 152
Rollie's (Sayulita), 124
Thierry's Prime Steakhouse (Puerto Vallarta), 76
Trío (Puerto Vallarta), 78–79
Vitea (Puerto Vallarta), 81
Xitomates (Puerto Vallarta), 79–80

FROMMER'S® COMPLETE TRAVEL GUIDES

Alaska
Amalfi Coast
American Southwest
Amsterdam
Argentina & Chile
Arizona
Atlanta
Australia
Austria
Bahamas
Barcelona
Beijing
Belgium, Holland & Luxembourg
Belize
Bermuda
Boston
Brazil
British Columbia & the Canadian Rockies
Brussels & Bruges
Budapest & the Best of Hungary
Buenos Aires
Calgary
California
Canada
Cancún, Cozumel & the Yucatán
Cape Cod, Nantucket & Martha's Vineyard
Caribbean
Caribbean Ports of Call
Carolinas & Georgia
Chicago
China
Colorado
Costa Rica
Croatia
Cuba
Denmark
Denver, Boulder & Colorado Springs
Edinburgh & Glasgow
England
Europe
Europe by Rail
Florence, Tuscany & Umbria

Florida
France
Germany
Greece
Greek Islands
Hawaii
Hong Kong
Honolulu, Waikiki & Oahu
India
Ireland
Israel
Italy
Jamaica
Japan
Kauai
Las Vegas
London
Los Angeles
Los Cabos & Baja
Madrid
Maine Coast
Maryland & Delaware
Maui
Mexico
Montana & Wyoming
Montréal & Québec City
Moscow & St. Petersburg
Munich & the Bavarian Alps
Nashville & Memphis
New England
Newfoundland & Labrador
New Mexico
New Orleans
New York City
New York State
New Zealand
Northern Italy
Norway
Nova Scotia, New Brunswick & Prince Edward Island
Oregon
Paris
Peru
Philadelphia & the Amish Country

Portugal
Prague & the Best of the Czech Republic
Provence & the Riviera
Puerto Rico
Rome
San Antonio & Austin
San Diego
San Francisco
Santa Fe, Taos & Albuquerque
Scandinavia
Scotland
Seattle
Seville, Granada & the Best of Andalusia
Shanghai
Sicily
Singapore & Malaysia
South Africa
South America
South Florida
South Pacific
Southeast Asia
Spain
Sweden
Switzerland
Tahiti & French Polynesia
Texas
Thailand
Tokyo
Toronto
Turkey
USA
Utah
Vancouver & Victoria
Vermont, New Hampshire & Maine
Vienna & the Danube Valley
Vietnam
Virgin Islands
Virginia
Walt Disney World® & Orlando
Washington, D.C.
Washington State

FROMMER'S® DAY BY DAY GUIDES

Amsterdam
Chicago
Florence & Tuscany

London
New York City
Paris

Rome
San Francisco
Venice

PAULINE FROMMER'S GUIDES! SEE MORE. SPEND LESS.

Hawaii

Italy

New York City

FROMMER'S® PORTABLE GUIDES

Acapulco, Ixtapa & Zihuatanejo
Amsterdam
Aruba
Australia's Great Barrier Reef
Bahamas
Big Island of Hawaii
Boston
California Wine Country
Cancún
Charleston
Chicago
Dominican Republic

Dublin
Florence
Las Vegas
Las Vegas for Non-Gamblers
London
Maui
Nantucket & Martha's Vineyard
New Orleans
New York City
Paris
Portland
Puerto Rico
Puerto Vallarta, Manzanillo & Guadalajara

Rio de Janeiro
San Diego
San Francisco
Savannah
St. Martin, Sint Maarten, Anguila & St. Bart's
Turks & Caicos
Vancouver
Venice
Virgin Islands
Washington, D.C.
Whistler

FROMMER'S® CRUISE GUIDES

Alaska Cruises & Ports of Call	Cruises & Ports of Call	European Cruises & Ports of Call

FROMMER'S® NATIONAL PARK GUIDES

Algonquin Provincial Park	National Parks of the American West	Yosemite and Sequoia & Kings
Banff & Jasper	Rocky Mountain	Canyon
Grand Canyon	Yellowstone & Grand Teton	Zion & Bryce Canyon

FROMMER'S® MEMORABLE WALKS

London	Paris	San Francisco
New York	Rome	

FROMMER'S® WITH KIDS GUIDES

Chicago	National Parks	Toronto
Hawaii	New York City	Walt Disney World® & Orlando
Las Vegas	San Francisco	Washington, D.C.
London		

SUZY GERSHMAN'S BORN TO SHOP GUIDES

France	London	Paris
Hong Kong, Shanghai & Beijing	New York	San Francisco
Italy		

FROMMER'S® IRREVERENT GUIDES

Amsterdam	London	Rome
Boston	Los Angeles	San Francisco
Chicago	Manhattan	Walt Disney World®
Las Vegas	Paris	Washington, D.C.

FROMMER'S® BEST-LOVED DRIVING TOURS

Austria	Germany	Northern Italy
Britain	Ireland	Scotland
California	Italy	Spain
France	New England	Tuscany & Umbria

THE UNOFFICIAL GUIDES®

Adventure Travel in Alaska	Hawaii	Paris
Beyond Disney	Ireland	San Francisco
California with Kids	Las Vegas	South Florida including Miami &
Central Italy	London	the Keys
Chicago	Maui	Walt Disney World®
Cruises	Mexico's Best Beach Resorts	Walt Disney World® for
Disneyland®	Mini Mickey	Grown-ups
England	New Orleans	Walt Disney World® with Kids
Florida	New York City	Washington, D.C.
Florida with Kids		

SPECIAL-INTEREST TITLES

Athens Past & Present	Frommer's Exploring America by RV
Best Places to Raise Your Family	Frommer's NYC Free & Dirt Cheap
Cities Ranked & Rated	Frommer's Road Atlas Europe
500 Places to Take Your Kids Before They Grow Up	Frommer's Road Atlas Ireland
Frommer's Best Day Trips from London	Great Escapes From NYC Without Wheels
Frommer's Best RV & Tent Campgrounds in the U.S.A.	Retirement Places Rated

FROMMER'S® PHRASEFINDER DICTIONARY GUIDES

French	Italian	Spanish

CLOSED due to accidental demolition

WEGEN BISSIGEN EICHHÖRNCHEN GESCHLOSSEN

CERRADO CABRAS

Κλειστό Μετεωρίτες

POOL CLOSED プールも 閉鎖中 ELECTRIC EELS

Hotel closed for facelifting

FERMÉ POUR RAISON DE GRÈVE DES BONNES

FECHADO! POR CAUSA DE ATAQUES DOS CROCODILOS

I don't speak sign language.

A hotel can close for all kinds of reasons.

Our Guarantee ensures that if your hotel's undergoing construction, we'll let you know in advance. In fact, we cover your entire travel experience. See www.travelocity.com/guarantee for details.

travelocity

You'll never roam alone.